The Social Costs and Rewards of Caring

DERMOT CLIFFORD
Archbishop of Cashel & Emly

Avebury

Aldershot · Brookfield USA · Hong Kong · Singapore · Sydney

Published by
Avebury
Gower Publishing Company Limited
Gower House
Croft Road
Aldershot
Hants GU11 3HR
England

Gower Publishing Company
Old Post Road
Brookfield
Vermont 05036
USA

ISBN 1 85628 074 8

Printed and Bound in Great Britain by
Athenaeum Press Ltd., Newcastle upon Tyne.

Contents

362.6
C 631

142, 192

Foreword

One of the essential roles of social science research is to highlight and explore that which is taken for granted, or relegated to the margins, within prevailing orthodoxies. This book fulfils precisely that mission in a way which will be welcomed, queried and criticised according to the readers' interests and perceptions. It is a report of research which both complements and contrasts with much recent work on the way in which care in the community is organised and provided for elderly people and people with learning difficulties (mental handicap). The insights and perspectives which Dermot Clifford conveys are interestingly different because the work was undertaken in the sparsely populated rural areas of the Republic of Ireland, because the author is a Roman Catholic Archbishop with a distinctive view of social policy issues, but also because the questions posed give emphasis to some issues which have been touched upon but lightly in much contemporary research.

Care has always been provided by families in the community and the importance of social care has attracted episodic interest. In the past three or four decades, however, it has commanded increasingly consistent and urgent attention from public policy makers and analysts in most developed countries. In Britain, the Poor Law contributed significantly to a legacy of institutionalisation and to a post-war determination to reinstate community based care as the cornerstone of public policy towards vulnerable and dependent people. What the policy of community care long took for granted and neglected to explore in detail was that such care largely devolved upon the fine structure of society: the family and kinship system and networks of neighbours and friends. Hidden within that fine structure lay a sharp division of labour and a strong pattern of inequality: women did the work of caring and they tended to pay a measurable, not to say high, price for the privilege. For privilege read duty? A new orthodoxy about the implications and outcomes of community care emerged from research conducted in the nineteen-seventies and nineteen-eighties and from the feminist theoretical framework within which it was often, though not invariably, located. The caring role was seen to be onerous financially, socially and even in terms of the physical and emotional wellbeing of the carers. This emphasis on the costs of caring could not fail to highlight the compelling structure of values and expectations which must underpin such a demanding role.

Dermot Clifford cites and acknowledges the important intellectual contribution of feminist research in this book before turning to explore the motivations of carers in great detail and to ask what positive experiences as well as costs might be associated with the task of long-term caring. The samples of carers of elderly and mentally handicapped people are quite large - impressively so for an unfunded piece of personal research. The similarities and differences between rural Ireland and the predominantly urban face of Britain revealed in similar studies are continually intriguing. They even affect the research method: nowhere else in Europe could one draw a defensible sample from the First Friday visiting lists used by parish priests!

Such cultural - and religious - differences have always to be borne in mind in interpreting findings. The strong influence of religious belief on carers' attitudes and behaviour cannot be minimised or ignored. But even this clear point of contrast with other, more secular, western societies is one of degree rather than of kind. The Christian heritage runs strongly through the highways and byways of social policy theory and practice; it is useful to have it figure so clearly, powerfully and unambiguously. The cultural forces which promote the acceptance of a duty to care - and not to count it as a duty - is never more clearly outlined than in the words of some of these devout carers. But inherent and pervasive as social obligations are in any culture, they are not the whole story. What Dermot Clifford also uncovers is a strong and persistent vein of love and affection, learning, self-discovery and fulfilment, as well as self-sacrifice among his sample of carers. Social science ought not only to diagnose pathology, social ills and dysfunction; this study helps us view caring in the round as a human and social activity precisely because it highlights pleasures as well as pains, the genuinely reciprocal as well as the altruistic and the socially obligated.

Unfortunately, to suggest that caring may bring

compensations as well as costs, and therefore to publish this study, is a politically sensitive and controversial act. The policy implications of research cannot be ignored (although to anticipate them too fully can promote self-censorship and imbalance). It is all too possible that the consequences of financial exigency and of medaciously inegalitarian policies can be 'legitimated' by reference to the fact that carers in some situations feel no compulsion to dwell on the sacrifice they make or may even prefer to emphasise the positive effects of their caring experience. But to acknowledge the positive as well as the negative dimension of caring must not be allowed to become a source of moral succour to the Gradgrinds of social policy making. Dermot Clifford has himself used his research to argue, not without success, for better financial support for carers in the Irish Republic. We should not need to conceive of social care as an unremitting burden in order to recognise the ethical, not to mention the purely practical and instrumental, case for adequately and publicly supporting vulnerable and dependent people and their carers. This is the essential message of the large body of contemporary research and writing on social care - to which Dermot Clifford's book makes its distinctive but complementary contribution.

Adrian Webb

Loughborough University

1 Background

Since I am using the 'life history' technique on others in this study, perhaps it is only fair that I should begin with a brief autobiographical sketch. I was a late vocation to Social Administration! I had been a priest for eight years when my bishop, Dr. Eamonn Casey, assigned me to the London School of Economics for postgraduate studies in 1972.

When I landed in Holyhead the policeman at Immigration eyed me and my Irish registered car with some suspicion. "What is the nature of your business in this Country, Sir". "I've come to do some studies, Officer". "And what, may I ask is the subject of your studies?" "Social Administration", I replied. There was a long pause. For an awful moment I thought he was going to ask me to define this strange discipline. "Oh, *Social Administration*", he said, "I see, I wish you luck". I was waived on.

I was welcomed to the L.S.E. by Professor Brian Abel-Smith and the Staff, most of whom were younger than I was. My tutor, Adrian Webb, certainly was, but he very sportingly took up the challenge of teaching someone with no background whatever in the Social Sciences. He had a vital virtue, rarely found in bright young men – patience. I feel I may have tried it sorely in the early days.

My previous studies were more of a hindrance than a help at first. There was, for example, 'the literature' to which they kept referring. To one for whom this term conjured up poetry, novels and great authors the 'literature' was somewhat of a come-down. It was found to consist of

1

assorted books, articles, monographs, mimeographs, reports, green papers, white papers, occasional papers, Fabian tracts, and much else, many of which were almost impossible to track down.

There seemed to be a propensity to gloom in much of the writing. It made for sad reading generally. There was the "plight" of the elderly, the "cycle of deprivation" and "social malaise". Further hazards included the "poverty trap", the "wage-stop" and the "four week rule". There was just one Shakespearian touch - the title of a book, "Sans Everything". Luckily I was soon advised that one was not required to read everything, but rather to "examine the literature" which is, of course, an art in itself.

Seriously, the subject seemed to be very much dominated then by material issues. It was heavily preoccupied and understandably so, with the rediscovery of poverty among the elderly and families. But material well-being seemed to be the sole objective of social policy. The human spirit tended to be neglected and forgotten. That there could be a 'poverty of the spirit' among the materially well off did not merit any attention. This serious gap was pointed out by Mother Teresa of Calcutta, [1] "You have a Welfare State. But I have walked your streets at night and gone into your Homes and found people dying unloved. Here you have a different kind of poverty. A poverty of the spirit, of loneliness of being unwanted. And this is the worst disease of all, worse than tuberculosis or leprosy".

In any case Social Administration then concentrated almost exclusively on the production and delivery of specific social services. It seemed to me then that the subject could well broaden its horizons beyond material well-being and develop a social policy of the "human spirit". First impressions ...?

An honourable exception to this narrow way of thinking was Richard Titmuss who returned to lecture in the Lenten term though suffering from terminal cancer. He made a deep impression on me. He took up the broad philosophical questions. He argued for the primacy of altruism over self-interest in human relationships. He communicated deep personal conviction and compassion for people. His commitment to values did not lessen his demands for rigorous scientific method. The tight material framework had its place but it was to be the servant not the master. These lectures were his last; we attended his Memorial Service in June 1973.

As part of my course I undertook a study on Social Stigma in Ireland during my summer holidays. The designing of the survey, and the experience of interviewing gave me my breakthrough in understanding Social Administration. As I moved from house to house and listened to story after story I realised that I was dealing with the building blocks of the subject. Indeed, every person had a unique story to tell. Many of the tales were sad. But the human spirit has a capacity to survive and to overcome adversity. There is

2

the lighter side too, the humour and the sense of fun which form an essential part of the survival kit of the disadvantaged. Oscar Lewis had captured this aspect in the 1960's with *The Children of Sanchez* as did Dominique Lapierre in the 1980's with *The City of Joy*.

The study on Stigma, which included three hundred interviews, and formed part of my M.Sc examination was subsequently published in Ireland [2] and in Britain [3].

On my return to Ireland, I became Secretary to the Diocese of Kerry and also Social Policy Advisor. I also took up the post of part-time lecturer at University College Cork, at the invitation of Professor Damien Hannan.

A study on Poverty had been carried out in the early part of 1974 in the Kerry Diocese and I helped publicise the findings at Seminars which were held in the ten towns [4]. The elderly emerged as the most deprived group in this study. Their incomes were frequently below the poverty line, their housing tended to be old, run down and lacking in amenities such as running water and indoor toilets. And a substantial minority were reported to be isolated and lonely.

This last fact took most people by surprise. Kerry people prided themselves on their good neighbourliness and community spirit. It had been taken for granted that nobody was left out of its strong networks of family, relatives, neighbours and friends. Furthermore, there were new Community Care proposals emerging from the recently formed Health Boards and voluntary bodies were to be coordinated with statutory through Community Councils. Many refused to believe that a large section of the elderly could possibly be lacking in human companionship.

So, in 1977, I undertook a further study into the question of Loneliness among the over 65s. A large sample was selected in the Diocese which includes all County Kerry and eleven parishes in County Cork. Four hundred and seventy eight interviews were completed; 15 per cent of the respondents said they were lonely "always" or "often" and a further 20 per cent said they were lonely "sometimes".

The study was intended to be action directed. The findings received national coverage in the media over Christmas 1977. The main aim now was to stimulate good neighbourliness and informal visiting in the first place and, in the second place, young volunteers were to be trained to visit the frail elderly in their area along the lines of Hadley, Webb and Farrell's *Across the Generations* [5]. Pilot schemes were set up in schools and in parishes. I published articles in the two principal journals for priests and religious [6,7,8] and in the national and local press.

During 1978, I became interested in the work of voluntary organizations in England and attended the A.R.V.A.C. Conference in London at which Philip Abrams spoke on "Neighbourhood Care and Social Policy". I subsequently followed the development of his ideas and his research until his untimely death in 1981. As a sociologist he brought a fresh approach and he questioned many of the current assumptions of Social Administration.

The most striking finding in the study on loneliness was the relationship between it and incapacity. The greater the degree of incapacity the more likely the old person was to feel lonely. It was this finding which led me to concentrate on the frail elderly who generally lived with their families. Up to this point I had thought that only those who lived alone were in need of greater companionship.

During those years, I established links with the Statutory Services and was at regular meetings with the Director of Community Care, the Medical Officer of Health and the President of the St. Vincent de Paul Society, the main voluntary organization engaged in the care of the elderly and the poor. Each year we organised a Seminar on Community Care. Our guest speaker on one occasion was Clare Wenger, who presented research into the care of the elderly in rural Wales. This proved most interesting from a comparative point of view and I subsequently kept contact with the Research Unit at the University College of North Wales, Bangor.

My study of the frail elderly soon made me realise how much they depended on their carers. Indeed not only *they* depended on these dedicated people but the whole community depended on them. Were it not for them, the residential sector would most probably be swamped with demand for places.

In the early 1980's, I became aware of the impetus for social justice and equality in the area of Community Care in the British literature on Carers. The work of Land [9] and Finch and Groves [10] pointed out that the carers were almost always women and they were unpaid. What was more, they were frequently *expected* by society to sacrifice careers and work outside the home in order to care for elderly relatives or handicapped children. As well as financial costs, there were heavy costs to their health also, as they carried out the daily grind of caring with, it appeared, little or no help from husbands, children, relatives, or neighbours. Occasionally, the rewards to carers were mentioned but the costs and injustice to women carers were what was mainly emphasised. Since no study of carers had ever been done in Ireland, I became curious to examine the attitudes of carers here.

My interest in the mentally handicapped resulted from taking up an invitation from the Franciscan Sisters of the Divine Motherhood in 1976 to come and reside at their Childrens' Home, St. Mary of the Angels at Beaufort, nine miles from my place of work in Killarney. I took on the role of Chaplain there. Soon I became involved in the lives of the children and their parents who were encouraged to visit regularly. The complex included a school which was attended by children from the Home and others who came in buses as day pupils from a wide area round about. In 1983 I

4

published an article on the gifts of the handicapped and on their place in the Christian Community [11]. The work of Jean Vanier had a major influence on me in this area.

The mothers were almost always the principal carers of the handicapped children and I soon realised their great need for support from family and community in their difficult caring role. In fact, very little had been published on the care of the handicapped here [12,13].

It was from this background that the idea formed and grew of a comparative study of the carers of the frail elderly and the mentally handicapped in the Diocese of Kerry. It combined my own two main areas of interest, it followed fairly logically from my earlier research and it allowed me to break new ground in social research in Ireland. So, here I am, eighteen years on, adding my own contribution to "the literature" of Social Administration. I hope it will be read or at least examined!

'NOTES'
1. Mother Teresa of Calcutta, "Sayings of the Seventies" *Observer*, compiled by Cross, C. London.
2. Clifford, D., 1975, "The Public, the Client and the Social Services", *Social Studies*, Maynooth.
3. Clifford, D., (a) "Stigma and the Perception of Social Security Services", *Policy and Politics*, Vol. 3 No. 3
4. Clifford, D., 1975 (b), "The Poor in Town and Country", *Social Studies*, Vol. 4, No. 1
5. Hadley, R., Webb, A., and Farrell, C., 1975, *Across the Generations,* George Allen and Unwin, London
6. Clifford, D., 1979, "How Lonely the Aged?", *Intercom,* Vol. 10 No. 10, Catholic Communications Institute, Dublin
7. Clifford, D. 1980, "Old age hath yet his honour and his toil", *The Furrow,* Vol, 31 No. 9
8. Clifford, D., 1983 (b) "And ready to greet Him when He comes again?", - Attitudes of the elderly to death.
9. Land, H., 1978, "Who cares for the family?", *Journal of Social Policy,* Vol. 7 Part 3
10. Finch, J., and Groves, D., 1980, "Community Care and the Family: A Case of Equal Opportunity", *Journal of Social Policy,* Vol. 9 No. 2 pp.487-514
    Finch, J., and Groves, D., (eds.), 1983, *A Labour of Love,* Routledge and Kegan Paul, London
11. Clifford, D., 1983 (a), "This is my ball and you can play with it", *The Furrow,* Vol. 34 No. 7
12. "Major Issues on Planning Services from Mentally and Physically Handicapped Persons", 1981, *National Economic and Social Council,* Government Publications, Dublin
13. "Community Care Services: An Overview", 1987, *National Economic and Social Council,* Government Publications, Dublin.

2 The Irish context

I shall now seek to situate the study within the Irish context. I shall briefly outline the historic background, the demographic patterns and the development of the social services for the elderly and the handicapped, with special reference to the Health Board area in which the study was conducted.

Richard Titmuss [1] once compared the social services of a modern industrial society to a train journey. His point was that the social services are integral to a modern State and not "things apart" or of "marginal interest". "They are not things one sees out the train window, they are part of the journey itself". Continuing his analogy, the Irish train has, over the past one hundred and fifty years or more, run parallel to its English counterpart. It was under British Rail until 1921. Although it is a much shorter train it has met with much the same problems as the English train, over-crowding, delays and breakdowns. In the very recent past, carriages have been removed. The Irish train drivers and passengers have always kept a close eye on the progress or otherwise of the British trains. Very occasionally, the Irish have been ahead.

To understand the social services in Ireland today, one has to begin with the Poor Law Ireland Act 1838 and follow its subsequent history. [2] The new Poor Law Act of 1834 was imposed on Ireland despite the fact that the Irish Commission specifically recommended against its introduction. George Nichols, on visiting the Country briefly, rejected this recommendation and introduced the Workhouse System throughout the land.

This was Ireland's first statutory social service and within a few years one hundred and sixty three workhouses had been built. As in England, the severity of the Workhouse System was gradually modified over the years but to-day's social services for the elderly, handicapped, children and mentally ill branched out from its main line. So too did the income maintenance service.

The Famine of 1846 and 1847 so overwhelmed the Workhouse System that police frequently had to push back starving crowds who begged for admission in these years. A temporary relaxation of the workhouse test was forced upon the Poor Law Commissioners and outdoor relief was granted as a temporary measure through the Irish Poor Relief Extension Act of 1847 or the Soup Kitchen Act as it was popularly called. In fact, this temporary concession was never revoked and the outdoor relief of that time became the Home Assistance service when the Irish Government took over in 1921. This continued to be the main income maintenance system for the very poor until it was further modified by the Supplementary Welfare Act 1975. With the foundation of the Irish Free State in 1922, the workhouses were re-named County Homes and became the residential homes for the elderly poor. It was not until 1968 that the Inter-Departmental Committee on the Care of the Aged advocated that, "the concept of County Homes should be abandoned".

In the health area the pressure from famine and accompanying cholera brought about the Dispensary System for the whole country. The Medical Charities Act of 1851 set up seven hundred and twenty three Dispensary Districts each having a General Practitioner. This gave the sick poor, free medical care and free medicines at their homes or at the dispensary. The very sick were moved to Fever Hospitals, which were in or near the Workhouses. This service remained virtually unchanged until 1970 when the Health Act of that year provided a Choice of Doctor Scheme. From the dispensaries, a Domiciliary Midwifery Service developed in 1859 which was not subject to the Workhouse Test. This, in turn, had some influence on the development of the State Hospital Service and the area of preventive health. County Infirmaries, small local hospitals, grew side by side with Workhouse Union Hospitals. The Workhouse Hospitals were open to the sick also without the Workhouse Test from 1862 onwards.

The break-up of the mixed workhouse took place somewhat earlier in Ireland than it did in England with the boarding-out of children through the Relief of the Destitute Poor in Ireland Act of 1862. The mentally handicapped began to be rescued from the workhouses also with the founding of Stewart's Hospital in Dublin in 1869. It still cares for this group.

The services which branched out from the mainline Poor Law received minor adjustments when the Irish Free State was

8

founded in 1922 and occasional re-adjustments up to 1970. The 1960's saw the first up-turn of the Irish economy for more than a century. This was the result of a boom in the world economy as well as the policy of inducing foreign investment and foreign industries to Ireland. Emigration, which had been a constant drain on the population since the Famine, began to be reversed for the first time in the early 1970s. From 1973 to 1979 there was a net immigration with the return of many who had gone to England or America in the forties and fifties. The population, which had consistently fallen from 1847 to 1971, began to increase for the first time. Some of the newly created wealth was invested in the Free Education Scheme 1966 and the Free School Transport Scheme 1967 for the Post-Primary sector.

But it was in the area of Health that the most important developments took place from the point of view of this study. The Health Act 1970 [3] rationalised the health and community services. It took under its wing the General Hospitals, the Special Hospitals for the handicapped and the mentally ill, as well as Community Care, which includes the personal social services for the elderly, the handicapped and the mentally ill. The 1970 Health Act was based on the recommendations of four separate Reports : (a) The White Paper on *The Health Services and their Further Development,* 1966 [4]; (b) *The Commission of Inquiry on Mental Hendicap 1965 [5];* (c) *The Inter-Departmental Committee on Care of the Aged 1968 [6];* (d) *The Commission of Inquiry on Mental Illness 1966* [7].

It is interesting to search out the references to Community Care in these influential documents. The White Paper on *The Health Services and their Further Development,* which was the blue-print for the 1970 Health Act, said:
"the Government's general aim is to encourage old people to stay at home and to endeavour to ensure that assistance will be available where needed to enable them to do so without causing hardship to the aged or too heavy a burden on their relatives. Primarily, this assistance will form part of the ordinary pattern of the health services... and this should adequately meet the medical and allied needs of most of old people."

The *Commission of Inquiry on Mental Handicap* had this to say:
"It is accepted as a general principle that community care (i.e. care provided outside residential centres) is therapeutically better for a handicapped person, permits of a fuller development of his personality and avoids the difficulty of adjustments to normal life which is frequently experienced after prolonged care in a residential centre. It is desirable, therefore, that community care should be provided so that, where possible, the mentally handicapped can be retained in their own homes or in suitable family care."

The *Inter-Departmental Committee on Care of the Aged* was unequivocal on the need for community facilities and the avoidance of institutional care:

"The vast majority of the aged live in the community and many families make great sacrifices to look after their aged relatives. Even with such sacrifices it is beyond the power of the family in most cases to provide for all the needs of the aged – these needs can be met only by a partnership between the family and the voluntary organisations... so the Committee's recommendations regarding the services which should be provided are based on the belief that it is better and probably much cheaper to help the aged to live in the community than to provide for them in hospitals or other institutions."

The *Report of the Commission of Inquiry on Mental Illness,* 1966, recommended a movement away from custodial care to "rehabilitation and restoration to the community as far as possible". In this way they were giving official recognition to a trend which was already well under way as the total number of patients in Mental Hospitals had fallen from 21,075 in 1958 to 15,392 at the time of the Report with a corresponding increase in out-patient treatments over the same period.

Both the Committee on the Care of the Aged and the Committee on Mental Handicap were well aware that some institutional care would continue to be needed. The Care of the Aged Committee advocated moving away from the large County Home institutions and the provision of Welfare Homes for the ambulant with Long-Stay Hospitals for those who needed long-term care. They recommended that each area should have a Geriatric Assessment Unit. Likewise, the Commission of Inquiry on Mental Handicap realised that extra places would be needed in residential homes for children who needed to have some early training or schooling.

A second important emphasis in all these Reports was the role of the voluntary bodies. The White Paper on the Health Services stated:

"Voluntary Organizations can often provide the most effective home aid. It is important that their efforts should be encouraged by support and assistance from Public Authorities, and, if all the services are to be provided effectively then there should be close co-ordination between those working voluntarily and appropriate Public Officials."

The Report on the Care of the Aged recommended that:

"Local Authorities should take an active role in encouraging voluntary bodies providing services for the aged and should support them financially."

It also recommended that Social Service Councils should be set up to achieve co-ordination of statutory and voluntary services and disseminate information in regard to the available services and should foster the development of community services.

A further Report by McKinsey, *Towards Better Health Care* 1970/1971 [8], recommended that the Programme Manager for Community Care would "communicate the nature of the target of the community care programmes and agree with the heads of voluntary agencies on the funds they are to receive to ensure that there is agreement about specific contributions the voluntary agencies will make to reach these targets and to encourage the effective operation and co-ordination of these organizations".

The voluntary sector [9] has always been very strong in Ireland. The religious organizations and others have played a major part in the provision of services for the poor, the elderly and the disabled. After the 1970 Health Act many areas have voluntary Care of the Aged Committees, meals on wheels services, visitation services and so on. These are frequently funded by the Health Board to provide the services.

In the area of mental handicap, the major part of provision is through Religious Orders who have run the residential homes and very often provided the day-care services as well. These Orders have usually had the support of groups like Parents and Friends of the Mentally Handicapped. The Orders have received most of their funding from the Department of Health since the 1970 Health Act. Sometimes, they employ Social Workers who are again funded through the Department of Health. Members of these Religious Orders can be involved at the policy-making level within the Department of Health. It is they who have pioneered advances in the service including the provision of small group homes, workshops and training centres and the supervision of flats for adult mentally handicapped.

A Report commissioned by the National Economic and Social Council and carried out on their behalf by Sheila O'Connor, *Community Care: an Overview,* [10] summed up the assumptions which ran through all the Reports mentioned above.

"(1) Community Care is better than institutional care;
(2) Community Care is probably cheaper;
(3) The voluntary sector has a significant contribution to make and it should be fostered."

She goes on to point out that the commitment to Community Care did not result in increased resources to that sector. The share of the total expenditure n Community Care actually fell from 23.4 per cent in 1976 to 22.2 per cent in 1985. During that time, the share of the General Hospital Programme increased from 48 per cent to 51.2 per cent. However, the programme for the handicapped, including mentally and physically handicapped, rose from 7.6 per cent to 9.9 per cent during the same period. It is generally recognised that the General Hospital and District Hospital systems have been over-used and that, because they are seen as important sources of employment they continue to take the

lion's share of the available finances. When local
hospitals are closed, even small sub-acute hospitals, there
is always strong public protest. The people see the closure
of their hospitals as a blow to the health services at local
level. But when cutbacks took place in the health services
with the closure of many hospitals over the past three
years, instead of an extension of Community Care, which one
would expect there were severe cutbacks in this sector also.

Services for the elderly in the community

The two main services relevant to the elderly in the
community are those of the Public Health Nurse and the Home
Help service. There is, of course, the General Practitioner
service which replaces the old Dispensary Doctor with the
Choice of Doctor Scheme. All elderly who have the non-
contributory old age pension are entitled to a medical card,
to free visits from their general practitioner and to free
drugs from the chemist. Forty per cent of the population as
a whole have these free services at the present time.
The social workers who are employed by the regional Health
Boards tend to spend almost all their time with child care
and with family problems. A number of social workers are
also employed by the Religious Orders in the mentally
handicapped area. But the Social Work Service does not
reach the elderly.
In their case the public health nurse is the key person.
She gives nursing care where necessary and is usually the
person who organises home help and acts as the referral
agent to hospitals, day care centres and welfare homes. The
public health nurses are a long established service and now
number 1,153 with additional superintendent public health
nurses in each County. The public health nurse gives
intensive care to 3 per cent of the over sixty fives
throughout the country. The ratio of 1:2,616 population was
recommended by the Working Party on the Workload of Public
Health Nurses in 1975. The ratio varies greatly from one
Health Board area to another, however. For example, it
stands at 1:2,233 in County Leitrim and at 1:3,014 in Dublin
City. The ratio in the Southern Health Board area, where
this study was done, is 1:4,191, the highest of all the
Health Board areas in this respect. The variations would
seem to have very little to do with variations in actual
need. The reverse may well be the case. O'Connor stated
that they were markedly under-staffed in some areas. With
the recent cutbacks in the health services the training of
public health nurses has come almost to a standstill.

The Home Help Service

The 1970 Health Act empowered but did not require Health
Boards to provide a Home Help Service. Prior to 1970, some

local authorities operated their own schemes but on the introduction of the 1970 Health Act, the Minister for Health allocated funds for this purpose to the Health Boards. Voluntary agencies have been very much involved in this area also. It would seem that considerable flexibility is allowed in the manner in which the Home Help Service is organized in the different areas.

In practice, almost all the home helps are part-time. In some of the Health Board areas, neighbours are given a small payment to provide a lunch and do some housework for an old person next door. In the Southern Health Board area various pilot schemes are in operation. In one, a local woman, usually a housewife, has a group of four or five elderly people whom she visits a few times a week. She is supervised by a Home Help Organizer who recruits the home helps. The results seem promising in this particular rural area. The public health nurse is the one who organises and supervises the Scheme in other areas.

In 1983, 2 per cent of those over sixty five were receiving home help and 75 per cent of the recipients were living alone. O'Connor sees the Home Help Service as very inadequate. She found it particularly difficult to get precise information on the extent and nature of the help given by voluntary bodies, volunteers and neighbours. She found that the level of training, support and remuneration were generally uneven and unsatisfactory. There were large variations in resource distribution. As well as this, she pointed out, "at present, the Home Help Service is available almost exclusively to elderly people living alone. There is considerable reluctance to provide the service to people living with relations. This reflects the widespread reluctance, not only in Ireland but also in Britain, to support caring relatives".[12]

There are a number of other services which are worth mentioning briefly. The over sixty sixes who are in receipt of the non-contributory old age pension are entitled to free travel on public transport, to free television licences and to free rental on their telephones. There are fuel allowances and electricity allowances for those who live alone. In these areas, I think that the Irish train is somewhat ahead of its British counterpart.

The most recent Report on the care of the aged came from a Working Party appointed by the Minister of Health in 1986 with the following terms of reference:

"Accepting that the overall objectives of services for the elderly are:-
(a)   to enable the elderly person to live at home, where possible, at an optimum level of health and independence,
(b)   to enable those who cannot live at home to receive treatment, rehabilitation as near as possible to home.

the Working Party is asked to review:
(i)   the role and function of existing health and
        welfare services in serving these objectives,
(ii)   the appropriateness of existing health and welfare
        services,
(iii)   the comparative effectiveness, efficiency and cost
        of alternative models and settings,
(iv)   the planning norms for services both residential
        and community."

The membership of the Working Party included civil servants, medical, psychological and social work personnel and administrators of Community Care in the Health Boards, a geriatrician and a representative of the National Council for the Aged. Their findings were presented to the Minister for Health in October 1988 with an accompanying letter which included the following three points:
(a)   that the dignity and independence of the elderly
        can best be achieved by enabling them to continue
        to live at home with, if necessary, support
        services provided by the State;
(b)   that when ill or disabled, the elderly are
        entitled to the same standard of treatment
        available to the rest of the population even if
        services have to be organized in ways that meet
        particular needs;
(c)   that when admission to long term care is
        unavoidable, such care should be of the highest
        standard and should respect the dignity and
        individuality of the elderly person."

This Report, *The Years Ahead: A Policy for the Elderly,* [13] endorsed fully the commitment of the 1968 Report to the desirability of Community Care but it adverted also to the difficulties experienced by carers and it pointed out ways in which statutory services should be expanded to give more support to carers. It did not advert to O'Connor's criticisms of the services although it proposed detailed policy and financial improvements for the elderly and their carers.

The Kerry Diocese: Area of the present study

The Diocese of Kerry includes all of County Kerry with its population of 120,000 and ten rural parishes of County Cork with a population of 20,000 approximately. It is situated in the south west of Ireland and is within the Southern Health Board region. Together with its central area (the two main towns of Tralee with its population of 20,000 and Killarney with a population of 8,500) there are three peninsulas, Dingle, Iveragh and Castletownbere. These are scenic areas and very popular with tourists but, in common with the greater part of the West and North West of Ireland,

14

these areas have suffered greatly from unemployment and emigration and migration to the cities. The population of County Kerry has constantly declined since the Famine. In 1901 it was 165,726; in 1926 it had fallen to 149,127 and by 1971 it was at an all time low of 112,722. During the next decade it began to increase for the first time to 120,281 in 1979, but even then it was the two main towns of Tralee and Killarney and their environs which increased, while the three peninsulas continued to lose, if at a slightly slower rate.

Despite the high birth rate throughout all the years, emigration depleted the ranks of those between 18 and 25 one generation after another. This leads to a disproportionate percentage of over sixty fives in many rural areas. In Ireland as a whole 10.7 per cent of the population are over sixty five. In the rural counties it is much higher. County Leitrim has 17.6 per cent over sixty five, County Mayo 15.9 per cent, County Roscommon 15.6 per cent, County Sligo 14.2 per cent, County Donegal 14 per cent, County Kerry 14 per cent. County Kildare, on the other hand, which is situated near Dublin has only 7 per cent over sixty five. Within County Kerry, which has 14 per cent over sixty five, there are great variations from the towns to the rural areas. In the Dingle peninsula, 16 per cent are over sixty five, in Iveragh peninsula 18 per cent are over sixty five. The small parish of Tahilla, near Sneem, has 28 per cent. The south coast of England or the retirement areas of Florida would find it difficult to match this figure. When one adds to this the fact that County Kerry has the fourth lowest density of population in Ireland one begins to have an idea of the challenges which face the delivery and provision of social services in these far-flung parts. Most of them do not have train services or even regular bus services. Many of the elderly live a long distance from towns and from their G.P.s. In the Western Health Board, for example, two fifths of the elderly live more than five miles from their G.P. This would be true also of much of the Southern Health Board area. Voluntary bodies tend to be centred in towns also and services like meals-on-wheels and transport to and from day-care centres turn out to be very expensive. The studies of Wenger and her co-workers in North Wales describe similar problems of distance and inaccessibility.

Apart from a few passing references and the most recent Report (1988), very little has been mentioned in the Irish literature about the need for supporting the carers. It has been acknowledged that families very often make great sacrifices to look after an elderly or handicapped member, but nowhere was the support of the carer mentioned as a priority. Neither was there any reference to the fact that it is mostly women who are carers. It was pointed out by O'Connor that the Home Help Service, in particular, is centred almost exclusively on the elderly who live alone. She also points out that, "basic to the promotion of individual welfare is information on the range of needs, not only of dependent people, but also of those who are providing informal care, in particular, families. Information on dependent people in terms of services that facilitate community living is limited. Information on informal care and on the motivation and expressed needs of those who provide it has not been collected until very recently. Similarly, information on the voluntary sector in Ireland is limited". [14]

In fact, in 1987, the National Council for the Aged, an organization set up by the Irish Government, examined the extent and nature of caring for the elderly in two studies [15]. No comparable study has yet been attempted on carers of the handicapped. In respect to the literature at any rate, the Irish train has fallen greatly behind its British counterpart. I am happy, however, to be on board and urging the driver to speed up a little!

'NOTES'

1. Titmuss, R.M., 1958, *"Essays on the Welfare State"*, Unwin University Books, London, Preface.
2. Burke, H., 1987, *The People and the Poor Law in 19th Century Ireland,* W.E.B. (Women's Education Bureau), England, gives an account of the development of social services from the Poor Law Act (Ireland) 1838, the first public social service. Its foundations are still discernible in the services to-day.
3. Hensey, B., 1972, *The Health Services of Ireland,* 2nd. ed., The Institute of Public Administration, Dublin, covers the different developments in health policy up to the 1970 Health Act.
4. *The Health Services and their Future Development,* 1966, Government Publications, Stationery Office, Dublin.
5. *Report of the Commission of Inquiry on Mental Handicap,* 1965, Government Publications, Stationery Office, Dublin.
6. *The Care of the Aged,* 1968, Report of an Inter-Departmental Committee, Government Publications, Stationery Office, Dublin.
7. *Report of Commission on Mental Illness,* 1966, Government Publications, Stationery Office, Dublin.
8. *Towards a Better Health Care,* 1970, McKinsey & Co. Dublin.
9. See *Directory of Social Service Organizations,* 1980, National Social Service Council, Dublin, for a list of national and local voluntary organizations which help in this field.
10. O'Connor, S., *Community Care Services An Overview:* 1987; National Economic and Social Council, Dublin.
11. *Survey of Workload of Public Health Nurses,* 1975. Report of a Working Party, Government Publications, Stationery Office, Dublin.
12. O'Connor, S., 1987, op.cit., p.54
13. Report of the Working Party on Services for the Elderly (1988), *The Years Ahead: A Policy for the Elderly,* Government Publications, Stationery Office, Dublin.
14. O'Connor, S., 1987, op.cit., p.33
15. (a) O'Connor, J., Smith, E., and Whelan, B., *Caring for the Elderly,* Part I, *A Study of Carers at Home and in the Community,* 1988, National Council for the Aged, Dublin.
   (b) O'Connor, J., Smith, E., and Ruddle H., 1988 *Caring for the Elderly,* Part II, *The Caring Process, A Study of the Carers in the Home,* National Council for the Aged, Dublin.

3 Review of literature

Community Care like other concepts in Social Administration such as social class, alienation, social stigma, loneliness and poverty, is elusive, difficult to define or make operational. Perhaps, its vagueness is the cause of its long-standing popularity. When Douglas Houghton stated in the 1950s that, "There are three institutions in Britain about which no hard word can be said, the Crown, the Church and the National Assistance Board", he could, with a little foresight, have included Community Care.

Part of its strength and most of its weakness comes from the pentecostal quality which enables it to be understood by very diverse interest groups, each in its own language and accepted on its own particular terms. It means all things to all people and very particular things to some. The result is an ideal which all accept, but, a reality which has not even remotely lived up to the ideal, thirty years after it began to emerge on an alternative to institutional care.

Nevertheless, the concept has been clarified and developed since it was popularised in relation to the Mental Health Act 1959. And it has been tested in practice in a number of local projects carefully monitored and yielding promising results. Even though it has been a slow developer its time may yet come. Its retarded development was due in no small measure to its near starvation of public finance.

Community Care began as a reaction to and a move away from

the grim Poor Law institutions which became increasingly
unacceptable after World War II.   Perhaps, the horror
aroused by Nazi concentration camps played a part in the
wish to replace large institutions of all kinds, whether for
children, the mentally ill, the handicapped or the elderly.
The publication of Townsend's "*The Last Refuge*", [1] the
scandal at Ely Hospital, Cardiff, Bowlby's "*Child Care and
the Growth of Love*" [2], Robb's "*Sans Everything*" [3],
Morris's "*Put Away*", all seemed to confirm the belief that
the sooner such institutions were demolished the better.
    Webb and Wistow [5] rightly situate this move within a
more complex framework: "The first post war commitment was
to move away from the institutional heritage of the Poor Law
by building new smaller homes.   The second development was
the expansion of domiciliary and day-care services: small
dwellings for one or two person households and sheltered
housing, as alternatives to residential homes.   The third
was concern to reduce the need for long-stay care of the
elderly in hospital and to avoid the silting up of beds in
both acute and geriatric wards.   In the case of mental
illness and handicap, this issue of hospital beds was at the
heart of policy from the very beginning."   Then there was
the further objective of avoiding unnecessary public
expenditure on formal services.
    One ought also to mention the discovery of the phenomenon
of "institutionalisation" [6] as a kind of social paralysis
which grows on the inmates of large institutions after some
years confinement.   So there was, what Webb and Wistow
describe as a "confluence" of factors, at work in the
proposed move from institutional to Community Care.
    As early as 1961, Titmuss [7] was alerting the public to
the dangers of sending patients out of hospitals into a
community which did not have anything like adequate
domiciliary services.   They were "off the books" as far as
the health services were concerned but they were often
abandoned and uncared for.   In a purple passage Titmuss
described Community Care as "the everlasting cottage-garden
trailer".   He worried, "we may pontificate about the
philosophy of Community Care; we may feel righteous because
we have a civilised Mental Health Act on the statute book
but unless we are prepared to examine at this level of
concrete reality what we mean by Community Care, we are
simply indulging in wishful thinking.   To scatter the
mentally ill in the community before we have made adequate
provision for them is not a solution; in the long run even
for H.M. Treasury...   At present we are drifting into a
situation in which by shifting the emphasis from institution
to community - a trend which in principle and with
qualification we all applaud - we are transferring the care
of the mentally ill from trained staff to untrained staff,
ill-equipped staff or no staff at all."
    An important clarification of the concept of Community
Care came with Bayley's [8] distinction between Care *in* the
Community and Care *by* the Community.   This was to give, as

he put it, "more substance" to the term. Care *in* the Community was the Government's official services operating outside large institutional settings, conceived of and operated independently of the people who happened to live in the area round about. Care *by* the Community meant that ordinary people in the community were part of the caring process and were involved as family, neighbours, voluntary bodies or volunteers. "A view of Community Care which takes account of the complexity of human organization and the realities of our political and administrative system entails consideration of society at four levels: (a) the client and his family which merges into (b) the social network of family, kin and neighbours (c) the social worker and the local authority services which may or may not include (d) some form of residential care". Here we have a continuum of care between informal and formal sectors of Care and a recognition that residential care formed an integral part of any comprehensive service. Bayley hoped to develop a sensitive interweaving of formal and informal but possibly underestimated the difficulties involved.

Abrams [9] was soon to deny that there was any such continuum, in fact he maintained, in his influential article of 1977, that the formal system tended to undermine and erode the informal. He cited various studies to prove that community or neighbourhood care almost always boiled down to care by family or kin. Neighbours came a very poor third according to Abrams. He was critical of the romantic notions of natural good neighbourliness as portrayed in the Bethnal Green accounts of Young and Wilmott, [10] attributing this to the fact that they were more often kin than neighbours. Indeed the same charge has been made about the account of mutuality in the Ireland of the 1930s in Arensburg and Kimball's classic study, where again, many of the neighbours who exchanged help were, in fact, kin [11]. Abrams maintained that Community Care just does not happen in the modern setting. Although he modified this view in the light of his later studies, [12] Abrams' challenge in this area was valuable since it forced social scientists to question any easy assumptions about the automatic existence of Community Care. Henceforth it could not be presumed to exist unless proven by research. For Abrams [13] the situation was that, "...we must start off from the finding that in the typical social setting of contemporary British society, Community Care is typically volatile, spasmodic and unreliable; very much *not* a social fact."

He saw the only realistic prospect for Community Care as existing within family and kin in the first place and in the second within moral communities such as Churches. The motivation for such care, he claimed, would be empathy, sense of duty and reciprocity. This latter resulted in a "calculative involvement" on the part of helpers. "Reciprocity is at the heart of the caring relationship in Community Care. One can only wonder at the extent to which the question of what the caring agent gets in return for

20

care given has been neglected in earlier research. *"Across the Generations* takes a useful step in this direction as far as volunteers working with the elderly are concerned. And there are other indications that caring for others can be an important means of obtaining care for oneself for certain groups - especially the chronically underemployed middle aged of both sexes - and that members of such groups are thus available as potential caring agents. But we need to know a good deal more about the rewards for care."

Abrams thus rejected the notion of Care by the Community as an army of neighbours rallying around automatically. This simply does not happen any more in a culture where privacy is such a prized value. So, for all practical purposes he narrowed down Community Care to the family in the first instance then to kin and finally to moral communities. The social division of care had gone a further step.

About the same time, Moroney [14] undertook a very influential investigation into Community Care policies in Britain and concluded also that the family bore the main burden of Community Care. He examined the existing data on families with frail elderly dependants and mentally handicapped children and he supplemented this information with interviews with academics, social service administrators and families. He posed three fundamental questions: (a) Are families less able and willing to care for their dependent members than they were? (b) If more families want to get rid of their dependent what are the likely costs in terms of social policy? (c) How far is social policy itself influencing family attitudes and responsibilities?

His conclusion was that the social services in Britain were not supporting care within the family. They tended to "substitute" for it when it was absent or when it had broken down under the burden. The residential sector swallowed up the major part of the budget for a small percentage of the elderly and mentally handicapped while domiciliary services were directed predominantly to those who had no family network. Meanwhile, the families who were struggling to look after a dependent person were given no help until their capacity to continue had been eroded or collapsed altogether. The social services behaved somewhat like a life-guard who looked on from the shore while one swimmer struggled to rescue another and only came to their assistance when both had gone under. He then fished them out and undertook to revive them both.

In fact, Moroney [15] subsequently expressed the view that the social services penalised families if they cared and rewarded them when they ceased caring by taking over full-time care of the cared-for person and sometimes the carer as well. He laid the blame in part on the social worker's training on the pathology of the family, but also on a deep-rooted ambivalence about the family's role. This conclusion was borne out by the Equal Opportunities Commission (1982)

[16]: "There is considerable evidence to suggest that the failure to consider family needs as well as those of the dependent creates such problems for the carer that she may eventually be unable to continue caring. Isaac's study revealed that less than half of all patients admitted to a geriatric hospital in Glascow were hospitalised solely for medical reasons; the ill-health of the carer, caused by the prolonged strain of caring, or her inability to give up work, were more significant factors."

When Community Care, understood as care within the family, became part of the conventional wisdom in the early 1980s, the Conservative Government seized upon it eagerly. Mrs. Thatcher and her Ministers quickly assumed the high moral ground with exhortations to self-reliance, non interference by the State in the family domain and in a short time their moral tone was higher even than that of the bishops! For example, one distinguished prelate only avoided being sent to Coventry by the fact that he happened to be the Bishop of that city already! He had merely pointed out that the State had definite obligations to the deprived. Mr. Patrick Jenkins [17] summarised the Conservative Government's philosophy of Community Care for his benefit and for others who had ears to hear. "There has been a tendency to believe that as statutory services grow, as more services are provided by the public authorities, so the community can safely entrust their cares and their concerns for the elderly and others in need to the town hall and Whitehall and need not themselves bother much. I was a little saddened to see a letter in 'The Times' last week from a distinguished prelate arguing precisely this fallacy. He argued that the nation's failure to afford the level of statutory services we might wish betokened a lack of Christian compassion on the part of the authorities. He simply could not be more wrong. His letter seemed to me ... to (say) ... that caring is the job of the State and not of the people ... The primary responsibility rests in the community; the statutory services are there to provide a framework, a back-up and social help in particular circumstances. It really is not and cannot ever be the other way round - the statutory services as the central provider with a few volunteers here and there to back them up. That simply does not represent the reality and we delude ourselves if we think that that's what it could or should be."

Here one has come from the acknowledgment of the *fact* that most care of dependants actually comes from within the family to the assertion that the family *ought* therefore to do all the caring. Community Care as located in the family then becomes a lofty excuse for the State's cutting back on services and ignoring carers until they qualify for "special help in particular circumstances".

Mr. Jenkins spelled out this philosophy even more fully on another occasion. [18] "The Government's approach to the personal social services is founded on the simple fact that the frontline providers of social care always have been and will continue to be, the family and the community". And according to Mrs. Thatcher herself; "... it all really starts in the family, because not only is the family the most important means through which we show our care for others. It's the place where each generation learns its responsibility towards the rest of society... I think that the statutory services can only play their part successfully if we don't expect them to do for us things that we could be doing for ourselves." Walker [19] notes that this ideology has been translated into policy towards the elderly: "It is the role of public authorities to sustain and where necessary develop - but never displace informal and voluntary care and support. Care *in* the community must increasingly mean care *by* the community."

So by the late 1970s "Community Care" had come to be identified very much as family care. The 1980s were to usher in another searching analysis of caring in the work of a host of feminist writers beginning with Land [20], then Finch and Groves [21, 22] and continuing up to the present time. These writers bring the debate from the *social* division of caring within the community to the *sexual* division within the family. Here one finds that, for a variety of reasons, the main burden of caring almost invariably falls on the shoulders of a female carer. Our detective work to discover the "real carer" has taken us from vague notions of community, to the family and finally to a woman within the family. Had we borne in mind the ancient rule of thumb for readers of detective stories, "cherchez la femme", years of searching could have been avoided! While this obviously is an over-simplification, it does strip down the notions of Community Care to its essentials. This helps to clarify. Research does redress the balance somewhat in favour of family members, spouses and other relatives, neighbours and friends.

The main arguments of the feminist writers are valid. The majority of carers are women, they do not generally get the degree of help which they ought from family members, from neighbours or from domiciliary services. Their labour is largely unpaid or poorly acknowledged. Welfare payments, where granted to carers, are mere tokens of the work done. Graham [23] summed up the carers' contribution: "it is only visible when it is not done".

It is surprising now to find that so little attention was paid to the social and emotional costs to the carers. Part of the reason was that the emphasis in the care of the elderly was on the elderly who were in institutions or those living alone in the community. It took a long time to realise that the majority of the very frail elderly were being cared for in the family. Titmuss [24] did advert to "hard pressed daughters" who may themselves be pensioners or nearly retirement age and Abrams [25] wrote of carers who "experienced anger and frustration". He advocated urgent study of the needs of carers which he described as "peculiarly unexplored territory".

Seldom has the call for research and clarification been met so swiftly, though Abrams did not live to see more than the beginnings of the analysis and research on the needs of carers and on the social costs and rewards of caring which came mainly from feminist writers in the 1980s. This analysis situated the joys and sorrows of carers within the overall context of injustice to women within the family, in the workplace and within Western society generally. This injustice is deeply rooted in the culture and traditions of Western societies the feminists claim. The traditional notions of family and community no longer correspond to the reality of life in urban settings. Yet social services and income maintenance services still operate on the assumption that nothing has changed.

Finch and Groves and others maintain that the assumptions shared by politicians and policy makers in relation to the family are based on the outmoded Judeo-Christian model of family. There is also the "cultural designation" of women as the natural carers and this remains very strong. The converse is that men are not expected to act as carers. It is not generally assumed that they will be able or that they ought to be able to look after their elderly or handicapped relatives. The financial dependence of women on men within the family is another result of these outdated assumptions about the role of women and this applies particularly to female carers who are frequently forced to forego work outside home because of their caring role. Caring thus boils down for the feminist to unpaid labour in the home. Thus the word "community" is for Wilson [26] "an ideological portmanteau for a reactionary, conservative ideology which oppresses women by silently confining them... I suggest that we abandon the word community altogether – it is only one of the veils of illusion in which we are cocooned."

The State, through its income maintenance policies and its domiciliary services, the argument continues, serves to reinforce traditional ideas of family, community and women's dependent role. One is back to something very like the philosophy of the Conservatives on the obligation of the family to care, except that the family now reads female carer. Finch and Groves [27] expressed it as follows: "Thus community policies ... can easily become policies which create a moral imperative to care, imposed upon women to whom nature and chance have assigned a frail or handicapped relative. Such a situation is clearly disadvantageous to women in terms of the promotion of equal opportunities." The consensus of feminist writers is that the model of family on which present-day social policies are based is as outdated as the notion of "village life" as sometimes looked back to with nostalgia. This refers to the notion of the caring community based on close personal relationships, constructive methods of social control, the passing on of wisdom between the generations, mutual respect and patriarchal authority. Wilson [28] relates these ideas to

the sociology of Talcott Parsons on family and community and
the Chicago school generally which postulate a polarity
between family values and urban values. These in turn, are
reflected in Parsons' description of the division of roles
within the family between husbands and wives. The man is
moulded by the rational formal world of work which he
inhabits while the woman's role is one of warmth, feeling
and the intimacy of the mother and home-maker. This has led
to the notion that women are "natural" carers while men are
neither suited by nature or training to the caring role.
Wilson describes this view as a "deeply conservative view of
a necessary polarity between the sexes" and says it was
already fully fledged in the Victorian period. Because of
this antiquated kind of thinking she suggests that the
concept of community as used by social administrators,
policy planners and politicians "is riddled with reactionary
implications especially with a vision of family which is
incompatible with women's liberation."
The Equal Opportunities Commission (1984) came to much the
same conclusion. It stated: "In recent years a number of
important studies have ... examined the reality of Community
Care and the demands placed upon the carers. These have
been reviewed in two earlier publications, *Caring for the
Elderly and the Handicapped* and *Who Cares for the Carers?*
It is clear from the evidence presented in these, firstly
that the costs (physical, social and emotional) to the
carers are often very great and, secondly, that these costs
are by no means evenly distributed across the community.
The majority of carers are women, who are often coping alone
with severely dependent elderly relatives to the detriment
of their own health, their standard of living and their
social lives. Many carers receive little help from other
family members or the community and most receive little or
no support from services. In the face of an increasing
burden of dependency between now and the end of the century,
it is essential to ensure that the available resources are
used to the best advantage. This should not mean exploiting
those individuals who are prepared to care". [29]
The Commission went on to describe the cultural
expectations which regard the man's wish to remain at home
and care for a dependent relative and the woman's wish to
work outside the home rather than care for a relative as
equally "abnormal". "To what extent", asks the Commission,
"are society in general and the Health and Social Services
in particular, re-inforcing and perpetuating traditional
values and social roles in caring relationships and is this
working to the detriment of women carers?" [30] The studies
of the Equal Opportunities Commission (1984) confirmed that
the majority of carers are women (59 per cent) and that they
receive little help generally from husbands, family or
anyone else. "As long as they were prepared to continue
without complaint other relatives and friends did not
enquire too closely. When help was provided it was usually
from close relatives such as husbands. [31]

142, 192

The Commission also reported discrimination against women carers in favour of elderly living alone and in favour of men carers by the domiciliary services including home helps and meals on wheels. There is a presumption that women can cope and that men cannot which is mediated by a set of expectations that it is appropriate for women to undertake a heavier burden of care than might be expected of men.

Since 60 per cent of women under retirement age are economically active in Britain the question of opportunity cost and wages foregone because of caring is an important one. Baldwin and Glendenning [32] examined it and found that, "severe disability in a child is associated with marked differences in women's participation rates, hours of work and earnings; and these disparities increase as the child gets older." Only 35 per cent of mothers of disabled children were economically active as compared with 59 per cent of mothers in the FES control group. They advocated greater flexibility for carers, male and female, who wish to combine work outside the home with the caring role.

Baldwin [33] did a further study of the extra financial costs to families who care for dependent children at home. This very detailed examination of day to day costs led her to conclude that the financial impact of the child's condition was considerable and pervasive. She advocated increases in benefits and an "expenses benefit" for carers to offset the extra expenses invariably incurred. Baldwin seems to favour a Fabian approach rather than a radical reformation of the system and this is what carers in her study seem to desire also. There remains, however, the conclusion of the Equal Opportunities Commission (1980), "It is socially unjust that those who perform the vital task of caring for the elderly should have to forfeit employment opportunities and employment rights to do so". [34]

Even leaving aside the problem of the costs borne by carers, the balance sheet of Community Care is uncertain. The issue of whether Community Care is necessarily less demanding on the public purse than residential care is complicated. There is no doubt that there has always been an *assumption* on the part of Governments that it is cheaper, certainly in the short run. There can be no doubting that it is more costly to look after an elderly person or handicapped child in a residential setting than it is when he/she is looked after at home without any help or support from social services. This is the care *by* the community, informal care and "its hallmark", according to Webb and Wistow [35], "is that it does not involve the State in expenditure – or is believed to involve only marginal expenditures." When it comes to care *in* the community, where the State is involved in expenditure on various services, the relative costs of such care and full-time residential care are difficult to estimate. This is true mainly because the State has never made adequate services available in the community in terms of personnel such as social workers, public health nurses, home helps and paid volunteers. It is only when the State is prepared to put sufficient money into keeping frail elderly and mentally handicapped children in the community, who have hitherto been forced into residential care, that realistic comparisons can be made. One must face the costs of providing *comparable* levels of care in the community.

The Kent Community Project operated to a budget of two thirds of the cost of residential care for each frail elderly person it kept in the community. They kept within the limits and even had a little to spare in the early years of the experiment. The most recent studies of the Project confirm continued success within these self-imposed financial constraints.[36] Perhaps this should be the target of Governments, but unfortunately when there have been cutbacks in public spending they have affected the Community Care side as much, if not more, than the residential. More often than not in the case of the elderly and the mentally handicapped, as Webb and Wistow[37] point out, "the parents are faced with the choice of placing their child in residential (or hospital) care or carrying on unsupported in the home."

Rimmer[38] argues that if the present philosophy of shifting the burden of care from the State back to the family continues, women will suffer disproportionately. She points out that most of the costs to the carer are never computed in the economics of Community Care. This would involve what Abrams[39] described as a "language for translating psychological costs into cash terms". He believed that if such cost-benefit analysis could be done it would prove that Community Care would prove a great deal more expensive than residential care.

The social costs to the carer include emotional stress, physical fatigue, worry about the cared-for person and the future, curtailment of social life, strain on carers' marriages as well as interference with work outside the home. Bayley[40] documented many of these as early as 1973 and they have been confirmed in recent studies such as that of Nissel and Bonnerjea,[41] who describe how some women had to give up work with the loss of badly needed family income while others tended to combine work and caring which gave rise to patterns of arriving late to work or being worried all day about the elderly cared-for person. Glendenning[42] found a high incidence of loneliness and isolation among carers. The Equal Opportunities Commission (1982) [43] lists these social costs under the headings of emotional, social and effects on employment opportunities. These are set out in detail and they touch upon all the costs already mentioned with the addition of depression, strained family relationships especially between wife and husband, lack of money and lack of space to entertain friends.

While the costs to the carer are amply documented, the rewards to the carer have received considerably less mention in the literature. The balance, Vincent [44] states, is being restored. She points out that, while earlier

27

literature tended to stress the costs of caring to individual women carers, the rewards are beginning to be recognised more in recent times. This is due, she says, to "feminist analyses of female roles and experiences".
In the early literature the rewards rarely received any mention and when they did, they tended to be viewed as the bait which lured the carer into the caring trap. For example, Baldwin and Glendenning:[45] "It would be wrong, however, to overlook the fact that the care of a dependent child has its own compensations and that many women with severely disabled children derive substantial rewards from this specialised task. These pleasures and satisfactions rooted in feelings of love and protectiveness are reinforced by "public opinion", and by ideological values attached to motherhood and the family by contemporary social welfare institutions and practices."
Pitkeathley [46] begins on a promising note: "Because caring can be such a distressing experience it is tempting to begin any account of what carers feel with a long list of distresses but we would do well to remember that caring can bring joy, too, and it can certainly bring happiness in helping carers feel that they are fulfilling a duty or returning love, given to them in the past, or even in just fulfilling an obligation". Then follows an account of a carer who expresses satisfaction in her role of looking after her handicapped daughter: "It may seem a bit odd to you but we still find some fun between us when we remember some funny incident... There are times ... which make it all seem worthwhile..." But Pitkeathley comes in immediately; "These joyful experiences seem rare enough. More frequently carers say, "Caring has made me a physical and mental wreck..." This is the last we hear of rewards.
Graham [47] warns that because of the separate analysis of caring as labour and love by sociologists and psychologists respectively, "its more distinctive and most compelling qualities have been lost". The rewards to caring are among the missing. The Equal Opportunities Commission [48] did mention the rewards: "Despite the social and economic restrictions experienced by carers, there is no doubt that for many people the emotional rewards of caring far outweigh the disadvantages. However, the existence of intangible advantages does not justify the continuation of policies which ignore the basic rights of women..." Mention of rewards is almost always accompanied by immediate qualifications.
Considering the evidence on caring, one would not expect writers to be "over the moon" about the rewards of caring, but, I believe, that the other side of the moon, in this case, the unexplored side of caring, needs to be examined even though it is invisible and "intangible" as the Report put it. Surely the rewards to the carer are one of the main reasons why carers continue to bear such costs? I believe that when they are better understood and fully acknowledged without qualification we will be in a better position to

improve support services for carers.

Recent writers such as Briggs and Oliver [49] describe caring as "the claustrophobic atmosphere of twenty four hour a day servitude" which produces "a tinder-box of resentment, anger and rebellion". Mace and Rabins [50] deliver an American verdict on caring with their title, *The 36-Hour Day*. For Graham [51] it is an "act of female sacrifice and supreme selflessness". The Equal Opportunities Commission [52] concludes its examination of the effects of caring upon the carer: "The rewards of caring are more likely to be forthcoming when the caring role is freely chosen by the carer, and she is welcomed by her charge ..."

An important contribution to clarifying the concept of caring was made by Parker [53]. In a short space he did for "tending" what Bradshaw once did for "need". He identified four practical features: duration, intensity, complexity and prognosis.

(a) *DURATION:* how long the commitment is likely to last must be an important consideration for someone undertaking the caring task. People are naturally cautious about committing themselves to an open-ended caring situation. In informal care, there are no fixed hours, no set times off.

(b) *INTENSITY:* the degree of tending may vary from fixed tasks done once per week to being on all twenty four hours a day to feed, wash, lift and comfort, thus probably interrupting a whole range of other activities such as employment, leisure and education.

(c) *COMPLEXITY:* how far are special skills required? Caring can involve administering special diets, insulin injections, various medicines and coping with confusion and anger in a cared-for person. "Relationships with and around dependent people can become complicated even when the physical tasks are simple".

(d) *PROGNOSIS:* Is more or less care likely to be required as time passes? Parker points out a difference between caring for young and old. In the case of the young a steady reduction in need can be expected while the elderly are likely to deteriorate progressively. "It is crucial to include the idea of prognosis", he concludes.

Parker's searching analysis of the concept of "tending" enables us to appreciate the differences which can exist from one caring situation to another. The degree of variation is enormous. For many, caring is light but for a minority the burden can become unbearable. The carers also vary in age, health and in their motivation. Parker made explicit what must be the doubts and fears of those who face the caring task for the first time.

A number of practical experiments in Community Care have been set up and monitored. The best known is the Kent

Community Care Project mentioned earlier [54]. There is also the Gofal System [55] in North Wales, the patch-based community of Hadley [56] and a variety of good neighbour schemes described by Abrams [57]. These are locally based service delivery systems which provide a more familiar and accessible service to the community than the conventional social services normally do. In all the schemes "natural carers" are identified and supported.

The Kent Community Care project overcomes Parker's problems of "duration" by providing back-up care so that the carers of the frail elderly can take breaks at definite times. Contracts are drawn up with local people to do specific tasks. The elderly were assessed as people requiring residential care before the experiment commenced. The Gofal System involves the same kind of contracts for similar small financial payments. Another unusual feature of the Kent Community Care project is that the social workers were given control over the budget.

This is always a difficult bridge to cross between a Social Service Department and social workers in the field. Administrators are always most reluctant to issue what is suspiciously like an "open cheque" to social workers. The Kent experience was to illustrate this reluctance: "Despite the decentralisation of the budget in terms of allocation it did not prove possible also to decentralise its distribution. Hence a considerable amount of time has been consumed in continuing negotiations with Central Office Treasurer's Department over the administration of contract payments." Such difficulties confirm Abrams' doubts about the existence of a continuum between formal and informal care. There are several bridges to be crossed between professional and lay people and between administrators and both, before understanding and trust can be established. The Kent Community Project seems to have negotiated the crossing successfully in the end.

The upper limit of two-thirds of the cost of corresponding care in a residential home to be spent on any individual client proved to be slightly more than was in fact necessary. But the Kent scheme has a further attraction. It shows clearly that while Community Care is not exactly welfare on the cheap, it is, nevertheless, cheap welfare when compared to the extra cost involved in comparable institutional care. It is at this price or somewhere near it that Community Care must be accepted as a "good buy" by Social Service Departments. Recent indications also confirm that the Kent Community Care Project has been successful in keeping elderly people in the community when they would otherwise have been in residential care. [58] Almost twice as many of the frail elderly in the Project sample were still at home after one year as in the comparison group.

The Gofal Scheme, as described by Wenger, [59] showed how the community began to become involved as the contracted helpers began to be assisted by spouses, children and neighbours. Relatives who had held back lest they become trapped, now came forward when they found that they would not be on their own and left to do everything for the cared-for person.

Such controlled social experiments in Community Care have proved the value of formally assigning helpers manageable tasks which do not overwhelm or isolate them. The small payments are not meant to be more than an incentive, but obviously they count with the helpers and with their network. They prime the pump, as it were.

So Community Care has developed from the vague notion that everybody would be helping everybody, everywhere, at all times, to a situation in which specific people perform well-defined tasks for frail elderly, at set times and for a small payment. Much of the vagueness is banished and with it go many of the doubts and fears.

Before leaving the practical experiments and they are a growing phenomenon both in the U.K. and in the U.S.A. [60], I should like to include an experiment of a different kind. This is the Jean Vanier [61] Community, l'Arche. Here small groups of handicapped people are befriended by "assistants" who are largely unpaid or underpaid and who enter into a relationship of friendship with the handicapped. As Parker noted, "tending beyond the superficial level, is likely to establish close relationships, affection and a sense of obligation. These are not easily abandoned." Vanier and his assistants set out deliberately to foster the growth of the handicapped through sharing a common life. Work, meals, prayer and recreation are in common. Relations with the local community are fostered to counteract prejudice against the handicapped. Being with the handicapped is more important than doing things for them according to Vanier. His work is based on profound respect for the dignity and potential of the handicapped who have their own particular gifts - gifts of the heart mostly, though not exclusively when one considers handicapped people like Christopher Nolan and Davoren Hanna who have written prize-winning poetry and prose despite the most crippling physical disabilities from birth.

Vanier's assistants find that they learn a good deal from their contact with the handicapped and, not least, they learn about themselves and their "brokenness", as Vanier describes their own needs for friendship and search for meaning in their lives. The idiom in Vanier is very different from much of the literature which describes caring as a "burden", "a daily grind, "a bleak form of servitude". According to Vanier, the carer also grows through the experience in the Community. There is a two-way process of enrichment. The handicapped are not written off as useless, the assistants are assumed to have their emotional and social needs too.

Describing his personal experience in the first months after he went to live with two mentally handicapped men near Paris in 1964, Vanier says: "I had to learn that l'Arche was not just my project but also Raphael's and Philippe's and

that many others were to come to l'Arche and put down roots
there. I had to discover something about welcome and
respect for people, something about liberation of hearts and
patience. I had much to learn about myself and my faults
and defects, my need to dominate and command after spending
eight years in the Navy. I had to learn about human growth
and suffering, about sharing and about the ways of God. [62]

Other accounts [63] agree that these communities are
happy. Their only therapy is, "family living together,
where we share, work and pray, suffer and celebrate
together, where we grow together in love, in hope and in
freedom of heart". Such a project involves the risk which
people take when they "venture out from behind their
frontiers and meet others, discover their beauty and learn
from them." "Is this a dream or Utopia?", asks Vanier. The
context is that of close relationships, of belonging. It
involves reciprocity, giving and receiving. It involves
self-sacrifice. But if its costs are high, so are its
rewards. "So the Community takes on a wider meaning. It is
lived not only among its own members but in the larger
community of its neighbourhood, with the poor and with all
those who want to share its hope. So it becomes a place of
reconciliation and forgiveness where each person feels
carried by others and carries them. It is a place of
friendship among those who know that they are weak but know
that they are loved and forgiven. Thus community is a place
of celebration". [64]

Such descriptions would seem far-fetched were it not that
they are now well established in a variety of countries
including France, England, Belgium, Canada, Ireland,
Denmark, India, Haiti, Honduras. While it is clear that
such living demands a degree of commitment not easily given
by the ordinary person, it does highlight a vital dimension
of caring which seems to go largely unnoticed in the other
literature; that of service and sharing within a moral
community as a genuinely self-selected life-style. Vanier's
own life could be described as one of male sacrifice and
supreme selflessness.

But to return to the main literature, the concept of
Community Care has been gradually developed and clarified
over the past thirty years. The practical experiments at
local level have given promising results, initially at
least. The problem has been that Governments have never
been willing to commit the level of finance which would
permit Community Care to reach its potential.

The recent work of Dalley [65] rounds off this literature
review in an intriguing manner. She calls for a return to
"collective care". She reacts against the family and the
"familist ideology" in much the same way as the proponents
of Community Care reacted against Poor Law institutions in
the post Wold War II days. Family care of elderly and
handicapped, Dalley claims, "is much favoured by Governments
as a money saving device and it depends on 'compulsory
altruism' on the part of women." Women are forced by the

prevailing ideology of familism to sacrifice themselves as unpaid carers. This is bad for the carers and bad for the cared-for. Dalley quotes from the *"Gift Relationship"* in which Titmuss demonstrated that, "for the gift to be safe, that is non injurious to the recipient, it had to be freely given." [66]

She then proposes a socialist alternative to community/family care which divides the burden of caring across the whole of society. More particularly, caring would be shared by family, neighbours, the local community and the social services in a flexible manner. The family itself would have to admit the collective spirit and fall in with the others in communal facilities. There, dependants would be cared for in solidarity, instead of the isolation and loneliness of the family setting. Collective provision would relieve carers from much of the strain experienced at present. It would also make for better relations and a higher standard of care.

Dalley surveys many forms of collectivism in different societies and in different eras of history. She wishes to avoid the stigma of the Poor Law institutions on the one hand but on the other she warns that we must "beware of domesticity". [67] Consequently, child care, housework and the care of the elderly and handicapped should be socialised. "The feminist alternative", Dalley concludes [68] "is of a society which willingly takes a collective responsibility for all its members, which values the activities of caring and recognises the worth both of those cared for and those doing the caring. 'Unpaid', 'voluntary' or 'informal' care is not given a higher moral value than care provided by the collectivity - such care is too often the outcome of *compulsory* altruism and is exploitative of both giver and receiver."

The review of the literature might lead one to conclude that fashions change even in Social Administration, that institutions are out in one era and back in again in the next! This would be a quite unfair accusation against a discipline which has never gone in for colour or show! What has occurred is a development in the understanding of Community Care as changes in society and in the family forced clarification of the concept. Secondly, while social research in the sixties and seventies focussed almost exclusively on the cared-for, more recent studies have focussed on the carers, thus giving us a new perspective. The feminist movement has introduced a new and challenging ideological element to the debate on Community Care.

However, one important question has not been answered in the literature to date. Given the high costs to carers, why do they continue with their task? The literature on costs must clearly predict that care by the community, i.e., care within the family, by a woman on her own very often, must be in rapid decline. Yet the fact remains that the vast majority of frail elderly and mentally handicapped are cared for outside of institutions. The family is proving itself to be an extremely resilient caring agent. How are we to account for this?

Perhaps, the answer lies on the other side to the balance sheet – the side which has never been adequately filled in to date? Perhaps the benefits or rewards side makes up for the costs in whole or in part? The durability of care can in theory be accounted for in three ways:

(a) Carers have a sense of duty which stems from family, moral or religious values;

(b) Carers experience rewards for caring which make up for the costs or even outweigh them perhaps. There is a trade-off, conscious or unconscious, on the lines of the calculus mentioned by Abrams who stressed repeatedly that reciprocity was the main motivation in Community Care;

(c) Self-sacrifice, frequently mentioned in the feminist literature and in Vanier is the driving force. Self-sacrifice transcends duty and rewards. It is a "hot" concept while duty is a "cold" one. In the end carers will probably express it in terms of love.

I shall address these questions in the final chapters and I should hope to throw new light on the dynamics of caring. Do carers stay at their posts because of a sense of duty or because of rewards experienced or again because they undertake it in a spirit of self-sacrifice? If all three factors are at work what weighting is to be given to each? A satisfactory answer to these questions would fill a present gap in the literature and would make an original contribution to Social Administration. One gap in the British literature, in particular, would be filled. This is the failure to date to properly document the rewards to the carer and to accord them their true weight in accounting for the durability of care. A second gap will be filled in the Irish literature by a study on carers which breaks new ground in relation to the mentally handicapped and where the first study on the carers of the frail elderly by the National Council for the Aged was published in 1988. [69]

The formidable task for academics and social policy makers is to create the public demand for a Community Care system which actively mobilises, organises and supervises formal and informal systems, and commits the necessary finance to it. Public demand for such an operation might then register with the politicians of a present or a future Government. The economics of Community Care should also commend themselves to any Government which looks beyond the short-run. It will cost money but it will be cheaper in the long-run than residential care. One is seeking to build up the political will for as big a break-through as the Labour Government achieved in Britain in setting up the N.H.S. in the years after World War II. What is needed now is an option for Community Care on its economic and social merits rather than by way of a reaction to Poor Law institutions or of saving money in the short run or of falling in love with

the concept itself which, so far, has flattered to deceive.
Then, and not till then will Titmuss' "cottage garden
trailer" really come to flower!

'NOTES'

1. Townsend, P., 1962, *The Last Refuge,* Routledge and Kegan Paul, London.
2. Bowlby, J., 1963, *Child Care and the Growth of Love,* Hammondsworth, Penguin Books.
3. Robbs, B., 1967, *Sans Everything,* Nelson, London.
4. Morris, P., 1969, *Put Away,* Routledge and Kegan Paul, London.
5. Webb, A.L., and Wistow, G., 1987, *Social Work, Social Care and Social Planning: The Personal Social Services,* Since Seebohm, Longman, London.
6. Tizard, J., 1968, *Community Services for the Mentally Handicapped,* Oxford University Press.
   SEE: Goffman, E., 1961, *Asylums,* Anchor Books, Doubleday and Co., New York.
7. Titmuss, R., 1968, *Commitment to Welfare,* George Allen and Unwin, London, Ch.ix.
8. Bayley, M., 1973, *Mental Handicap and Community Care,* Routledge and Keegan Paul, London, p.19.
9. Abrams, P., 1977, "Community Care: Some Research Problems and Priorities", *Policy and Politics,* Vol.6 No.2.
10. Young, M., and Wilmott, P., 1986, *Family and Kinship in East London,* with new Introduction by Young and Wilmott, Peregrine Books, London.
11. Arnsberg, C.A., and Kimball, S.J., 1940, *Family and Community in Ireland,* Harvard University Press.
12. Bulmer, M., 1986, *Neighbours: The Work of Philip Abrams,* Cambridge University Press, Cambridge.
13. Abrams, P., 1977, op.cit.
14. Moroney, R.M., 1976, *The Family and the State: Considerations for Social Policy,* Longman.
15. Moroney, R.M., 1980, "*Families, Social Services and Social Policy*", U.S. Dept. of Health and Human Service, Washington.
16. Equal Opportunities Commission, 1982, *Who Cares for the Carers? Opportunities for those caring for the elderly and handicapped,* A survey Report, p.19.
17. Jenkins, P., Speech to Age Concern, 1980. Quoted in Webb, A.L., and Wistow, G., op.cit. p.273.
18. Jenkins, P., 1981, *The Guardian,* April 8th. Quoted in Walker, A., (ed.), 1982, *Community Care: The Family, the State and Social Policy,* Basil Blackwell and Martin Robertson, Oxford, p.1.
19. Walker, A., (ed.), 1982, op.cit.
20. Land, H., 1978, "Who Cares for the Family?", *Journal of Social Policy,* Vol. 7 Part 3.
21. Finch, J., and Groves, D., 1980, "Community Care and the Family: A Case of Equal Opportunities", *Journal of Social Policy,* Vol.9 Part 4.
22. Finch, J., and Groves, D., (ed.), 1983, *A Labour of Love,* Routledge and Kegan Paul, London.

23. Graham, H., in Finch, J., and Groves, D., (ed.), 1983, op.cit. p.26.
24. Titmuss, R.M., 1968, op.cit.
25. Abrams, P., 1977, op.cit. p.141.
26. Wilson, E., in Walker, A., (ed.), 1982, op.cit. p.54.
27. Finch, J., and Groves, D., 1980, op.cit. p.503.
28. Wilson, E., in Walker, A., (ed.), 1982, op.cit.
29. Equal Opportunities Commission, 1984, *Carers and Services: A Comparison of men and women caring for dependent elderly people,* A Survey Report, p.7.
30. Equal Opportunities Commission, 1984, op.cit. p.8.
31. Equal Opportunities Commission, op.cit. p.27.
32. Baldwin, S., and Glendenning, C., in Finch, J., and Groves, D., (ed.), 1983, op.cit. Ch.3.
33. Baldwin, S., 1985, *The Costs of Caring: Families with Disabled Children,* Routledge and Kegan Paul, London.
34. Equal Opportunities Commission, 1980, *The Experience of Caring for Elderly and Handicapped Dependents,* A Survey Report.
35. Webb, A.L., and Wistow, G., op.cit. p.72.
36. Davies, B., and Challis, D., 1987, (a), *Matching Resources to Needs in Community Care,* Gower, London ALSO.
    Davies, B., and Challis, D., 1987, (b), *Case Management in Community Care,* Gower, London.
37. Webb, A.L., and Wistow, G., 1982, op.cit.
38. Rimmer, L., "The Economics of Work and Caring", in Finch, J., and Groves, D., 1983, op.cit.
39. Abrams, P., 1977, op.cit. p.143.
40. Bayley, M., 1973, op.cit.
41. Nissel, M., and Bonnerjea, L., 1982, *Family Care of the Handicapped Elderly: Who Pays?,* Policy Studies Institute, No. 602, London.
42. Glendenning, C., 1986, *A Single Door,* Allen and Unwin, London, Ch.10.
43. Equal Opportunities Commission, 1982, op.cit. p.5.
44. Vincent, J., 1988, *"Carers Survey",* Unpublished Paper, Loughborough University.
45. Baldwin, S., and Glendenning, C., in Finch, J., and .Groves, D., (ed.), 1983, op.cit.
46. Pitkeathley, J., 1989, *It's My Duty, Isn't It? The Plight of Carers in Our Society.* Souvenir Press, London & Canada.
47. Graham, H., in Finch, J., and Groves, D., (ed.), 1983, op.cit.
48. Equal Opportunities Commission, 1982, op.cit. p.7.
49. Briggs, A., and Oliver, J., 1985, *"Caring: Experiences of looking after Disabled Relatives",* Routledge and Kegan Paul, London, p.119.
50. Mace N.L., and Rabins P.V., 1981, *The 36-Hour Day.* The John Hopkins University Press, Baltimore.
51. Graham, H., in Finch, J., and Groves, D., (ed.), 1983, op.cit.
52. Equal Opportunities Commission, 1982, op.cit. p.7.

53. Parker, R., 1981, "Tending and Social Policy" in Goldberg, E.M., and Hatch, S., *A New Look at the Personal Social Services,* Policy Studies Institute, London, pp.26-30.
54. Challis, D., and Davies, B., "A New Approach to Community Care for the Elderly", 1980, *British Journal of Social Work,* Vol. 10 No.1, pp.1-18.
55. Wenger, G.C., 1984, *The Supportive Network,* George Allen and Unwin, London, pp.190-191.
56. Hadley, R., and McGrath, M., 1980, *Going Local: Neighbourhood Social Services,* National Council for Voluntary Organizations, London.
57. Abrams, P., Abrams, S., Humphrey, R., and Snaith, R., 1981, *Action for Care: A Review of Neighbour Schemes,* Volunteer Centre, London.
58. Davies, B., and Challis, D., 1987 (a), op.cit. which demonstrates the success of the Kent Project in a number of ways. For example, 69 per cent of the Project sample but only 34 per cent of the comparison group were still at home after one year.
59. Wenger, G.C., 1984, op.cit. pp.190-193.
60. Davies, B., and Challis, D., 1987, op.cit.
61. Vanier, J., 1979, *Community and Growth,* Darton, Longman and Todd (Translation), London. Revised edition 1989.
62. Vanier, J., 1982, (Introduction and Conclusion), *The Challenge of l'Arche*, Darton, Longman and Todd, London, p.2.
63. See Clarke, B., 1974, *Enough Room for Joy,* Darton, Longman and Todd, London.
    also, Spink, K., 1990, *Jean Vanier & l'Arche, A Communion of Love*, Darton, Longman and Todd, London.
64. Vanier, J., 1979, op.cit. p.248.
65. Dalley, G., 1988, *Ideologies of Caring: Rethinking Community and Collectivism,* Macmillan Education, London.
66. Dalley, G., 1988, op.cit. p.18.
67. Dalley, G., 1988, op.cit. p.57.
68. Dalley, G., 1988, op.cit. p.149.
69. O'Connor, J., and Riddle H., 1988, *The Caring Process: A Study of Carers in the Home,* National Council for the Aged, Government Stationary Office, Dublin.

4 Methods

The Previous study on Loneliness influenced my approach to the present study. In the Loneliness study I had cocked a giant ear at the needs of the elderly in the Kerry Diocese. I was alerted to the problems of the sub-group of over 75s, who generally lived with relatives and reported more loneliness and boredom than those who lived alone. [1] Incapacity was the important factor here. Infirmity increased with age and the inability to take an active part in the social life of the area caused much unhappiness.

My attention began to be directed to the caring relatives who were frequently spouses or siblings. But it was only very gradually that I realised that these caring relatives, whatever their age, could be under many pressures resulting from their caring task.

This thorough investigation gave me a feel for the over 65 age group and was a most interesting comparative study for me since I had studied the work of Shanas [2], Townsend and Wedderburn [3], Hadley and Webb [4], Tunstall [5] and later Wenger [6], Power [7], and Kivett [8] on loneliness among the elderly in England, U.S.A., Denmark, Wales and Ireland. It also served, in effect, as a pilot study in the context of the present study of carers. A pilot study of 474 interviews must be somewhat unusual in this field! But it did mean that the present study was carried out against an empirical background on the lives of the elderly in the area in which I had grown up and worked as a priest for twenty years.

The two interviewers used in the loneliness study, both young women, were students of mine in their final year of their degree course at University College Cork and this project formed part of their fieldwork training. Among the sample of over 65's, 15 per cent admitted that they were "always or often lonely" and 20 per cent said they were "sometimes lonely". 70 per cent thought that loneliness was a problem in the country generally and 60 per cent thought that there were a lot of lonely people in their own area. 56 per cent felt that some of their neighbours suffered from loneliness. Cross-tabulation showed a direct and significant relationship between attribution to others and eventual admission of ones own loneliness. The questions were the standard ones used in the literature up to then. They were strategically placed about half way in the interview after more general questions had been broached and rapport established.

More recent writers such as Wenger [9] have questioned the value of the standard questions on the grounds that they rely totally on self reporting, that the subject carries stigma and, therefore, is unlikely to be admitted in all cases. Spouses, for example, might feel compelled to deny this feeling lest they be disloyal to their partners. Wenger [10], though using the standard questions for comparative purposes, has designed a set of eight indirect questions on whether the persons felt they had sufficient companionship, whether they had people in whom they could confide and call on in a crisis and so on. In fact, Wenger found a higher incidence on this aggregate score than she did on the standard questions. She found that married women reported a good deal of loneliness, a finding which had not come up before. Wenger also questioned just what being "lonely sometimes" amounted to. We would all, if we were honest, probably have to admit that we are sometimes lonely.

Granted the validity of many of her points, it must be said that, while there may be a tendency to underreport in some cases, there may also be a tendency to over-report, for example, in cases of bereavement where it would be disloyal to the departed spouse not to admit to loneliness. To this must be added the possible bias of interviewers in search of loneliness and worried lest they come back to their Director empty-handed.

What comes through from internal examination of the results of the Kerry Diocesan Study was that the group that declared that they were "lonely sometimes" were consistent in their responses to a whole range of questions on issues of companionship, the desire to see a visiting service set up, their attitude to death and their actual participation in work and the social life of their communities. When asked if they would like more company, 51 per cent of the total sample said they would, 66 per cent of those who said they were "sometimes lonely" said "yes" and 91 per cent of those "always/often lonely" said "yes". A 75 per cent overlap occurred between those who were "sometimes lonely" and those who declared they were "often bored". Boredom certainly carries no social stigma since three year olds in the modern world frequently profess to be overwhelmed by it! 36 per cent of the sample were "often bored", 75 per cent of the lonely were bored. And 75 per cent of those who were often bored were lonely. The comparison of the different studies is reported in Table 4.1. It should be kept in mind that there were some variations in the actual wording of the standard questions on loneliness. Also, Hadley and Webb's sample were referred as very frail elderly in the first place and thus were more likely to suffer from loneliness while Power's sample all lived alone. Power's study, done on behalf of the St. Vincent de Paul Society, involved interviews done in Northern Ireland and in the Republic, a rare achievement since the "troubles" began in 1969.

TABLE 4.1   Comparison Of Various Studies On Loneliness

% Lonely

		Always/ Often	Some- times	Never/ Rarely	Total lonely
Denmark: Shanas et al.	1968	4	13	83	17
U.K.: Shanas, Townsend et al.	1968	7	21	72	28
U.S.A: Shanas et al.	1968	9	21	70	30
U.K.: Tunstall, Four Areas	1966	9	25	66	34
U.K.: Hadley & Webb	1975	29	42	29	71
Ireland: North and South, Power	1979	14	25	66	39
North Wales: Wenger et al.	1980	5	20	75	25
U.S.A. Rural: Kivett	1979	16	42	43	58
Ireland, Kerry Diocese: Clifford	1977	15	20	65	35

When Townsend tried to account for the difference between Denmark on the one hand, and the U.K. and the U.S.A. on the other, he described how a more formal pattern of relationships existed in Denmark than in other countries. The Danish old people were accustomed to privacy all their lives and so had less need of friendship having been more independent in their lifestyle. He concluded that the difference between them and the other two nations in the study was one of "emphasis" rather than of "kind". [11] The comparative studies are intriguing for the social scientist but I cannot delay any further over them here.

The second important finding in this study was the association between loneliness and physical incapacity. The more incapacitated the person, the more likely he/she was to be lonely. It was striking. Incapacity was measured on the Townsend-Wedderburn [12] and Sainsbury [13] model of a set of activities value-judged to be central to normal living for elderly people in modern society. These can be classified as "personal" and "household" tasks. From 2.5 per cent to 4 per cent found great difficulty with personal tasks but the degree of difficulty rose with the more complicated household tasks such as cooking, bringing in fuel, washing clothes etc. where the numbers in difficulty rose to 25 per cent. Loneliness and the degree of incapacity were very closely related. The greater the degree of incapacity the more likely the old person was to be lonely. For example, among those who found "no difficulty" in dressing 30 per cent were lonely, of those who experienced "some difficulty" 72 per cent were lonely and where "great difficulty" was experienced 90 per cent were lonely.

This led me to the conclusion that there was a small sub-group of frail elderly whose physical and social needs were far greater than the general body, who, by and large, enjoyed a degree of independence and integration above what I had expected from the British and American literature. Of course, much of the literature in the 1960s and the early 1970s was inclined to dwell on the minority of elderly who suffered from extreme mental and emotional deprivation and the image of the elderly tended to be based on those in long-stay institutions of the "Last Refuge" kind. The balance has been restored in the last five or six years with most writers beginning their first chapter with a strong rejection of the earlier stereotype. [14]

The sampling method

For the purpose of the present study I needed to find a sample of elderly people who were very likely to be frail and housebound and therefore likely to be dependent on carers to a considerable degree. The use of Baptism registers as in the Loneliness study would have yielded too few people of this kind for the present purposes. An alternative approach had to be found. The one actually adopted was almost certainly unique in the history of Social Administration and could only have been relied upon in a country like Ireland where religious practice is exceptionally high. The sample was drawn from the list used by priests in their first Friday Communion calls to the

42

housebound elderly because this proved to be the best guide to the frail elderly.

This method had the added advantage of enabling me to identify a sample of people who had not self-selected themselves as being in a special need or difficulty. So, it seemed reasonable to assume that this approach would enable me to identify "normal" carers rather than those who were under pressure and had communicated this to one of the agencies. Recent studies such as that of Ungerson [15] selected twenty one carers from lists supplied by the Social Service Department of carers who had contacted them while Lewis and Meredith's [16] sample was to some extent self-selected. The forty one respondents in the latter were located "via the National Council for Carers and their Elderly Dependents, the Association of Carers, a letter to a local newspaper, a Social Services Department of a London borough, the manager of a Part III home, a hospital carers' support group and by personal contact". Ungerson [17] summed it up neatly: "Carers are notoriously difficult to find".

In the study on Loneliness, the two most regular official visitors to the homes of the elderly were the priest and the public health nurse. The social workers work almost exclusively with families and in child care. The priest visited 15 per cent at least once per month, while the public health nurse visited 9 per cent at the same intervals.

The priest's monthly visit to the elderly is known as the first Friday Communion Call, a pastoral practice dating back to the early part of this century and universal throughout Ireland. The Irish have been traditionally very faithful to Sunday Mass at which attendance is obligatory unless illness or incapacity or other serious difficulties prevent it. In practice, according to research done by the Church itself [19] and by Irish Marketing Research, the over-all attendance is approximately 90 per cent. Among the older rural people (51+) it ran as high as 95 per cent. When health and mobility decline beyond a certain point, the old person drops out and either he/she or the family inform the priest and thenceforth he comes on the first Friday of each month with Holy Communion. Ceasing to attend Sunday Mass is a land-mark in the old person's life and most are reluctant to surrender to what must be the final phase of life. Even among the most incapacitated group in the Loneliness study, 14 per cent had attended Mass the Sunday previous to the interview.

It therefore seemed to me to be a reasonable assumption that a further study involving the frail elderly might find its most reliable sample from the First Friday lists of the priests. The Church of Ireland ministers were invited to send names from their congregation but only a very small number of names were submitted. It is possible, of course, that a small number of elderly have lapsed and such people would have been missed out by this sampling method. I believe that their number would be very small. They would however be very likely to be isolated or lonely.

When incapacity was measured on a scale from 0 to 14 on the lines developed by Sainsbury (1974) using a list of personal and household tasks, it was found that the frequency of the priest's visit increased with the degree of severity. The monthly First Friday call stands out.

TABLE 4.2   Incapacity And Priest's Visits

Incapacity	Weekly	Monthly	Few Times per year	Yearly	Never	N.A.
0 Score	0.3	4.8	4.8	3.8	80.8	5.4
1-7 Score	0.0	13.8	8.0	5.7	70.1	2.3
8-14 Score	2.8	40.3	8.3	8.3	40.3	0.0

(n = 474)

The alternative would have been the public health nurse's visiting list, but since the public health nurse was under examination in the study, this seemed inappropriate. It seems certain too that there are not enough public health nurses in many areas, the ratio of nurses to population being lower in the Southern Health Board area than in any of the other seven areas. The public health nurse is thought to give intensive care to 3 per cent of the elderly, as a whole as mentioned earlier.

The General Practitioner might have been called upon but issues of confidentiality would arise. I believe furthermore, that social scientists must have faith in the measuring tools of their discipline for all its "vaguearies" and value judgements. The carer, is in many ways the best informed person on the health and well-being of the cared-for. The carers once identified, could be presumed to have what Webb and Hobdell [20] described as the "authority of relevance" in the case of their charges. But the priests' Communion list was felt to be a very good way of getting to the frail elderly and from them to the carers.

A harmless enough question appeared at the extreme right-hand margin of the question on incapacity in the Loneliness study. It asked those who had "great difficulty" or those who "had to be helped" with personal or household tasks, "If you can't, who helps?" Like Richard Titmuss and the train journey, this marginal question turned out to be an integral part of the next journey if not the first. What seemed to be a side issue then, i.e., the caring person, was to become the subject of my next study. What seems very strange ten years on is the fact that the responses were coded as "spouse", "child", etc. without a mention of the sex, let alone gender, of the carers! Moroney [21] who was writing around the same time has since been taken to task by Ungerson [22] for referring throughout his book to "family care" and never to "woman care". He was described as "implicitly extremely anti-feminist". The sources from which help was received are listed in Table 4.3.

TABLE 4.3   Source Of Help For Incapacitated Elderly
In Loneliness Study

(n = 474)

%

Person who helps when task cannot be performed:	Spouse	Child	Other Relative	Neighbour	Volunteer Voluntary Organiz- ation
Dressing	0.2	–	–	–	–
Washing	0.4	0.2	–	–	–
Making cup of tea	0.8	1.3	0.6	0.2	–
Cooking a hot meal	4.0	4.0	1.5	0.6	1.3
Doing light house- work	5.7	5.9	2.1	0.8	0.6
Doing heavy house- work	7.0	10.1	2.5	1.7	0.4
Washing clothes	9.3	10.8	2.8	1.9	0.8
Carrying in turf/ coal	1.9	12.0	2.8	1.9	0.2

The sample of elderly then were selected from the lists submitted by 50 priests from 18 parishes chosen at random from the 54 parishes of the Diocese. Two Church of Ireland ministers submitted five names. The priests were also asked to state, if possible, whom they considered to be the main caring person. In this they were not always very precise nor was it possible to be in some cases. But the involvement of priests made it possible to seek further information in doubtful situations.

A total of 1170 names were put in alphabetical order and one in nine names was selected by random choice. Of this 130, eleven had died in the months between selection and the interview, two had gone to a residential home, one to a long stay hospital and three refused to acknowledge that they had any carer. There were no refusals on the part of carers where they could be identified. In all, 122 interviews were done but 9 were not valid either because the cared-for person had died or gone to a residential home. It was decided to interview those for general interest and a few of them are mentioned later on in the study. It is interesting

45

to find that Lewis and Meredith [23] did their study on carers who had ceased to care for some time and built up "caring biographies" of daughters who had cared for mothers.

The sample of handicapped was drawn from a list compiled by statutory and voluntary organizations in the area just before I began this study. It included all the moderately and severely handicapped, those in day schools and those in three Training Centres. I then chose a random sample from the list. I am confident that I have a representative sample of moderately and severely mentally handicapped in the Kerry Diocese. There were no refusals from the carers of the mentally handicapped. In fact, they welcomed the opportunity to talk about their experiences and their problems. A total of 86 interviews were completed with the carers of the mentally handicapped. Altogether, there were 208 interviews ranging from two to three hours in length. Of the 208, nine were not included in the analysis as mentioned earlier.

One of the problems encountered was that a small number of the elderly when approached said that they did not have a carer. They insisted on their independence and said they needed no assistance. One man aged eighty four said he kept a gun in case of night attack, another said that "nobody looks after me except Almighty God". A third, aged eighty two, on whom I called, took offence at the very suggestion that he needed a carer. "Do I look decrepit", he asked. His son and daughter lived in England and phoned him regularly. When I gained his confidence by allowing him to tell his life story at some length, he confessed that he had a paid home help. Before I left he asked if I could use some influence to have the home help paid by the Health Board! Three of the sample were ruled out when they claimed to have no carer.

Otherwise, the elderly very readily identified their carer who was contacted and interviewed. Occasionally, it was not easy to decide who the real carer was. For example, and 86 year old man who was crippled with arthritis had a son who lived with him in the home and a married daughter who lived a mile away. The son worked at night in a factory and naturally spent most of the day in bed. The daughter came and cleaned the house and got the old man's meals. The daughter was the one chosen as the carer.

The questionnaire and the interviewing

After the usual background information, a short life-history was strategically placed in the questionnaire. The "life history" technique was suggested to me by Malcolm Johnson [24] when I called on him prior to designing the questionnaire. His idea was to give the interviewees full freedom to outline their life stories in their own way. The main events as seen by the individual can be far more relevant than the structured sets of questions usually administered by interviewers with regular schedules. Johnson would make the life history the major part of the interview with a few starter questions at the beginning and some prompting along the way.

I decided to include a shortened version, to limit the life history to that part relevant to the caring task, e.g., the mother's story from the birth of her handicapped child, the moment she discovered that the child was handicapped and her experiences since then. Or, in the case of a carer of the elderly, how the caring task was initially entrusted to her and the story since then. This technique yielded rich rewards as individuals willingly told their stories with feeling and vivid memories. Not all the interviewers were equally successful in getting the carers "to talk", but overall, this question added a unique dimension to this study. I feel that this was a very worthwhile approach and it seemed also to open up the interview as it established rapport. More than one third of these "life histories" are reproduced in Appendix 1.

The questionnaire then went on to examine the degree of help needed by the cared-for person and the actual "daily grind" of caring. Then the actual help received from others was examined, that of spouse, children, neighbours, friends, social services and voluntary bodies. Further sections dealt with the motives for caring, the joys and sorrows, costs and rewards as the carer saw them. Some questions were asked about the State welfare payments received and about the carer's attitude to employment outside the home. The question of the carer's leisure activities, holidays and breaks was examined. The cultural expectation that caring is more appropriately a woman's role than a man's role was gone into a different ways. At the end the interviewer was asked to comment on the carer and on whether it was likely that the caring would be continued. The questionnaire is reproduced in Appendix 2.

I included two vignettes in the questionnaire. I had used this technique in the previous study on social stigma [25] and found it useful as a method of eliciting sensitive information. Respondents showed considerable powers of problem solving and in the process revealed personal feelings which would be difficult to tap through direct questions. I felt that this tool ought not be omitted on this occasion although I used it sparingly.

The two vignettes went as follows:

(i)   (Ask women)
       Suppose a good friend of yours came to you with this problem. She had a job as a secretary in an office in town, but now her mother has got a stroke and needs continual care for the foreseeable future. Should she give up her job and mind her mother? Or should she seek some other way out?
       How would you advise her in her dilemma?

(ii) (Ask men)
      Suppose a good friend of yours came for advice. His
      mother has had a stroke and needs continual care for
      the foreseeable future. He works in a drapery shop.
      Should he give up his job and mind his mother? Or
      should he seek some other way out?
      How would you advise your friend in his dilemma?

The interviewing involved a great deal of travelling in
this sparsely populated area. The interview team included
two ladies, with experience in research with the Economic
and Social Research Institute, Dublin. A third was a Social
Science graduate, Ms. Mary Clifford who had helped with
previous studies also. A fourth was a priest with training
in Counselling. I did some of the interviews myself also.
I directed the team and discussed the finished schedules
with them as they went along. The E.S.R.I. interviewers
were extremely accurate in recording responses but had no
experience in the life history technique. However, this
aspect improved with practice and any initial weakness was
compensated for by the strength of others in the team.
The participation of priests as interviewers in this study
gives rise to the question of whether the carers might have
responded differently to lay interviewers than they did to
priests. In fact, the priests did 26 interviews out of the
208 and all their interviews were with carers of the
elderly. It is possible that on certain questions the
carers might answer to please the priest and that they might
be loathe to express their dislike of the caring task
knowing the Church's teaching on duty to parents for
example. On the other hand, it could be argued, the priest
is one in whom people trust with confidential information,
so perhaps, they would confide more in him than in lay
interviewers.
Cross-tabulation on a large number of issues where bias
might be expected, showed that there was no significant
difference between attitudes of carers as expressed to
priests and to lay interviewers on almost all issues. For
example, there was no significant difference on the question
as to whether the carer felt a sense of duty to look after
the cared-for person; nor on whether preparing the house for
the priest's first Friday visit caused extra work for the
carer. The same applied to the question about caring
placing a strain on the carer's marriage and on the question
of regret on the carer's part that she was not in full-time
work. However, on reporting on disagreements with the
cared-for person, the carers were more likely to admit their
loss of temper to the lay interviewers than to the priest (s
= .02). But on the question as to whether religion or
family was the greater source of their sense of duty there
was no significant difference between responses to priests
and lay interviewer.
At the end of the day, I felt very happy to have done this
original work, a comparative study of carers of two groups,

the frail elderly and the mentally handicapped, in an Irish setting. It was also the logical conclusion to previous studies and fitted in well with my pastoral experience. Just when the interviews were being completed, I was promoted and had to bid farewell to Kerry. I set out to do something I had never bargained for, to work for the Kingdom of God outside the Kingdom of Kerry!

'NOTES'

1. Clifford, D., 1977, *The Kerry Diocesan Study on Loneliness,* Unpublished.

Loneliness and Family Integration

Living with:	% Lonely	Living with:	% Lonely
Spouse & children	12.0	One child only	45.2
Spouse & one child	16.8	Non relatives	50.0
Spouse only	17.5	Brother or sister	55.8
Two or more children	33.0	Living alone	58.4
Male child & his		Living with other	
nuclear family	34.4	relatives	60.01

(n = 474   s = .0000)

2. Shanas, E., Townsend, P., Wedderburn, D., Friis, H., Milhij, P., Stehouwer, J., 1968, *Old People in Three Industrial Societies,* Routledge and Kegan Paul, London.
3. Townsend, P., and Wedderburn, D., 1965, *The Aged in the Welfare State,* G. Bell & Sons Ltd., London.
4. Hadley, R., Webb, A.L., and Farrell, C., 1975, *Across the Generations,* George Allen and Unwin, London.
5. Tunstall, J., 1966, *Old and Alone,* Routledge and Kegan Paul, London.
6. Wenger, G.C., 1984, *The Supportive Network,* George Allen and Unwin, London.
7. Power, B., 1979, *Old and Alone in Ireland,* St. Vincent de Paul Society, Dublin.
8. Kivett, V.R., "Discriminators of loneliness among rural elderly: implications for intervention", *The Gerontologist,* Vol.19 No.1 pp.108--115.
9. Wenger, G.C., 1985, "Loneliness: A pattern of measurement", *Unpublished paper.*
10. Wenger, G.C., 1981, "The Elderly in the Community: family contacts, social integration and community involvement", Working Paper No.18, Social Services in Rural Areas Research Project, University of North Wales, Bangor.
11. Townsend, P., in Shanas et al., op.cit. p.271.
12. Townsend, P., and Wedderburn, D., op.cit. Ch.1.
13. Sainsbury, S., 1970, *Registered as Disabled,* George Bell & Sons, London.
14. See Wenger, G.C., (1984), op.cit. Ch.1 or Pyke, M., (1980), in *Long Life,* J. M. Dent & Sons Ltd., London
Wenger states:
"When we hear about old people we are usually told about their difficulties. This is because most research had focussed on the problems of the elderly. This book is different in that it takes as its subject retired people living in their own homes in the community and for the most part coping capably... it

hopes to challenge the negative stereotype of old age..."

Magnus Pyke gives a highly sympathetic and personal account of the positive aspects to being old in to-day's world. He states:

"In 1975, a large group of elderly people living in their own homes was studied in Scotland. It was found that the percentage needing some help in living a normal life was about a quarter of those aged between seventy and seventy four and about a third of those between eighty and eighty four. At the age of eighty five and over, most of them required support of one kind or another. Yet even so, three quarters of the over eighty fives - after twenty and twenty five years beyond the accepted age of retirement - retained their ability to cope with the ordinary affairs of daily life provided they had appropriate help." (Ch. 2 p.17)

15. Ungerson, C., 1987, *Policy is Personal*, Tavistock Publications, London.
16. Lewis, J., and Meredith, B., 1988, *Daughters who Care*, Routledge, London.
17. Ungerson, C., 1987, op.cit.
18. Clifford, D., 1986, "The First Friday Communion Call", *The Furrow*, Vol. 37 No.11.
19. *A Survey of Religious Practice Attitudes and Beliefs in the Republic of Ireland*, Research and Development Unit, Maynooth, Ireland, 1986.
    See also: "Religous Beliefs Practice and Moral Attitudes: A comparison of two Irish Surveys 1974 - 1984" Research and Development Unit, Maynooth, 1986. Mass attendance in Rural Ireland was 94.2 per cent in 1974 and 93.6 per cent in 1984. The corresponding urban figures were 86.0 and 76.7 respectively. Overall attendance in 1974 was 90.9 and 86.9 per cent in 1984. Among the oldest group (51+) the figures remained at 92 per cent for both urban and rural over the ten years. The fall off has taken place in urban areas and among the young age group (18-25).
20. Webb, A.L., and Hobdell, M., 1980, in Lonsdale, S., Webb, A.L., and Briggs, T., (eds.), *Teamwork in the Personal Social Services*, Croom Helm.
21. Moroney, R.M., 1976, *The Family and the State: Considerations for Social Policy*, Longman, London.
22. Ungerson, C., 1987, op.cit.
23. Lewis, J., and Meredith, B., 1988, op.cit.
24. Johnson, M., 1981, "Ageing Needs and Nutrition", Interview Document, *Policy Studies Institute*, London. also
    "Observations on the Enterprise of Ageing", *Ageing and Society*, Vol. 2 p.1, March 1982, Cambridge University Press.
25. Clifford, D., 1975 (a), "Stigma and the Perception of Social Security Services", *Policy and Politics*, *Vol. 3 No.3*.

5 The carers: basic data

In the case of the mentally handicapped, the carers were almost all women (97.7 per cent). In the case of the elderly, 72.6 per cent were women. The 27.4 per cent men who were carers of the elderly formed a lower proportion than those of the Equal Opportunities Study (1982) [1] where 41 per cent of the carers were male. In a study of Carers of the Elderly in Ireland by the National Council for the Aged [2] 82 per cent were female and 18 per cent male. In an American study by Horowitz [3], 70 per cent of adult children in caring roles were female.

Age of carers
There was no significant difference between the ages of the carers of the two groups in this study (s = 0.38) as can be seen from Table 5.1.

TABLE 5.1   Age Of Carers

Age of Carers	Carers of Elderly	Carers of Mentally Handicapped
	%	%
Under 30	2.7	6.0
30 - 35	5.4	11.0
35 - 50	36.9	49.6
50 - 65	31.6	28.6
65 - 75	18.0	3.6
75+	5.4	1.2

One has to be careful not to stereotype the carers any more than the elderly, as mentioned earlier, since their age span is also wide. One is less surprised by the age spread of the carers of the elderly who will naturally include many spouses and siblings as carers, but the ages of the carers of the handicapped is somewhat surprising and has some implications which will be mentioned later. Of course, when one remembers that some adult handicapped were included from Workshops and Training Centres this finding is not quite so unexpected. 25 per cent of the handicapped are over 18.

Occupation

The occupations of the carers were, in the main, given as "housewife". For the carers of the handicapped this was the case for 91.9 per cent as against 55.7 per cent for the carers of the elderly. This reflects the high level of unemployment in the area generally as well as the bind of caring for elderly or handicapped and other children very often. In the towns, some part-time work exists for such jobs as waitresses in tourist areas. But in the country, jobs are generally very scarce.

TABLE 5.2   Occupation Of Carers

% (n = 192)

Occupation	Carers of Elderly	Carers of Handicapped	Male	Female
Housewife	55.7	91.9	0.0	73.0
Farmer	12.3	1.2	44.4	1.3
Retired	10.4	1.2	25.9	5.1
Unskilled manual	5.4	–	7.4	5.1
Skilled manual	3.8	1.2	–	–
Intermediate non-manual	6.6	–	–	–
Lower professional	2.8	1.2	–	–
Higher professional	0.8	3.5	–	–

The participation of female carers in work outside the home is very small indeed. The question of their previous participation and their attitude to work outside the home will be discussed in more detail later.

Marital status

The two groups of carers differed significantly [2] in relation to marital status, almost all of the carers of the handicapped being married as will be seen from Table 5.3.

TABLE 5.3   Marital Status Of Carers

% (n = 119)	Carers of Elderly	Carers of Handicapped	Male	Female
Married	61.9	84.9	41.9	69.5
Single	31.0	2.3	51.6	23.2
Widowed	5.3	9.3	3.2	6.1
Separated	1.8	3.5	3.2	1.2

Relationship with cared-for-person

The Carers of the mentally handicapped are much less varied than those of the elderly in regard to their relationship with the cared-for person. The huge majority are mothers looking after their offspring. Table 5.4. shows the pattern of the relationships which are almost completely blood relationships apart from one relationship by marriage and one foster parent-child relationship.

TABLE 5.4   Relationship Between Carer And Cared-for
                     Handicapped Child

(n = 86)

CARER	CARED-FOR HANDICAPPED	%
Mother	Son	52.3
Mother	Daughter	41.8
Mother	Foster daughter	1.2
Father	Daughter	1.2
Sister	Brother	1.2
Sister-in-law	Brother-in-law	1.2

The elderly and their carers contained a much wider
variety of relationships including blood, marriage and
relationships of friendship and neighbourliness.

TABLE 5.5   Relationship Between Carer And
                          Cared-For Elderly

CARER	CARED-FOR ELDERLY	%	NUMBER
Daughter	Mother	16.5	19
Son	Mother	7.8	9
Daughter	Father	6.9	8
Son	Father	1.7	2
Wife	Husband	6.0	7
Husband	Wife	6.0	7
Grand-daughter	Grandmother	0.9	1
Sister	Sister	1.7	2
Sister	Step-sister	0.9	1
Sister	Brother	0.9	1
Brother	Brother	0.9	1
Daughter-in-law	Mother-in-law	9.5	11
Daughter-in-law	Father-in-law	4.3	5
Son-in-law	Father-in-law	0.9	1
Niece	Aunt	2.6	3
Niece	Uncle	2.6	3
Niece-in-law	Uncle-in-law	4.3	5
Sister-in-law	Brother-in-law	1.7	2
Sister-in-law	Sister-in-law	1.7	2
First cousin	First cousin	0.9	1
Female neighbour	Old person	4.3	6
Male neighbour	Old person	2.6	3
Home help (female)	Old person	6.9	8

The two common stereotypes of the unmarried daughter
minding her ageing parents, and that of the ageing wife
caring for her husband, are not borne out. The rate of
spouses as carers (12 per cent) seems low especially when
compared with the figure of the Equal Opportunities

55

Commission 1982 Study [5] which was 27 per cent. I am not sure how one can account for this wide divergence. National samples might be a guide. Perhaps the very high ages of the cared-for in this sample causes the lower rate of spouses as carers. In a very extensive survey of Carers in the U.S. by Stone and Cafferata [6] 29 per cent of primary caregivers were adult daughters, 23 per cent were wives while 13 per cent were husbands. The rate of neighbours as carers in the present study was 6.9 per cent as opposed to 11 per cent in the English study. Then there were the Home Helps who were carers for 6.9 per cent. The Equal Opportunities Commission Study excluded Home Helps. The reason for their inclusion in this study will be explained later.

It is worth examining the marital status of the daughters and sons who are the carers of their parents.

TABLE 5.6   Children Caring For Parents

	Daughters caring for Father or Mother	Sons caring for Mother *
Married	13.9% (16)	0.0% (0)
Single	7.8% (9)	6.9% (8)
Widowed	1.8% (2)	0.0% (0)
Separated	0.0% (0)	0.9% (1)

* There were just two cases of sons caring for their fathers.

From the table it seems that single sons are as often carers as either single daughters or spouses.

The breakdown between blood and marriage relationship was 48.8 per cent blood relationship, 34.4 per cent marriage relationship which includes 12 per cent of spouses while 13.9 per cent of cases involved neither blood or marriage relationship.

The carers of the handicapped were significantly more likely to be caring for other dependants than the carers of the elderly. 95.3 per cent of them look after others in the home as against 65.5 per cent of the carers of the elderly. In both cases approximately 50 per cent of the other dependants are under 15 years of age.

The majority of the carers of the handicapped live in the same house as the cared-for person 74.7 per cent. The remaining 25.3 per cent of the cared-for are in the residential schools, for five days of the week and return for weekends, mid-term breaks and school holidays. Among the carers of the elderly, 67.6 per cent live in the same house as the cared-for person, 26.1 per cent live in different houses from the cared-for person, 3.6 per cent are together during the day, and finally 0.9 per cent live together at the weekends.

Most of the carers and the cared-for had a number of relatives living in the neighbourhood with other relations further afield in Ireland and abroad, illustrating the migration and emigration which are common here. Table 5.7 summarises.

TABLE 5.7   Relations Of Carers

Miles	Less than 2	2-3	4-5	6-10	11-70	Siblings in Ireland	Siblings Abroad
%							
Carers of Elderly	49.4	10.3	11.5	17.2	11.5	82.4	75.7
Carers of Handicapped	38.2	14.7	17.6	10.3	19.1	80.2	70.9

Not quite half of the carers felt that they had a friend or helper who might be regarded as of special support. 42.1 per cent of carers of elderly and 40 per cent of carers of the handicapped said they had such a friend. These friends lived within two miles in 85 per cent of cases.

History of caring

The "life history" section came early in the interview when carers were asked to recall how they first came to assume the task of caring. After the 20-30 minutes spent on this "story", four or five specific questions were put if certain issues had not been mentioned already. From the accounts given by the carers of the elderly, 45 per cent of them always lived with the elderly person and it was "natural" that when he/she became feeble the carer assumed the role. For 35 per cent a crisis in the life of the old person, usually sickness, an accident or bereavement, caused the old person to come to live with the carer or occasionally the other way round. Another 7 per cent of carers returned from abroad to assume the caring role and 6 per cent gave up a permanent job in Ireland to do so.

With the carers of the handicapped, caring almost always began with the birth of the child and a number of the mothers found the discovery of the handicap traumatic. The caring began in very trying circumstances in some instances and even years later the carers spoke with deep emotion about their early experiences.

When asked if there were others who might have taken on the caring task at the time, only small numbers felt there was, 14.5 per cent in the case of the carers of the elderly and 4.9 per cent in the case of the handicapped. Among the carers of the elderly who felt this way, 50 per cent pointed to a sister while one or two mentioned a son, a daughter-in-law, a niece and a neighbour. But the majority felt that the task fell naturally to them, that there was nobody else who could have or ought to have assumed it.

When queried as to how it was to them rather than to someone else the caring was entrusted their answers, outlined in Table 5.8 below, reflected a sense of family obligations while other motives began to come through also. The most common reasons given by the carers of the handicapped were expressed as follows:

"I was his mother", "I was her mother and there was nobody else to take on the job"; "Who else would do it, I being her mother?"; "I was not prepared to put her into a residential school"; "He was mine"; "Since I was his mother the task naturally fell to me"; "She was one of the family and I was her mother, she was my child, she was my baby and my responsibility"; "I brought her into the world"; "I was there".

With carers of the elderly similar reasons were noted:

"She is my mother"; "He is my father"; "I was the only daughter and I lived with my parents so naturally I looked after them when they grew feeble"; "I had lived in the house with my parents-in-law since I married Sean"; "Dan is my husband so isn't it only natural that when he got old I should look after him"; "Because I was the last of the family at home, all the others had gone away"; "Jim worked for the family and always lived in the house, he helped in the farm and it was natural that he should stay on when he grew feeble"; "We are her daughters and she looked after us when we were young so we accept that we should help now when she needs care"; "Pat my uncle reared me. I was always in the house"; "I was single, with no one to think of only myself"; "I was the one at home and my sister came back here when her health broke down in England"; "I was his wife and I still loved him and nobody else could humour him only myself"; "Wasn't I her husband"; "Why should I throw him in some home when I'm able to do it?"

Neighbours said things like:

"I'm her nearest neighbour"; "Sure I know him most of my life and I was his neighbour".

A home help who was the carer said, *"I lived close to him always. As a home help, I know his needs as I always called there".* Another home help, *"I answered an ad. in the newspaper."* She had become a live-in home help to an elderly couple whose daughter works in Dublin.

TABLE 5.8   How Carer Was The One To Whom The
             Task Of Caring Was Entrusted

(a) Carers of Handicapped   (n = 86)

Reason Given	Number of Times Mentioned
Carer was child's mother	63
Carer was child's father	3
There was nobody else to look after child	6
Carer did not want anybody else to take her place	6
Carer was child's sister	2
Carer saw it as a duty	2
Other	4

(b) Carers of Elderly   (n = 100)

Close blood relationship mentioned (mother, father, sister, brother)	18
Carer was last member of family left at home; was youngest at home	18
Cared-for person had always been in house	13
Carer was only child/only daughter	5
Carer was single and at home	3
Carer was nearest neighbour	6
Carer was closest relative alive	4
Carer mentioned the personal qualities of the cared-for person which won them over	2
There was nobody else to take on task	7
Carer took on task as home help	7
Carer was appointed by member of family to take on task	2
Carer answered advertisement in the press	1
Other	11

These reasons for caring spring mainly from a sense of
family loyalty and the duties of its members to each other.
One of the factors often mentioned to account for help from
outside the family seems to apply within the family also.
Reciprocity which was noted by Abrams [7], applies as
reciprocity between the generations and was an important
factor here. With most, caring seems to be seen as their
natural role, part of family expectations. The word
"naturally" cropped up frequently in their responses. The
carers are reflecting a set of family and community
expectations which they for the most part accept as
reasonable.

For some of them the caring has been going on for twenty
years or more as Table 5.9 illustrates.

TABLE 5.9	Length Of Time The Carer Has Been Performing Caring Role					
%	0-5 years	6-10	11-15	16-20	21-30	30+
Carers of elderly	37.1	14.7	12.1	6.5	3.8	0.9
Carers of handicapped	15.6	30.0	26.4	14.4	10.8	2.4

There were crisis points for some when a decision had to be made about placing the cared-for person in a residential setting or keeping him/her at home. This was a more frequent occurrence for the carers of the handicapped and it could happen very soon after the birth of the child or at school-going age when pressure could be brought to bear by husband, doctors, other members of the family and teachers or priests occasionally. The opening of day schools and the provision of transport in the past twelve years has lessened this pressure. 46.6 per cent of the carers of the handicapped reported such a crisis. Only 13.5 per cent of the carers of the elderly reported a similar experience and it was due to illness on the part of the cared-for person or the carer in a few instances. In such cases doctors sometimes advised residential care. Carers could sometimes be stubborn. At other times they took the advice as being in the cared-for person's best interests. Some examples will illustrate the conflicts which faced the carers at these times. First the carers of the handicapped:

"Some people said we should put our child away but we could never part with him";

"The doctor suggested a home but my husband and I decided to look after her ourselves";

"We felt at first that we would never put her away but when she was about four years old we found it impossible to cope with her";

"I thought about a home. When she was three our doctor told us she shouldn't start any school until she is seven at least so she is still at home";

"Being worried about his future and not wanting to burden his sister with the responsibility I searched around and found a place in a home for him";

"My husband thought it would be better to put him in a home";

"Last November she was not well and was very depressed and I was not feeling well myself either. I found it hard to cope day and night";

"We didn't want to keep John at home, we wanted to give him every chance in life so we sent him to a home and school."

Short term care might well solve some of the difficulties mentioned.

With the carers of the elderly the feelings of the cared-

60

for person were given more importance.

"On a temporary basis we sent her into the District Hospital which is a long stay hospital but she wasn't happy there so my husband and myself decided to bring her out again and she remains with us";

"A nun wanted her to go into a home but we would not agree";

"About seven years ago she got old and became more feeble. My husband and I had to balance our responsibility between looking after her and our children. We decided however that she would stay at home despite the arguments for placing her in a residential home";

"When Kathy was in hospital she was extremely unhappy there. Her daughter had a full-time job so she decided that the best thing to do was get somebody to take care of her at home so I came to live with Kathy as a home help";

"When my father-in-law got violent and threatened visitors we decided that he had to be placed in a psychiatric hospital for a time".

I examined these difficult decisions and found that in the case of the elderly, in 30.8 per cent of cases it was the carer alone who made the decision, in 23.1 per cent it was the cared-for person who decided while in 42.6 per cent the decision involved other family members and occasionally doctors. With the carers of the handicapped it was much more likely that husbands shared in the decision making in the majority of cases. Only 12.5 per cent of these carers said they had acted alone in the decision. As a group, the carers of the handicapped were more likely to be married as we saw earlier thus enjoying more support in arriving at difficult decisions regarding the cared-for person.

I was interested in finding out if caring was a tradition within the carer's family so I asked if the carer's parents had looked after a grandparent, a handicapped child or a handicapped adult. The responses were as follows in Table 5.10

TABLE 5.10   Whether Carers' Parents Had
                       Looked After Others

(n = 199) %		Grandparent	Handicapped Child	Handicapped Adult
Carers of Elderly	YES	51.3	0.0	0.0
	NO	48.7	100.0	100.0
Carers of Handicapped	YES	29.1	3.7	2.4
	NO	70.9	96.3	97.6
		(s = .002)		

There was extremely little previous experience of caring for handicapped but from the figure of more than 50 per cent of carers of the elderly whose parents before them had been carers, as opposed to 29 per cent of carers of the handicapped, one suspects that example and tradition are being handed down in the case of the carers of the elderly.

In summary, then, the carers of the handicapped were almost all mothers while more than one quarter of the carers of the elderly were men. There was no significant difference in the age of the two groups. The carers of the elderly were a much more diverse group in their relationship with the cared-for person. When one excludes the men, the carers were almost all full-time housewives with only one in ten working outside the home even part-time. Very few of the carers felt that they had been unfairly cast in the role of carer. On the contrary, most seem to feel that they fell naturally into the part.

For a minority of the carers of the handicapped, the mothers, their initiation was traumatic. In a small proportion of the carers of the elderly caring was the result of a crisis such as illness. Even as they described their initial involvement, motives for caring began to surface. These seemed to be very much family based with good neighbourliness added in a minority of cases.

I now include four "life histories" or "caring biographies", the more correct description used by Lewis and Meredith. [8] These illustrate the carer's personal experience of the costs and rewards of caring as well as giving their underlying motivation.

Case A

James O'Donovan, 66, looks after his wife Joan, 68. His son and a brother-in-law live in the house with them.

"Over the past ten years my wife Joan's health began to deteriorate. She got diabetes and had to go to hospital. She neglected it. She didn't take the insulin every day as she was ordered. When one has diabetes there is little healing when one gets another ailment. Joan's leg was burned with boiling water. It got worse and there was little or no healing. Eventually the limb got so bad that it had to be amputated.

I did not feel good about the situation at that stage. It was a great shock to me to learn that my wife's leg had been removed. I was hopeful, however, when I learned that she would get an artificial leg. This hope did not last long. Joan's sight began to fail. One eye gave trouble and in the end, the sight went. It was nothing compared to the distress I felt when she lost all her sight. She was now totally blind. It was then she became totally dependent on me.

I felt that all this would be too much for me. I thought I could never cope. This all happened four years ago now. I never realised how much I was able to do. I began to wash her. Getting her up out of bed and putting her to bed was difficult at first, but soon it came naturally to me.

As time passed, I became more familiar with the situation. I was able to cope. It brought Joan and myself closer together. Our five children rallied round as well. There was a great sense of unity. Edward our son at home, is exceptionally good. I thank God for giving me the strength to do what I have to do."

Case B

Noreen O'Riordan, 52, lives with her husband and youngest child and looks after her mother, 91.

"About two years ago, my mother got a mild stroke and then, about a year ago, she got another very severe stroke. She lost the use of her limbs and became incontinent and soils. She lived with my brother until about eight months ago. He retired early thinking that, perhaps, he could look after her. I used to hate to go home to see her. She was so dirty, huddled over the fire. I hated to see her dirty. Then about eight months ago, she had to go to hospital. She was miserable there and cried all the time. I think she was disappointed that she should be thrown there and that none of her own would keep her.

My own family advised me that I couldn't manage her at all. They said I was mad. My husband and myself discussed it and we felt that we couldn't leave her there. My brother couldn't manage her any more and my other sisters have large families. Mind you, she and I were never too close. She was in fact much closer to my other sisters, though anytime she had been sick it was to me she always turned. In the beginning she broke our hearts. She didn't want to be here but at home. Visitors always came to see her, too many at times. Indeed I find it very hard on Sunday sometimes, when all the visitors turn up together. But the visitors used to be uncomfortable in the beginning because she used to want to go home with them. It frustrated me too, because I knew that no matter how much I did for her, changing her, cleaning her, she wasn't satisfied and would prefer to be thrown in a dirty heap at home. A few months ago then, I had to have a break so she spent ten days in Hospital. I needed the time to myself and my husband and myself planned to go away for a few days. As it happened we didn't go because I was in and out to see her every day. She was happy enough for the first couple of days but then the tears all started again. She was delighted to be out and to be leaving the hospital but she thought she was going home and she was very disappointed to find herself, in her own words, "landed here again". I feel

63

guilty about her as I feel she deteriorated very much
while she was there. She was put into a ward with very
old people who couldn't talk to her. The Staff didn't
have time to get around to her and she lost her footing
and it was gone altogether as a result. I think she's
getting much weaker now. She used to be great company
telling stories about the old days and so on. Now she's
beginning to wander a bit and her voice is weakening.
She used to come out here to the living-room and sit by
the fire but not anymore. Then for a while, she'd get
out on the chair for part of the day, but now five
minutes is about enough for her. Though the children
were deprived of their study room and many of the family
outings which we used to have, they are very fond of her
and love to bring in their friends to see her."

Case C

Ellen Harty, 41, is married with five children, the eldest
21, while Sean her youngest is 3½.
I was 37 when I became pregnant with Sean. It was a
great surprise as the youngest was twelve. But we were
delighted and the children were delighted and they told
all their friends they were getting a new baby. When he
was born I thought his head looked large and I said this
to the nurse. The doctor told my husband and then he
told me. I cried for two whole days. I cried for the
disappointment of my other children and out of fear.
After all, we were not getting any younger. Then we
brought him home and my mother died and my husband came
down with suspected cancer. We thought he was finished.
This was the worst time in my life. The neighbours came
in and told me I would be better off without this child
and I had to ask one neighbour to please leave my home.
One neighbour said, "he looks like a little old
Chinaman". Miraculously, my husband got better. The
tumour disappeared. He got a clean bill of health.
More and more, Sean began to change our lives. He was
very sickly, and he had a very large tongue which used to
choke him. When he was two we became members of the
Down's Syndrome Association which issues a Newsletter.
There was an article in one of the Newsletters by a
Professor Browne who said that Down's Syndrome sufferers
who had long tongues should have an operation to shorten
them, thereby allowing them to swallow more easily. Sean
had this operation last August. We think he is the first
one in Ireland and certainly he is the first one in this
county to have this operation and he is now eating solid
food. The children adore him and we are all so proud of
him. We know he is an intelligent child. You can't
imagine how affectionate he is and all we want now for
him is that he will be able to reach his full potential.
He is included in all our activities and he knows he is

the centre of attention. We want the best for all our children and we hope to make Sean as independent as possible and we have great hope for the future as we know that new discoveries are being made all the time in this area."

Case D

Eileen Begley is 49. She has four children. Her daughter, Tima is 10.

"I never got over the shock of having a mentally retarded child. Looking back now I can honestly say it wasn't so much the shock of having her. It was more the way I was told. The paediatrician threw it at me. That is how I can only describe it. He said, "your child is a mongol and what can you expect at your age". I think I fainted at that stage. However, there was a nun there who was very kind to me and I regretted that she didn't get a chance of breaking the news to me. I was 39 when she was born. Most mothers have a fear of having a handicapped child, but I must confess that the thought never entered my head. I already had three children and I had given birth to each of them without any trouble. So I had no reason to believe that this would be any different. Before she was born I used to play a lot of golf and I was anxious to have the baby so that I could get back to golf and to my friends again. That was ten years ago and I haven't been able to play since. I was left out of hospital after three days and they kept the baby two weeks for me. I told them I didn't want to bring her home, that they could do what they liked with her. At that stage if a tinker going the road wanted her, I'd have given her away. The nun at the hospital told me not to leave her at the hospital too long because it was vital to form a bond quickly. I brought her home after two weeks, and for twelve months I didn't have any feeling for her at all. When she was around a year old, I was going to Dublin one morning and Tima was sick. I phoned the doctor and left my husband in charge and went off. I would never have done that with one of the others. When I came home, she was in hospital and was critical with pneumonia. The doctor was very annoyed at the fact that I had gone off to Dublin without a second thought. I spent the night with her in hospital and prayed that night that if she got well, I would make the best of things and would be a better mother to her. I haven't looked back since that night. Believe it or not, I am a better person because of Tima, less interested in material things and she has turned out to be the most loveable and kind of all my children".

'NOTES'
1. This study entitled, *Carers and Service: A Comparison of men and women caring for dependent elderly,* Charlesworth, A., Wilkin, D., and Dune, A., Equal Opportunities Commission 1982, provides some interesting comparisons. The study involved 157 cases.
2. O'Connor, J., Ruddle H., 1988, *Caring for the Elderly,* National Council for the Aged, Stationery Office, Dublin, p.78.
3. Horowitz, A., "Sons and Daughters as Caregivers to Older Parents: Differences in Role Performance and Consequences". *The Gerantologist,* 25, No.6, pp.612-617.
4. s = 0000 on Chi Square Test. To simplify from here on, unless otherwise stated "significant" difference will be taken to be s = 0000 on this test.
5. Charlesworth, A., et al., 1982, op.cit.
6. Stone, R., and Cafferata, G.L., 1986, *Caregivers of the Frail Elderly,* National Center for Health Service Research and Health Care Technology Assessment, 1988, *Research Activities* No.87.
7. Abrams, P., Abrams, S., Humphrey, R., and Snaith, R., 1981, *Action for Care: a review of Good Neighbour schemes in England,* Berkhamsted, Herts., The Volunteer Centre,
   In his first study of a Good Neighbour Scheme, Abrams emphasised reciprocity.
   "The notion of 'ordinary people wanting to help each other' rests on a simple expectation of reciprocity. Whether the return is made now or in the future, there seems to be a fundamental belief that help can earn help. The negative aspect of this, of course, is a rather overt belief that help *should* earn help, that payment is due."
8. Lewis, J., and Meredith, B., 1988, *Daughters who Care,* Routledge, London, p.14.

6 The cared-for persons: basic data

Of the 113 cared-for elderly, just slightly more than two thirds were women (68 per cent). The handicapped cared-for persons, on the other hand, were 54 per cent male and 46 per cent female. This is in line with the general pattern among the elderly in the developed world with women outnumbering men by two to one in the higher age groups. Within the elderly sample the higher age group predominated.

Advancing age is, in general, an indication of increased need for care and support from family, community and social services. It is generally agreed in the literature that the over 75s or, more recently, the over 80s [1], will be very unlikely to be able to cope without some help at least. Tables 6.1 and 6.2 show the elderly in this sample to be more likely to be over 80 than under it. The national figure for the over 75s was 36 per cent of all elderly in 1981, for over 80s it was 17 per cent [2].

Table 6.1   Age Of Elderly Cared-For Persons

Years	Number	%	Cumulative %
58	1	0.9	
63 - 64	2	1.8	2.7
65 - 69	9	7.7	10.4
70 - 74	16	13.8	24.2
75 - 79	20	17.2	41.4
80 - 84	29	25.0	66.4
85 - 89	26	22.4	88.8
90 - 94	11	9.5	98.3
95 - 97	2	1.7	100.0

(n = 113)

Table 6.2   The Old Elderly

% of Cared-for Elderly
persons aged:

90+	11.2 %
85+	33.6 %
80+	58.6 %
75+	75.8 %

The 86 cared-for persons among the handicapped go from 2½ to 44 years of age but the majority are under 14 (55.7 per cent) with the very great majority of the remainder under 30. A comparison between the cared-for persons ages and those of their carers is shown in Table 6.4. While there is no significant difference between the ages of the carers, the two sets of cared-for persons are at the opposite ends of the scale. Table 6.3. shows the ages of the handicapped cared-for persons.

Table 6.3   Ages Of Handicapped Cared-For Persons

Years	Number	%	Cumulative %
2½ - 7	14	16.2	16.2
7 - 14	34	39.5	55.7
14 - 18	16	18.6	74.3
18+	22	25.6	100.0

(n = 86)

68

Table 6.4   Ages Of Carers And Cared-For Persons:
Comparisons

	% Carers		% Cared-for Persons	
Years	Elderly	Handicapped	Elderly	Handicapped
1 - 19	0.9	0.0	0.0	76.7
20 - 44	36.9	44.4	0.0	23.3
45 - 64	40.5	54.0	2.7	0.0
65 - 74	18.0	3.6	21.2	0.0
75+	5.4	1.2	76.1	0.0
n =	113	86	113	86
%	56.8	43.2	56.8	43.2

s = 0.3811   s = 0.0000

The marital status of both groups is given in Table 6.5

Table 6.5   Marital Status Of Cared-For Persons

%	Elderly	Male	Female	Handicapped
Married	26.8	30.0	25.6	0.0
Widowed	45.5	30.0	51.2	0.0
Single	27.7	40.0	23.2	100.0

(n = 199)

These figures come very close to the national figures for
the over 75s which are: married, 28 per cent, widowed, 42
per cent and single, 25 per cent. [3]
    As with the carers, the majority of the cared-for persons
had been housewives while the men had been farmers or
unskilled manual workers for the most part.
    The relationship of the carers to the cared-for person has
been described in the previous chapter. It is worth while,
I think, to present the relationship from the cared-for
persons' perspective. Table 6.6 gives this picture.

Table 6.6   Relationship Of Elderly Cared-For To Carer

		%
Cared-for Person is	Mother of carer	24.1
" " " is	spouse of carer	12.5
" " " is	Father of carer	8.0
" " " is	Sister of carer	8.9
" " " is	Brother of carer	1.8
" " " is	Aunt of carer	2.7
" " " is	Uncle of carer	1.8
" " " is	Mother-in-law of carer	9.8
" " " is	Father-in-law of carer	5.4
" " " is	Grandmother of carer	0.9
" " " is	Sister-in-law of carer	1.8
" " " is	Brother-in-law of carer	0.9
" " " is	Neighbour/friend of carer	6.1
" " " is	Other relative of carer	6.3
" " " is	recipient of Home Help	7.1

The majority of the cared-for persons lived with their
carers with the exception of those handicapped (25 per cent)
who spent the five day school week in the residential centre
and 19.8 per cent of the elderly who lived alone.   This
seems to be a high figure in the case of the latter since
the national figure is only 18.4 [4] but in my previous
study of 1977 in this area 25 per cent of the over 65s lived
alone.   Both Wenger and Hunt had a higher figure for their
English and Welsh populations. [5]   Nevertheless the high
age of this sample would, one should have thought, make
living alone extremely difficult.   Even more surprising is
the fact that the majority of these elderly who live alone
are in their eighties.   Table 6.7 breaks down the twenty-two
cases.

Table 6.7   Age Of Elderly Living Alone

AGE	58 - 75	75 - 85	85 - 90	90+
n=22	22.7% (5)	45.4% (10)	27.2% (6)	4.5% (1)

The handicapped lived in significantly larger households
than the elderly as can be seen from Table 6.8

70

Table 6.8	Number Of People In House With Cared-For Person	
Household size	Elderly	Handicapped
	%	%
1	19.8	0.0
2	27.9	1.2
3	18.9	13.6
4	10.8	14.8
5	9.0	11.1
6	1.8	14.8
7	7.2	17.3
8	3.6	7.4
9	0.0	7.4
10	0.0	3.7
11	0.9	3.7
12	0.0	3.7
13	0.0	1.2

Relatives

Approximately half of the cared-for persons have a relative living within one mile of their home. In the case of the elderly this included a son for 20 per cent, a daughter for 12 per cent, a brother for 12 per cent, a nephew for 17 per cent and a first cousin for 16 per cent. Table 6.9 fills out the picture to include the relatives of the two groups of cared-for including siblings at home and abroad.

Table 6.9	Relatives Of Cared-For Persons						
Miles	Less than 2	2-3	4-5	6-10	11-70	Siblings in Ireland	Siblings Abroad
%							
Elderly	54.2	6.0	15.7	12.0	12.0	46.4	60.4
Handicapped	35.8	14.9	20.9	10.4	17.9	36.0	23.5

The carers identified a friend of the cared-for person who was of special support in 44 per cent of the elderly and 24.7 per cent of the handicapped. In this the two groups differed significantly but as seen in the last chapter, the carers had much the same proportion of such friends, approximately 40 per cent in each category. It would seem that the carers of the handicapped do not think their cared-for persons have very many real friends in the community.

The next task is to present a general picture of the degree of incapacity of the cared-for persons. This was done by means of questions on a list of activities believed to constitute normal living for a healthy active old person or growing child or young person in the case of the handicapped. The carer was asked to say whether the cared-for person could perform these activities alone or whether supervision or actual help had to be given in their performance. It can be assumed that there is nobody who knows the cared-for person's "form" better than the carer. The carer is "on the spot" day in day out. She will know the doctor's and the public health nurse's opinion of their state of health and will probably have hourly bulletins from the cared-for person on how he/she is feeling. The carer speaks, as I said already, with "the authority of relevance". She may, of course, be biased about the dependence of the cared-for person in certain cases. Table 6.10 gives the various personal and household tasks and the degree of independence or dependence of the cared-for elderly persons.

Table 6.10   Personal And Household Tasks
              Elderly Cared-For Persons

%

Does cared-for person have difficulty in:	Can do on own No difficulty	Under Super-vision	Only with help
Having all-over wash/bath	51.3	4.4	36.3
Washing hands/face	78.8	4.4	16.8
Putting on shoes/stockings	75.0	4.5	20.5
Doing up zips, buttons	70.5	8.9	20.5
Dressing other than above	71.4	9.8	18.8
Getting to and using W.C.	82.1	3.6	14.3
Getting in and out of bed	83.9	4.5	11.6
Feeding self	89.3	6.3	4.5
Shaving (men)			
Combing hair (women)	76.4	6.5	18.2
Cutting toenails	34.2	5.4	59.5
Negotiating steps/stairs	59.6	11.7	28.7
Getting around the house	80.6	5.6	13.9
Getting out of doors on own	51.5	14.1	34.3
The taking of prescribed medicine	40.5	22.6	36.9

The degree of dependence can be measured against Wenger's sample [6] where 7 per cent need help taking a bath or an over-all wash, 7 per cent need help getting out of doors on own, 5 per cent need help negotiating steps while only 3 per cent or less have to be helped with washing hands and face, putting on shoes and stockings, doing up buttons and zips, dressing, going to and using the W.C., getting in and out of bed, eating, brushing hair or shaving, getting around the house. Cutting toenails seems to present one of the most difficult problems for elderly people and in Wegner's [7] sample, 17 per cent had to be helped. In Hunt's study [8] it was 27 per cent.

It seems clear from the comparison between these two samples that the cared-for persons in this study are reported to display a much greater degree of dependence than a "normal" population of over 65s. Of course the accounts in one came from the elderly themselves who are thought to understate their disabilities and overstate their health as Anderson et al. [9] found with rural elderly. Tinker [10] puts forward the theory that since ill-health is associated with the negative stereotype of old age, elderly people refuse, as long as possible, to accept this label and continue to profess that they are well. Are the elderly more truthful to their carers than to social science interviewers? Are carers apt to exaggerate the degree of disability in order to show how much they are doing or even to feel that they are greatly needed? Or do carers sometimes produce dependence by doing too many things? These are interesting questions some of which will be teased out later.

When asked to rate the health of the cared-for persons, the carers described it as "Generally good", 41.6 per cent, "Fair only", 27.4 per cent, "Varies a lot", 15.9 per cent, "Poor", 10.6 per cent, "Very poor", 5.3 per cent.

Among the elderly in Wenger's [11] and Hunt's [12] studies less than 3 per cent are bedfast. In this study 7 per cent are bedfast. This was slightly less than the rate in the main residential home for Co. Kerry, St. Columbanus' Home, Killarney, former County Home and Workhouse originally. It has been modernised and new buildings have been added in the past twenty years. The comparative figures between the elderly in the community and those in this residential home are given in Table 6.11.

Table 6.11   Bedfast And Housebound Elderly

	Present Study	St. Columbanus' Home Killarney
Cared-for person is:	n = 113	n = 239
	%	%
Bedfast	7.1	9.4
Chair bound	10.4	10.6
Permanently housebound	38.4	91.5
Able to get up for up to two hours each day	6.7	10.6
Able to get up for six hours	16.2	16.6
Able to get up for normal day	77.1	54.7
Never able to go for short walk	29.4	-
Very rarely goes for short walk	28.4	91.5
Goes for a short walk once a week	5.5	8.5
Goes for a short walk most days	36.7	3.5
Not capable of being alone even for short periods	29.2	-

The comparison shows the elderly in the community to be more mobile generally than those in the residential home. The regime in St. Columbanus' Home is quite liberal and the residents may walk into town and do shopping or enjoy a drink. However, it seems that the vast majority of the residents (91.5 per cent) are unable to venture out at all. From a comparative point of view the significant figures are the sum of the bedfast and chairbound, 24.6 per cent for the elderly in this study as compared with 29.4 per cent of these in the residential home.

Continuing with Table 6.11, the 7.1 per cent who are bedridden plus the further 10.5 per cent who are chairbound and those who can only get up for two hours each day (6.7 per cent) constitute almost one quarter who must need a very high level of care. Considering also that 29.9 per cent are not capable of being on their own even for short periods, full-time care is required in the case of at least a third of the elderly cared-for persons.

The problem of incontinence will probably be thought to have been introduced in far too genteel a manner – the carers were asked "if there were problems of incontinence". 17.9 per cent said there were. The subject came up a number of times in the life histories where carers found this particularly trying. I felt that this area was a little bit too delicate, or should I say indelicate, for cross-examination and the interviewer might be regarded as too

74

inquisitive. This could damage rapport. So I decided to tread gently! In the case of the handicapped I felt I could be somewhat bolder.

When asked if the cared-for persons suffered from any specific disease 61.7 per cent of the carers said they did and mentioned at least one and sometimes combinations of different diseases. Arthritis was mentioned by 16 carers, diabetes 5 times; heart conditions, the after-effects of stroke, high blood pressure, hypertension and hardening of the arteries were each mentioned three or four times. There was one case of asthma, one case of Parkinson's disease, four were totally blind while a further six had only partial sight. Two suffered from severe deafness. Depression and nervous disorders were mentioned five times. "Senility" was mentioned in relation to two of the cared-for persons. Altzheimer's disease was not mentioned although it seems to be on the increase in Ireland as in the U.S. and U.K. and causes special difficulties for carers. Perhaps it was present as "senility". Norris [13] presents some extremely harrowing accounts by carers of the destructive course of this disease among their elderly parents and of the very stressful nature of caring for them either in the family home or in residential care. (See Life Histories No.9).

The elderly in this study are, as we saw, in the higher age brackets (80+) for the most part. Despite this fact many of them still retain a good degree of independence and are able to do many things for themselves and so many may not need a great deal of care and supervision. But there is a section, numbering over one third, who are in need of full-time care and attention. Without carers in the family or in the community it seems fair to say that they would be candidates for residential care.

The mentally handicapped cared-for persons

As mentioned earlier the 86 mentally handicapped were chosen at random from a list of all the known moderately and severely handicapped in County Kerry in 1985. The carers were asked a set of questions about their abilities and disabilities and their need for help with various aspects of daily living.

Bayley [14] found that there were two factors which proved crucial to decisions parents made to seek residential care for their handicapped child. The most important was behaviour problems. Bayley [14] states, "The behaviour of the subnormal was the most important single factor leading to hospital admission, dwarfing all others... in every group there were well over twice as many with a serious behaviour problem who were in hospital as there were at home." Behaviour problems included aggression, antisocial sexual behaviour, crime and problems with younger siblings. The other factors which predisposed parents or other carers to place their child in a hospital for the handicapped were the death or illness of a parent. Social reasons which include unsatisfactory home conditions, inadequate parental control and nursing problems came third among predisposing factors.

The responses of the carers to a number of questions relating to the cared-for person's abilities to perform different tasks are given in Tables 6.12 to 6.15.

Table 6.12   Continence

% (n = 86)	Frequently	Occasionally	Never
Wets at night	10.6	16.5	72.9
Wets during day	8.3	10.7	81.0
Soils at night	4.8	8.3	86.9
Soils during day	6.0	13.1	81.0

Table 6.13   Mobility

% (n = 86)	Not at all	Not Upstairs	Upstairs and Elsewhere
Walk with help	8.6	0.0	91.4
Walk by self	4.8	2.4	92.8

Table 6.14   Self Care

% (n = 86)	Not at all	With help	Without help
Feed self	2.4	8.2	89.4
Wash self	4.7	40.0	55.3
Dress self	3.5	36.5	60.0

Table 6.15   Personal And Household Tasks

%

Does cared-for person have difficulty in:	Can do on own No difficulty	Under Super- vision	Only with help
Having all-over wash/bath	29.8	33.3	36.9
Washing hands/face	65.3	24.7	20.0
Putting on shoes/stockings	56.5	10.6	32.9
Doing up zips, buttons	48.2	11.8	40.0
Dressing other than above	54.8	21.4	23.8
Getting to and using W.C.	69.4	21.2	9.4
Getting in and out of bed	90.6	4.7	4.7
Feeding self	90.6	5.9	3.5
Shaving (men); Combing hair (women)	61.0	15.3	23.7
Cutting toenails	15.7	7.2	77.1
Negotiating steps/stairs	85.4	6.1	8.5
Getting around the house	96.4	0.0	3.6
Getting out of doors on own	79.3	14.6	6.1
Taking prescribed medicine	83.3	-	16.7

The cared-for person's vision was described as poor in 21.2 per cent of cases and normal in 78.8 per cent of cases. With regard to hearing, 2.4 per cent were reported to be deaf or almost deaf, 4.7 per cent were said to have poor hearing and 92.9 per cent to have normal hearing. Speech was the next faculty to be examined. 9.5 per cent "never said any word at all", 34.5 per cent had odd words only (occasionally, these were choice words as it happens!) and 54.8 per cent spoke normally in sentences. 1.2 per cent could talk but didn't.

Coming to reading ability, 51.8 per cent could not read at all, 38.8 per cent could read a little and 9.4 per cent could read the newspapers. 47.1 per cent could not write, 45.9 per cent could write a little, 7.1 per cent could do their own correspondence. 38.1 per cent were unable to count, 51.8 per cent could count a little and 16.5 per cent understood money values.

Clarity of speech came next and 7.5 per cent of cared-for persons were said to be difficult to understand even by close acquaintances and impossible for strangers; 41.5 per cent were said to be easily understood by close acquaintances but difficult for strangers to understand and 50.9 per cent were said to be clear enough to be understood by everybody.

When a comparison is made between this sample and Bayley's, this group seems to have slightly less who are unable to walk at all (8.6 v 13.1). In regard to speech it is difficult to make a direct comparison with Bayley's handicapped. 25 per cent of his sample could not talk. In this study, 9.5 per cent could not say a word at all while

34.5 per cent could only say an occasional word. For one boy this word was "Capital" and it described all the things which pleased him. Another boy's only word was "Hot". The proportion of children suffering from blindness and deafness were similarly small in both studies.

Referring to incontinence Bayley [16] says, "Incontinence in children is more acceptable than in adults. Many of the children who were partly incontinent would be learning and becoming better controlled. In the adults, any incontinence probably meant incontinence for good, which is a daunting, expensive and exhausting proposal for the parents or others looking after the subnormal. It is easy to appreciate why a relative would be reluctant to take on a subnormal if he were incontinent." 19 per cent of Bayley's group were reported to be incontinent as against 28 per cent in this study on the general question mentioned earlier with regard to "problems with incontinence". From Table 6.12 it would seem, overall this group has slightly more problems of incontinence than Bayley's.

The important subject of behaviour patterns must now be examined since it can be so decisive as to whether or not the mentally handicapped will remain in the community. The responses on behaviour are given in Table 6.16.

Table 6.16   Behaviour Difficulties

	To a marked degree	To a lesser degree	No
	%	%	%
Hits out or attacks others	3.5	21.2	75.3
Tears up pages, magazines, clothing, damages furniture.	9.4	18.8	78.1
Extremely overactive, paces up and down restlessly, does not sit down for a minute.	10.7	17.9	71.4
Constantly seeking attention, will not leave adults.	8.3	27.4	64.3
Continually injures self physically, e.g., head banging, picking at sores, beating eyes.	4.7	3.7	91.8

It is difficult to estimate the extent and seriousness of these behaviour problems. Those who "misbehave" to a marked degree must surely be a handful for their carer and others. Those who do these things to a lesser degree are more manageable, one thinks, but it must be particularly difficult for carers in public with these cared-for persons. When asked what problems presented the greatest difficulties, carers put behaviour problems at the top of the list, speech difficulties next, then lack of mobility, and finally incontinence.

A point I thought worth investigating was whether the carers thought that the cared-for persons could do more for themselves than they actually do. I wondered if, perhaps, the carers might be making the cared-for more dependent than necessary. As might be expected neither set of carers agreed. Only 16.7 per cent of the carers of the handicapped and 3.7 per cent of the carers of the elderly felt that the cared-for could walk more often if they wanted to. What was very interesting was the different responses of the two groups to the question whether there were things which the cared-for persons did on their own, which while good for their independence, gave the carers more trouble than if they did them for their charges. Only 6.7 per cent of the carers of the elderly thought this to be the case but 44.2 per cent of the carers of the handicapped felt that this was the case.

Perhaps these carers are at some pains to develop independence in a way which the other carers are not? It seems that the carers of the handicapped consciously promote greater independence whereas those of the elderly were not so motivated. Carers of the elderly probably cannot look forward to progress in independence or only to temporary independence at best. But carers of the handicapped do look forward to improved performance as parents do in the case of normal children, and so they would be more tolerant and patient as part of the education or training process.

The carer was asked to recall the moods and the behaviour of the cared-for person during the week previous to the interview. The responses are contained in Table 6.17.

Table 6.17   The Behaviour And General Form Of The Cared-
              For Person Over The Previous Week

%

(n = 86)

	A lot	Some- times	Hardly at all/never
Restless	4.7	25.9	69.4
Irritable	3.6	29.8	66.7
Aggressive	3.5	20.0	76.5
Obstinate	10.7	48.8	39.3
Affectionate	91.8	7.1	1.2
Appreciative	77.4	16.7	6.0
Forgetful	7.1	41.7	51.2
Impatient	16.5	44.7	38.8
Cheerful	88.2	9.4	2.4
Repeating requests over again and again	34.5	27.4	38.1
Carer lost temper with cared-for person during past week	2.4	22.6	75.0
Carer had to restrain cared-for person	4.8	25.0	20.0
Carer was frightened of cared-for person	1.2	1.2	97.6
Carer was embarrassed by cared-for person	1.2	9.5	89.3
Carer found it difficult to leave cared-for person	7.2	26.5	66.3

While these responses show that the cared-for persons can
be annoying through "repeating things over again and again"
and though a certain amount of impatience and obstinancy
comes across, these are more than counter-balanced by the
very positive things said about them by the carers. There
seems to be a sense of loyalty at work here. One wonders if
the parents of normal children would give as high a rating
to them as these mothers of the the handicapped did. The
finding that a mere 2.4 per cent of the carers lost their
tempers often and only 22.6 per cent occasionally did so,
causes one to wonder how reliable this examination of
conscience is! However, we will see at a later stage that
the carers regard their development of patience and
understanding as one of the benefits which they derive from
caring.

A comparison between the 25 per cent who are in five day
residential care and those at home full-time showed no
significant difference in the measures on over-all health,
physical disabilities or general behaviour. The significant
differences were in relation to restlessness, irritability
and impatience. Those in residential care were reported to

have been significantly less restless, irritable and impatient than the others. And the carers had lost their tempers less with those in residential care than with the others. Since these interviews took place while the children were on their summer holidays, the differences may be due to less strained nerves on the part of the carers whose burden of caring may have been easier because they were not all the year round carers at the moment.

In summary, the elderly group are, by reason of their advanced age in the first place and by the carers' reports in the second, very dependent or most likely to become so with each passing year. About one third need full-time care. The other two thirds, while maintaining a fair degree of independence in daily activities, are all dependent to some extent and this dependence must necessarily increase in the majority of cases. Even without major crises the future must be one of increasing dependence.

The handicapped sample, not surprisingly, were a more active group physically than the elderly but here again there was a great deal of caring or "tending", as Parker [17] calls it, and supervision required from the carers. In so far as detailed comparisons can be made, the sample seemed to be generally in line with Bayley's British sample as regards their degree of disability and need for care.

By coincidence we found two carers in the elderly group who looked after both a handicapped child and an elderly person. There was also one case of a mentally handicapped girl who was a carer. (See Case Histories, 27, 74 and 76).

The study of carers which was conducted by the National Council for the Aged [18] in 1987 concluded that 17 per cent of the over 65s in the Republic of Ireland are dependent on their families for, as they put it, "a significant amount of care at home from a relation", as against 5 per cent who are in residential care. The remaining 78 per cent were leading independent lives. On the basis of 17 per cent of the total age group over 65 receiving care, the high average age of my sample would suggest that if I have erred in regard to their need for care, I have done so on the conservative side.

Lewis and Meredith [19] have identified three stages in the "caring sequence". Theirs is a useful contribution as it seeks to situate the carer in either (i) semi-care or (ii) part-time full care or (iii) full-time care. Sometimes these stages follow gradually with increasing age, at others a further stage is "triggered" by a crisis such as sudden illness or the death of cared-for person's partner. I would estimate that more than one third of the elderly in this study are at stage (iii), while the great majority of the remainder would be at stage (ii). In other words, there is a good degree of dependence here, sufficient to keep the carers occupied for most if not for all of the time!

'NOTES'

1. Wenger, G.C., 1984, *"The Supportive Network"*, George Allen and Unwin, London.
    "It seems apparent that the availability of supportive relatives is essential in keeping the majority of the over 80s in the community" (p.182).
2. *Census of Population,* 1981, Vol. 2, Central Statistics Office, Dublin.
3. *Census of Population,* 1981, op.cit.
4. *Census of Population,* 1981, op.cit.
5. Wenger, G.C., 1984, op.cit., p.8.
6. Wenger, G.C., 1984, op.cit., p.29.
7. Wenger, G.C., 1984, op.cit., p.30.
8. Hunt, A., 1978, *The elderly at home: a study of people aged sixty five and over living in the community in 1976,* Social Survey Division, OPCS.
9. Anderson, W., et.al., 1974, *Geriatric Medicine,* Academic Press, London.
10. Tinker, A., 1981, *The Elderly in Modern Society,* Longman, London.
11. Wenger, G.C., 1984, op.cit., p.27.
12. Hunt, A., 1978, op.cit., p.70.
13. Norris, J., (ed.) 1988, *Daughters of the Elderly,* Indiana University Press, U.S.
14. Bayley, M., 1973, *Mental Handicap and Community Care,* Routledge and Kegan Paul, London.
15. Bayley, M., 1973, op.cit., p.123.
16. Bayley, M., 1973, op.cit., p.120.
17. Parker, A., 1981, "Tending and Social Policy", in Goldberg, E.M., and Hatch, S., *A New Look at the Personal Social Services,* Policy Studies Institute, London, pp. 26-30.
18. O'Connor, J., Smith, E., and Whelan, B., 1988, *Caring for the Elderly Part I, A Study of Carers at Home and in the Community,* National Council for the Aged, Stationery Office, Dublin.
19. Lewis, J., and Meredith, B., 1988, *Daughters Who Care,* Routledge, London, pp.33, 180-182.

7 Help needed and provided

I shall now attempt to set out the actual degree of help needed by the elderly and the handicapped and the extent to which these needs are met by the carers, their spouses and others within and outside the family. I depend on the reliability of the carer's report in each case. The carer may, on the one hand, exaggerate her own role in the caring process in order to impress the interviewer and on the other hand she may exaggerate the contribution of the spouse or family or others out of a sense of loyalty, of not wanting to let the others down to an outsider.

The picture of care is built up with reference to a list of personal and household tasks some of which the cared-for person can do independently but others where he/she needs supervision or actual help to perform. In each case, the helper is identified. Table 7.1 shows the pattern of caring in regard to personal tasks. The "others" who help are further identified in Table 7.2.

TABLE 7.1   Cared-For Persons And Difficulties With Personal Tasks

%	ELDERLY							MENTALLY HANDICAPPED							
	Can Perform Task			Who Helps ?				Can Perform Task			Who Helps ?				
	On Own	With Super-Vision	Only with help	Carer alone	Carer & Others	Others in House	Others outside House	On Own	With Super-Vision	Only with help	Carer alone	Carer & Others	C.F.P. & Others	Others in House	Others outside House
Taking bath	59.3	4.4	36.3	34.8	8.7	7.2	13.0	29.8	33.3	36.9	42.4	4.5	34.8	4.5	0.0
Washing hands/face	78.8	4.4	16.8	29.6	7.3	3.7	0.0	55.3	24.7	20.0	23.2	0.0	35.7	1.8	0.0
Putting on shoes/stockings	75.0	4.5	20.5	34.5	6.8	5.3	0.0	56.5	10.6	32.9	13.0	0.0	46.3	1.9	0.0
Buttoning/zips	70.5	8.9	20.5	39.0	8.5	5.1	0.0	48.2	11.8	40.0	22.8	0.0	43.9	1.8	0.0
Dressing other than above	71.4	9.8	18.8	36.1	8.2	4.9	0.0	54.8	21.4	23.8	18.5	0.0	44.4	0.0	0.0
Getting to & using WC	82.1	3.6	14.3	22.2	7.4	3.9	1.9	69.4	21.2	9.4	19.6	0.0	27.5	0.0	0.0
Getting in & out of bed	83.9	4.5	11.6	19.6	5.9	5.9	2.0	90.6	4.7	6.7	6.7	0.0	11.1	0.0	0.0
Feeding self	89.3	6.3	4.5	14.9	10.6	0.0	0.0	90.6	5.9	3.5	2.4	0.0	17.1	0.0	0.0
Shaving/Combing hair	76.4	5.5	18.2	19.3	8.8	8.8	5.3	61.0	15.3	23.7	15.0	2.5	32.5	5.0	0.0
Cutting toenails	34.2	5.4	59.5	49.5	7.7	11.5	15.4	15.7	7.2	77.1	51.4	4.3	31.4	5.7	0.0
Up & down steps	59.6	11.7	28.7	34.0	17.0	11.3	1.9	85.4	6.1	8.5	9.1	0.0	18.2	0.0	0.0
Getting around house	80.6	5.6	13.9	23.3	9.3	4.7	2.3	96.4	0.0	3.6	2.7	0.0	5.4	0.0	0.0
Getting out of doors	51.5	14.1	34.3	45.0	13.3	6.7	6.7	79.3	14.6	6.1	6.8	0.0	20.5	6.8	0.0

84

Table 7.2

The Helpers : Relationship To Cared-For Persons

%	BATHING		WASHING		SHOES/STOCKINGS		W.C.		FEEDING		CUTTING TOENAILS	
	Elderly	Handi-capped	Elderly	Handi-capped	Elderly	Handi-capped	Elderly	Handi-capped	Elderly	Handi-capped	Elderly	Handi-capped
Father	0.0	53.8	0.0	73.7	0.0	69.2	0.0	75.0	0.0	57.1	0.0	43.8
Brother	10.5	7.7	11.1	5.3	11.1	3.8	12.5	0.0	20.0	14.3	0.0	9.4
Sister	0.0	19.2	11.1	15.8	11.1	23.1	12.5	16.7	0.0	28.6	3.2	15.6
Aunt	0.0	0.0	0.0	0.0	0.0	3.8	0.0	8.1	20.0	0.0	0.0	3.2
Son	15.8	0.0	22.2	0.0	22.0	0.0	12.5	0.0	0.0	0.0	20.7	0.0
Daughter	31.6	0.0	33.3	0.0	22.2	0.0	25.0	0.0	40.0	0.0	20.7	0.0
Daughter-in-law	5.3	0.0	11.1	0.0	11.1	0.0	0.0	0.0	0.0	0.0	3.4	0.0
Public health nurse or other official	26.3	0.0	0.0	0.0	0.0	0.0	0.0	0.0	0.0	0.0	20.7	6.3
	(n=19)	(n=26)	(n=9)	(n=19)	(n=9)	(n=26)	(n=8)	(n=12)	(n=5)	(n=7)	(n=29)	(n=32)

It can be noted from Table 7.1 that there is a good degree
of independence on the part of the cared-for persons. Only
a minority of 15 to 30 per cent need supervision or help
with many of the tasks in either group. Bathing and cutting
toenails cause greater difficulty. The elderly are less
mobile than the handicapped and need more help to get about.
    The carer is the person who gives most of the help with
these personal tasks. Among the others who help, the father
of the handicapped and the daughters of the elderly cared-
for are the ones most often mentioned. Sisters, brothers
and daughters-in-law come next. The public health nurse
performs two specific tasks for the elderly, i.e., bathing
and cutting toenails. But overall in the majority of the
personal tasks, either the cared-for person performs
independently or is helped by the carer alone.
    Turning to household tasks the picture alters however.
Table 7.3 outlines a set of household tasks and the help
required and received on the part of the elderly. The
carers of the handicapped were not included here.

Table 7.3   Household Tasks And Help Received
                        By Elderly

                        Who Helps?

	No help Needed	Carer Alone	Carer and Others	Others in house-hold	Others outside household
Cleaning house	12.4	76.1	1.8	3.5	0.9
Cooking	16.8	67.3	1.8	4.4	4.4
Washing dishes	17.0	67.0	2.7	11.6	2.7
Doing laundry	12.4	66.4	1.8	4.4	10.6
Making fires	16.2	61.3	1.8	12.6	1.8
Bringing in fuel	12.6	60.4	0.9	14.4	4.5
Gardening	3.2	48.5	0.9	26.9	14.0
Household repairs	1.9	32.4	0.0	33.3	26.7
Decorating	2.0	36.3	0.0	29.4	24.5
Shopping	4.5	74.1	1.8	8.0	5.4
Collecting pension	9.0	64.0	0.9	12.6	8.0
Budgeting	19.2	63.5	1.9	9.6	1.0

(n = 113)

The cared-for are far more dependent in regard to household tasks than personal tasks and the carer is again the main source of help. But in many of these household tasks the carer receives help from others - more so than with personal tasks. Husbands and sons assume prominence here. For example, help with bringing in fuel came from sons in 46.2 per cent of cases, for gardening it was 52.0 per cent, 46 per cent for household repairs, 43.2 per cent for decoration, 57.6 per cent for shopping, 55.6 per cent for collecting the pension. Perhaps this reflects the male role expectations within the culture? However, the sons helped with cooking in 23.5 per cent of cases, with cleaning in 25.0 per cent and with dish-washing in 31.3 per cent of cases; these activities would not be thought of as "men's work".

The contribution of spouses was examined in regard to the nature and extent of help given in Tables 7.4 and 7.5. The great majority of spouses do help but those of the carers of the handicapped seem to be more involved.

Table 7.4   Whether Spouses Help

%	Elderly	Mentally Handicapped
YES	72.2 (35)	91.0 (71)
NO	22.2 (12)	6.4 (5)
NO ANSWER	5.6 (3)	2.6 (2)
	(n = 54)	(s = 0.0000)

The nature of care given by the spouses here was classified as follows in Table 7.5

Table 7.5   Type Of Help Provided By Spouses

%	Elderly	Handicapped
Personal care	42.1 (16)	56.2 (40)
Minding	15.8 (6)	12.8 (9)
Outdoor activities	5.3 (2)	23.9 (17)
Other	36.8 (14)	7.0 (5)
	(n = 38)	(n = 71)

The carers then rated their spouses' help as shown in Table 7.6.

Table 7.6   Spouses Help Rated

Rating %	Elderly	Mentally Handicapped
Essential	51.1 (24)	63.9 (46)
Very Important	21.3 (10)	16.7 (12)
Important	8.5 (4)	9.7 (7)
Not Very Important	8.5 (4)	8.3 (6)
Non Existent	10.6 (5)	1.4 (1)
	(n = 47)	(n = 72)

Any inconsistency between the responses on spouse's help between Tables 7.4 and 7.6 may be due to the ambiguity of the "not very important" category in the ranking question. In fact, Table 7.5 shows that all 38 who said their spouse helped in the previous question were able to give details of the help given. Consequently Table 7.4 would seem to be a more reliable guide to the degree of spouses' help.

Other members of the family both within and outside the household were said to help with personal care and outdoor activities. These included children, brothers, sisters and other relatives of the cared-for person. Table 7.7 outlines the contribution of relatives living within the household.

Table 7.7   Help From Relatives Within Household

	Help Given		Nature of Help		
%	Elderly	Handicapped		Elderly	Handicapped
YES	82.1	95.2	MINDING	62.5	42.5
NO	9.5	4.8	HELP WITH ACTIVITIES	4.5	27.5
			PERSONAL CARE	0.0	10.0
	(n = 48)	(n = 68)		(n = 48)	(n = 68)

The help given by relatives who live outside the household is presented in Table 7.8.

Table 7.8   Help Given By Relatives
                  Living Outside Household

| % | HELP GIVEN | | | NATURE OF HELP | |
	Elderly	Handicapped		Elderly	Handicapped
YES	56.3	44.2	MINDING	53.6	53.8
NO	42.9	55.8	HELP WITH		
NO ANSWER	0.8	0.0	ACTIVITIES	6.0	25.0
			PERSONAL		
			CARE	7.1	8.2
			OTHER	33.3	13.0
	(n = 112)	(n = 86)		(n = 112)	(n = 86)

It would seem that by far the greatest part of personal caring comes from the carer and spouse in the case of the mentally handicapped cared-for persons and from the carer and others in the household in the case of the elderly. Using time diaries, Nissel and Bonnerjea [1] found in their study of care of the elderly within the family that the wives spent, on average, two or three hours per day on essential care while husbands spent a mere eight minutes. In the absence of time diaries in this study it is impossible to determine the actual amount of time spent in caring by spouses. The help which comes from relatives outside the home is largely "minding" for both cared-for groups, with an element of taking the cared-for person out of doors for various activities in the case of the handicapped.

The rating given by carers to the help received from relatives living within and outside the household can be seen in Table 7.9 which allows comparison between the various relatives and neighbours who help. The help from relatives within the home is rated higher than that of family members outside the home. But both are rated highly showing that the carers appreciate every help received. Family loyalty may be at work here also. In most cases, carers were not demanding or critical in regard to lack of help from relatives outside the home or from neighbours.

Later, we will see that the presence of the cared-for person is generally thought to be a force for unity within the families. When the carers were asked if they thought that family members outside the home ought to be doing more to help, less than 10 per cent in each group felt they should.

Table 7.9   Ratings Given To The Help Of Relatives And Neighbours

| | CARERS OF ELDERLY | | | | | CARERS OF HANDICAPPED | | | |
	Spouse	Family members in house	Family members outside house	Neighbours	Public Health Nurse	Spouse	Family members in house	Family members outside house	Neighbours
Essential	52.1	41.4	34.7	18.3	24.7	63.9	60.0	28.6	11.1
Very Important	21.3	32.8	32.0	39.0	24.7	16.7	32.9	47.6	33.3
Important	8.5	15.5	13.3	22.0	15.5	9.7	7.1	19.0	27.8
Not Important	8.5	10.3	20.0	8.5	35.1	8.3	0.0	4.8	19.4
Non-Existent	10.6	0.0	0.0	12.2	–	1.4	0.0	0.0	8.3

An interesting light was thrown on the help of relatives through responses to a question on how the carers coped with a crisis such as sudden illness of the cared-for person or an illness on their own part. After the doctor came spouses and relatives as helpers in crisis. Friends were lower down the scale and neighbours were not mentioned. Table 7.10 shows the sources of help in a crisis.

Table 7.10   Who Helped Carer With Crisis In The Past And To Whom Would They Turn In A Future Crisis

	Past Crisis		Future Crisis	
%	Elderly	Handicapped	Elderly	Handicapped
Doctor	67.9	69.0	44.5	42.0
Spouse or Other relative	14.0	27.0	37.0	48.7
Friend	12.5	4.0	12.0	3.9
Other	5.6	0.0	6.5	5.3

When asked who actually helped the carer the last time she had to stay in bed for a whole day, husbands scored high (33.3 per cent) with daughters, sons, brothers, sisters and very occasionally neighbours coming to the rescue. In a number of cases the carer made it clear that although she was ill she had to remain at her post.
"Although I was in bed I was well enough to get up and give the old lady the injection which is vital for her diabetes. My husband got the meals however."
"When I had Rachael I was only in hospital about three days. I was sore and stiff but I had to come straight home and start straight into looking after her and the others including Michael, the handicapped child."
"It happened once when the children were at home and they helped to look after Grandma. I was well enough to give orders from the bed."
Approximately 10 per cent of carers in both groups said they would have nobody on whom they could call in such a crisis.
Next came the help of neighbours. There was a significant difference between carers of the elderly and of the handicapped on this question as will be seen from Table 7.11.

Table 7.11   Whether Neighbours Help And
              The Nature Of The Help Given

Do Neighbours Help?   Nature Of Help

%	Elderly	Handicapped		Elderly	Handicapped
YES	56.6	32.9	MINDING	54.2	63.6
NO	42.9	67.1	OTHER	37.5	18.2
NO			PERSONAL		
ANSWER	0.5	0.0	CARE	8.3	-
			OUTDOOR		
			ACTIVITIES -		18.2

(s = .0036)

Neighbours' help consists in "minding" - being present, chatting and generally giving friendship and moral support to both carers and cared-for persons. Hannan [2] found that this function was an important one on the part of neighbours, in his study of small farmers in the South West of Ireland. The most important contribution which neighbours made and the one the farmers said they would miss most if they were to move from the area was "day to day pleasurable conversations". The help of neighbours was also ranked next in importance to that of relatives outside the home as shown in Table 7.9 above. While their help is clearly seen as of less importance than that of relatives either within the household or outside, only 9.0 per cent of the carers of the elderly and 5.0 per cent of the carers of the handicapped felt that neighbours should be doing more.

Neighbours are well regarded for their support even when they did not do much quantitatively. When they did give assistance they were very well regarded by the carers. The findings here on the carers' ranking of help received from family, kin and neighbours fits well with Bulmer's summary of Abram's studies. [3] "Something like nine tenths of the care given to those who in various ways cannot fend for themselves in our society is given by spouses, parents, children and other kin."

It is probably true to say that caring for elderly or handicapped is viewed primarily as the proper task of the family. On the other hand, neighbours in Ireland may be like the Welsh neighbours, described by Wenger, [4] as slow to interfere when an elderly person has a family of his/her own in the area. Families do not expect much more than interest, companionship and moral support from neighbours in the great majority of cases.

Help from statutory and voluntary services

Table 7.12 sets out the position of the cared-for in relation to visits from the various statutory and voluntary groups.

Table 7.12   Whether Different Officials
                    Visit Cared-For Person

%	Elderly Cared-for		Handicapped Cared-for	
	Yes	No	Yes	No
Doctor	76.6	23.4	11.5	88.5
Public health nurse	57.3	42.7	7.7	92.3
Social worker	0.0	100.0	23.4	76.6
Priest	94.4	5.6	5.1	94.9
Home help	12.3	87.7	0.0	100.0
Voluntary bodies	11.8	88.2	17.4	82.6

It is clear that the elderly receive more visits from almost all the statutory and voluntary representatives than the handicapped. This probably reflects the overall greater mobility and better health of the latter and, of course, it neglects to mention schools and training centres which play a very large part in the lives of carers and their handicapped cared-for.

The contrast between the priest's visits to the elderly and the handicapped is striking. One would have expected at least an annual visit in the course of routine parish visitation.

The two most frequent visitors to the elderly are the public health nurse and the priest. With the carers of the handicapped the social worker who is employed by the Residential Home through the Minister for Health is the most likely official person to call. Table 7.13 shows the frequency of the visits of the statutory and voluntary sector. As explained earlier, the social workers of the Health Boards work exclusively on family problems and consequently are not involved with the elderly. The social worker who is employed by the residential home, visits the families of the children regularly.

The Home Help Service is confined to the elderly and almost exclusively to the elderly who live alone. But in the very recent past families with children in this area have begun to receive a home help service when the mother is seriously ill and the children might otherwise have to be placed in residential care. This development seems promising.

Table 7.13

Frequency Of Professional Visits To The Cared-For Persons

	Elderly Cared-For				Handicapped Cared-For			
	Doctor	Public Health Nurse	Home Help	Priest	Doctor	Public Health Nurse	Social Worker	Priest
When sent for	68.0	14.8	11.5	2.0	100.0	87.5	52.8	88.9
Weekly	0.0	41.0	30.8	1.0	-	-	-	0.0
Monthly	25.0	26.2	50.0	86.7	-	-	8.3	0.0
Few times a year	7.0	18.0	7.7	10.2	-	12.5	38.9	11.1
n = actual number receiving any visit	100	61	26	98	51	32	36	27

The public health nurse is therefore the key statutory person in the care of the elderly while the priest is an important contact for the voluntary sector. The public health nurse visited 57.3 per cent of the elderly in the study. In the previous study on Loneliness among the over 65s in the same region, 11.4 per cent received visits from the public health nurse.

Within the group visited in the present study, 41.0 per cent received a weekly visit, 26.2 per cent a monthly visit, 14.8 per cent said they sent for her when they were in need and 11 per cent were visited a few times per year. This compares with 18 per cent in Wenger's Welsh sample and 8 per cent of Hunt's English sample [5] who had received home visits from the district nurse within the previous six months of the interview. Wenger found that those living alone in rural Wales were three times as likely to receive visits "despite the higher incidence of impaired health of those who live with others." [6]

The relative importance which the carers attached to the contribution of the public health nurse can be seen in Table 7.9. But there was a further dimension, namely, a contribution to the carer. 30 per cent of the carers felt that the public health nurse's visit helped them as well as the cared-for person. Moral support was the chief contribution together with some advice about personal care.

The most frequent services provided by the public health nurse were those of examining the patient, taking blood pressure, doing dressings, doing blood and urine tests, giving injections, checking on medicines and cutting toenails. The next most frequent task was washing or bathing the patient.

After these services, importance was sometimes attached to the chat which the nurse had with the cared-for person; though not by all, since one or two felt that the nurse did little else apart from chatting! But a few stressed the moral support which the nurse's visit gave to the cared-for persons and two or three acknowledged the same for themselves. The visits were described in the following terms.

"She comes and there's a general chat. My mother has a bunion problem and she dresses this for her."

"If Mary needs washing, she will wash her. She applies special ointment to the stump of her amputated leg; the nurse is excellent."

"She washes and dresses her and combs her hair and sees to all her personal needs."

"She takes her blood pressure, tests her urine and makes sure she is comfortable. She gives me sheets, paper sheets, and I have found these very helpful."

"She does nothing, only say, "hello, how are you?". She cuts her nails and brings her tablets when she wants them."

"She doesn't do anything. She just sits down on the chair and chats half the day."

95

"I only saw the public health nurse once, and as far as I could see, all she did was take her blood pressure."

"She doesn't have to do much for him because he is pretty good himself. I suppose she just checks him up to make sure he is alright."

"She is a lovely person and Tim enjoys her visits. She sees after him well."

"She bathes her, cuts her nails, takes her blood pressure."

"She does nothing much, just chats. Since about two years ago when my mother hurt her leg, the public health nurse has visited regularly to wash and dress the injury. She talks to her mostly. As she is a cousin of my mother's, it has become very much a social visit."

"She gives him injections. She cheers him up a lot. She takes his blood pressure."

"She calls, but she always calls in the morning and Jerry doesn't want to see anybody before 12.00 noon at the earliest. She talks in the window to him and he doesn't get much satisfaction out of it."

"He tells her his complaints. She advises him about different things. She is very good and very kind. However, it is her support and the support of her visits which make me feel that there is somebody behind me. She listens to my complaints and rings the doctor if she thinks this is necessary and she cuts his toenails."

"She gives her a bed-bath, takes her pulse and blood pressure. She is great. She takes her out of bed and tries to get her to walk."

"I am able to share my own problems with the public health nurse and this is a great support to me."

The public health nurse's help is perceived as important by the majority of the carers who experience her visits. She is important for the medical aid, the moral support and she also carries out a referral role to doctors and to residential sector when this form of care is deemed necessary.

Home helps

Only 12.3 per cent of the elderly have a home help; all are elderly who live alone. The home help is usually from within a few miles of the elderly person's home. The experience of the Health Board is that elderly people refuse to allow close neighbours to tidy or clean. The stranger is seen as less of a threat to privacy. The usual contribution is a weekly visit or a few times weekly at most. In two cases, there were full-time paid home helps who lived with the elderly persons.

Voluntary bodies

A surprisingly small minority of carers received direct help from voluntary bodies despite the strong tradition of this sector in Ireland. 11.8 per cent of carers of the elderly had visits from voluntary bodies including the St. Vincent de Paul Society, the Legion of Mary, a Meals on Wheels Service and the Wheelchair Association. In the case of the carers of the handicapped only 17.8 per cent received any direct help from voluntary bodies. The most frequently mentioned were the Parents and Friends of the Handicapped (9.3 per cent), the Down's Syndrome Association (3.5 per cent), the Wheelchair Association (2.0 per cent), the Faith and Light (Jean Vanier) Movement (2.0 per cent) and the Brittle Bones Association (based in Scotland) (1.0 per cent).

The Parents and Friends Association have been instrumental in securing two schools for the handicapped and have set up two workshops in the area. They did not receive as much mention as one would have expected from the carers. It is possible that carers are not clear on what the term 'voluntary organisations' includes .

The priest

Wenger [7] found that elderly people in North Wales received more visits from clergy than from any of the other professionals. She described the regular visits of clergymen of different denominations and, in particular, of the Non-Conformist ministers to the elderly in their homes and in hospital. She found that the clergy in North Wales were three times as likely to visit as the clergy in Hunt's study. [8] 50 per cent of the elderly in North Wales had received a visit in the past six months.

The situation in Ireland resembles that of North Wales in that clergy visit the elderly regularly in their homes and also in hospital. The Catholic custom of bringing Communion once a month, on the first Friday, has ensured that the elderly who are housebound are visited by the priest·on a regular basis.

In this study, 94.4 per cent of the carers said that the priest visited, 5.6 per cent said he did not. When questioned about the frequency of the priest's visit, the vast majority said that the priest came once a month. In the case of the elderly, 86.7 per cent said that the priest came once a month, 1 per cent said he came once a week, 2.0 per cent said he came when he was sent for and 10.2 per cent said he came a few times a year. It is clear that the monthly visit is the regular first Friday Call. When asked if they felt that the visit was important for the cared-for person, 94.4 per cent of the carers said they thought it was, 0.9 per cent thought it was not and 4.6 per cent were not sure. They were then asked to say why they thought it was important. The most frequent response was that the old person "looked forward" to the priest's visit on the first Friday. They described, in a number of cases, how preparations were made and how the old person often saw the visit as "the highlight of the month" for them. 30 per cent mentioned the fact that the elderly person looked forward very much to the first Friday Communion visit of the priest.

The second reason given was that "the old person was a religious kind of person", "a person with great faith", "a person who had always gone to Mass while they were able", and now saw this as a substitute for attending Mass. 28 per cent gave these as reasons. Some people simply said that "the old person loves to see the priest coming", or "likes to receive Holy Communion". 20 per cent mentioned this as one of their reasons for the importance of the priest's visit to the old person. Then, 18 per cent mentioned the fact that the old person received either a moral boost or was made very happy or consoled by the visit of the priest. The carers seemed to see both the religious significance of receiving the Sacrament and the social side of having a chat with the priest. There were three cases in which the carer felt that the reception of the Sacrament meant that the old person was prepared for death should it occur suddenly.

The carers gave their reasons in terms such as these:

"Mary is very religious. She likes meeting the priest every first Friday. It is one of the things she looks forward to every month."

"Because she always looks forward to it. It helps her a lot. It brings her out of herself."

"It's very important to every old person."

"He has a great chat with the priest and he'd keep him all day. He tells him about everything. He loves to meet the priest and feels better when he has Confession and Communion and when he gets his troubles off his chest."

"She would be very disappointed if he didn't call. This is the highlight of her life, to have Confession and Communion. She feels happy when she gets the Holy Communion."

"He looks forward to it so much, he loves the priest coming and it does him great good. He is a man of great faith. He loves receiving the Blessed Sacrament."

"She always liked going to Mass and now when she cannot go, she loves to receive Holy Communion at home. The day before he comes she'll say to me, "Tommy, have you the candle and holy water ready for the priest in the morning?'"

"She is a holy person. She likes receiving Holy Communion."

"He is a very religious man. He loves to receive the Sacraments."

"The Canon comes a few times a year and Denis receives Confession and Communion. He still goes to Mass *occasionally."*

"Religion is very important to old people. She pretends she doesn't want the priest, but worries if he's five minutes late."

"She was very holy and was always praying and looks forward to the priest's visit."

"She was always a great person for Mass. While she was able to get about she was never late. She'd like him to come every morning if he could. She's an exceptionally holy person."

"Since he can't get to Mass, he likes to have the priest come to the house."

"All old people look forward to the first Friday. It pulls her up and helps her morale. It renews her interest in the house and in her appearance when the visit of the priest is due."

"It makes her day and she counts the days until he comes. She loves getting Holy Communion."

"She feels very happy when she expects him and after he's gone she's very happy too. She looks forward to it. It's a big occasion for her. She likes to see the priest even though she is not over religious."

"It's very comforting for my mother-in-law to have the priest visit her."

"We enjoy the first Friday. All three of us receive and it is lovely."

"She is a very religious person and devotes most of her time to prayer. She looks forward to the priest's coming and feels very well afterwards."

"She looks forward to the day. It is a great interest for her, preparing the house and getting the candles ready."

"I think he really couldn't care less whether the priest comes or not."

It is clear from these comments that the first Friday Communion Call has both a religious and social function in most cases for the cared-for persons. To a lesser extent, it helps the carer also.

Thirty three of the carers of the elderly said that they liked the priest's visit and personally looked forward to it. They felt that the coming of the priest and the bringing of the Communion were in themselves pleasant events and they liked them. Ten of them mentioned the fact that the visit of the priest gave them moral support. It showed that the Church was interested in them and in the sick. It gave the carer an opportunity of chatting with the priest and of being reassured of the importance of their task of caring. Four people mentioned that they received a "spiritual boost" from the visit. Four others mentioned the reassurance that, should the old persons be taken suddenly, they would have received the Sacraments. It should be mentioned that the tradition here is that when somebody is taken ill suddenly, the priest is sent for at the same time

as the doctor, so that the Last Rites can be administered.
However, the most common reaction from the carers was the
effect the visit had on the old person. It was this which
gave them the greatest satisfaction with the priest's visit.
Seeing the old person happy and in good humour and obviously
consoled gave the carer, in turn, reason to be happy and
grateful. Thirty two of the carers of the elderly mentioned
this.

Though the priest's visit caused some extra work for the
carers in that they have to tidy the house, prepare a table
cloth and candles, and the elderly person also in many
cases, nevertheless, when asked whether the First Friday
visit created any difficulties or any extra work, only 3.7
per cent said it did, 96.3 per cent said that it did not.
This showed an overall attitude to the priest's visit which
was very positive.

In summary, it would seem that the carers set great value
on the help received from spouses, family members within and
outside the home, neighbours and social services statutory
and voluntary. From the actual amount of help reported one
would be tempted to think that the carers over valued the
help of others. This would be to omit the dimension of
moral support and the reassurance that help would be
available in a crisis. Family and community loyalty is a
factor also as is the cultural set of expectations within
which the carer lives and which she largely accepts as
"givens".

An interesting finding is what the carers thought would
happen to the cared-for person if they were no longer
available. The results are shown in Table 7.14.

Table 7.14   If The Carer Were Not Available Any Longer
              What Did She Suppose Would Happen To The
                        Cared-For Person

%

Who would look after Cared-for person?	Elderly (n = 112)	Handicapped (n = 86)
Other family member (excluding spouse)	40.5	32.5
Husband specifically mentioned as carer	7.5	31.3
Residential Home	37.7	25.5
Neighbour	3.7	0.0
Self-help, i.e., cared-for person could manage alone	3.7	0.0
Home Help (paid)	1.8	1.8
Don't know	0.9	2.3
Other	2.8	2.3

There was more reliance on family members, including spouses in the case of the carers of the handicapped, to continue the caring outside the residential sector. Neighbours did not count for very much when full-time caring was involved. Theirs is a very secondary role. The primary caring role rests with the family.

'NOTES'

1. Nissel, M., and Bonnerjea, L., 1982, *"Family Care of the Handicapped Elderly : Who Pays?"*, Policy Studies Institute, London, p.4

2. Hannan, D., and Katsaiouni, L.A., 1977, *"Traditional Families? From Culturally Prescribed to Negotiated Roles in Farm Families"*, The Economic and Social Research Institute, Dublin, p.85.
    The findings of this study indicate that a once thriving mutual aid system has declined to a residual level. Neighbours are not privy to secrets and confidences. They are not approached for financial loans. Their main function now is for conversation and exchange of news. But the farmers said they would miss their neighbours even more than their relatives if they had to move to a new County.

3. Bulmer, M., 1986, *Neighbours : The Work of Philip Abrams,* Cambridge University Press, Cambridge.

4. Wenger, G.C., 1982, *Personal Communication*

5. Hunt, A., 1978, *"The elderly at home : a study of people aged sixty five and over living in the community in England in 1976"*, Social Survey Division, OPCS, (Unpublished tables).

6. Wenger, G.C., 1984, *The Supportive Network,* George Allen and Unwin, London, p.54.

7. Wenger, G.C., 1984, op.cit., p.63.

8. Hunt, A., 1978, op.cit., (OPCS, Unpublished tables).

8 Dynamics of caring

One of the most important sections of this study was an exploration with carers of the social costs and rewards of caring. The question of what motivates them and what keeps them going was examined, as were their fears for the future.

Since Motivation is a key issue in the dynamics of caring, I shall examine it first. We saw earlier that carers saw their task as "natural" in the context of family relationships and to a much lesser extent in the context of community relationships. The carers were asked how the task had fallen to them and their answers reflected a sense of family obligation which they seemed to accept without much question in most cases.

They were asked the direct question as to whether they assumed the caring role out of a sense of duty. 60 per cent in each group said they had. Then they elaborated:

"It is my duty, that's all"
"It is my duty to look after my own children surely"
"His father always felt that we should look after him"
"It's a mother's duty to look after her children"
"I have a responsibility to all my children including the handicapped child"
"Mary is my wife and I felt obliged to do my best to look after her"
"I felt it was my natural duty to look after my mother in her old age"
"I knew that my husband was very anxious that I would look after his mother"

"I should look after my own father, surely"
"It's bound to be my duty. You can't expect a neighbour to do it for you if you don't do it yourself"

These replies acknowledge the duty to care for family members, elderly and handicapped, as a normal part of family life.

The next most common type of reply was that there was "really nobody else to do it". This shows that the carers see themselves as the last line of defence but they are not complaining too much. In fact, in a previous question, the vast majority did not feel there was anything unfair about the fact that they were left minding the child or the elderly person. They simply saw the caring task as falling to them in accordance with tradition and all round expectations.

"There was no one else to look after her"
"She had nobody else but me left. 'Twas a foregone conclusion that I should look after her"
"There was no other choice but to take charge"
"In my case it had to be; there was no one else to care for her"
"I felt nobody would care and love her as we did"
"I go to that townland every day and twice during the winter; nobody else calls to that old lady so I feel I have to do it"
"Well, all the rest of the family are in England"
"Sure, the poor man had nobody else after his wife dying"
"There was nobody else to look after her so I said as I was the youngest I'd try and keep the place together"
"The fact that he was here in the house when I came and who else could be expected to do the job"
"Yes, there was no one else there. If I didn't who would?"
"I'm the only one she has in the locality. She is my husband's mother and I would feel bad if I didn't do it".

Another frequent response was to appeal to family relationship as a sufficient explanation.

"He was my child"
"She was my child. I wanted to do the best for him"
"She was my daughter and I had to look after her and no more about it"
"Sure, you couldn't see your mother not looked after, could you?"
"He is my own"
"He was Sean's father and I became part of his family when I married and I cared a lot for him"
"I'm his wife and it's my duty"
"He is my neighbour. I am nearest to him, I'm only down the road. He was always a good neighbour"

Another set of responses was to express a love of the cared-for person as the motive.

"I love my child and I like minding him"
"I have cared for him because I love him"
"We have as much love for her as for the rest of them"
"Because she is my sister and I care for her very much"
"She is my wife and I love her and I feel it is a privilege to look after her while my own health holds out"

A small number gave reasons which stemmed from religious convictions. This was true in particular in the case of the carers of the handicapped.

"If God gave him to me it was to take care of him and not throw him away. Anyway, you could not throw away your own child no matter what kind they are. God gave him to us"

"God sent him to us so we were bound to take care of him"

"He was my child, God sent him to me and I was bound to do what I did"

"I see it as my Christian duty to support a neighbour in need"

Some answers involved a mixture of the reasons given above, and occasionally, the carers of the elderly gave serial altruism as their motive.

"I feel I will be old myself some day and hope someone does the same for me"

"I am better able to do it than the rest because if I was in the same position I would like someone to do the same for me"

"He looked after me when I was young so it is only natural now that I would look after him when he is old"

"I feel I owed his mother this much because my mother-in-law was good and kind to me always"

"Well, I was always good to her, but she was such a good mother and she didn't have an easy life"

The various explanations given for feeling a sense of duty are given in Table 8.1.

Table 8.1   Sense Of Duty Elaborated Upon

	Number of times mentioned	
	Carers of Elderly	Carers of Handicapped
Sense of duty re-stated	15	12
Close family relationship given as reason for caring: mother-child, brother, sister, wife, aunt, uncle	14	22
Nobody else available or willing to do it	12	7
Carer loves cared-for person or likes looking after him/her	4	5
Carers felt it was no trouble	9	6
Cared-for person is regarded as one of the family	3	4
Religious motives expressed	2	4
Carer speaks of reciprocal debt owed to parent because of being looked after as child	9	0
Unwillingness to send cared-for person to residential setting	4	4
Duty as good neighbour	2	0
Other	4	4
Unable to give reason	2	1

Since some tended to mention more than one reason the percentages are not given for each case. The empathy, affect and sense of duty which Abrams [1] identified as important factors are in evidence here. So is reciprocity which he stressed even more. The reasons are very much family based.

When we examined whether the sense of duty was to the cared-for person or to someone else only 10 per cent of the carers of the elderly and 1.3 per cent of the carers of the handicapped said it was to someone else - to husbands in the case of wives who looked after husbands' parents for example.

The family was reported to be a stronger source of this sense of duty than religion. Table 8.2 shows that the choice was in favour of family among carers in both groups.

Table 8.2   Whether Religion Or Family Was The More
             Important Source Of Their Sense Of Duty

%

n = 178	Carers of Elderly	Carers of Handicapped
Family more important	35.3	60.5
Religion more important	24.5	7.9
Both equally important	40.2	31.6

(s = 0.01)

Family motives were significantly more frequent in the
case of the carers of the handicapped. Perhaps the more
frequent contact which the carers of the elderly had with
their priests could explain this? Or, perhaps, the closer
blood relationship on the part of the carers of the
handicapped, mother-child most often, made the family the
stronger force in this case.
The carers did not seem to be excessively motivated by
social control factors such as possible criticism from
family, neighbours or clergy if they failed in this task.
Table 8.3 gives the picture.

Table 8.3   Whether Carers Felt They Would Be Severely
             Criticised If They Failed To Carry Out Their Task

Severe criticism expected from:	Carers of Elderly		Carers of Handicapped	
%	Yes	No	Yes	No
Family	37.3	62.7	47.1	52.9
Neighbours	38.1	61.9	38.6	61.4
Clergy	17.3	82.7	22.5	77.5

The neighbours do indeed exercise a considerable degree of
influence as critics, almost as great as the family overall.
But then in a community where everybody knows everybody
else, the carers are naturally somewhat sensitive to
neighbours' opinions, probably much more so than in an urban
setting (see Life Histories, Case No. 41). In the earlier
study [2] on Social Stigma, recipients of welfare payments
felt that they suffered a great loss of face before
neighbours who inevitably came to know of their situation.
They experienced a much higher degree of embarrassment
before neighbours than before family. The gossip of
neighbours in rural Ireland has been a topic much written
about by novelists, a good example being, *The Valley of the
Squinting Windows* by Brinsley McNamara.

A final question, well on in the interview, probed the carers' motives yet again. "If you were asked the crucial question, 'why do you do it and why do you continue to care when it becomes very difficult', how would you answer?" The earlier questions may have caused the carers to ponder on their motives, or the building up of rapport with the interviewer may have helped to overcome initial shyness, but they now began to bring expressions of love for the cared-for person to the fore. They also tended to give two or three reasons together, as for example, *"I do it because he is my father and I love him and there is no one else to do it".* These responses are outlined in Table 8.4

Table 8.4   Why Carer Continues When It Becomes
                              Very Difficult

Reasons given and number of times mentioned	Carers of Elderly	Carer of Handicapped
Love of cared-for person mentioned or feelings of special affection	24	34
Cared-for person is really no trouble	16	15
Sense of duty felt	18	12
Close blood relationship given	13	16
Carer enjoys the task and wants to continue	19	11
No one else to do it	3	3
No choice in the matter	3	3
Cared-for person's needs stressed	0	4
Other	5	5
Religious reasons given	3	2
Philosophic reasons given	3	3

What emerges here is a positive attitude which goes beyond a mere sense of duty. There is a playing down of the difficulties, "no trouble", and a declaration on the part of many that they enjoy the caring role despite its difficulties.

"Because I love him like nobody else"
"We all love Maura. We all look forward to the weekends when she comes home because we love her and want to care for her."
"She is my child and I don't want anyone else to care for her. I love her more than the rest. We love her and she is a child of God."
"Because she is adorable"
"She is very lovable. I feel that I will have her when all the others are gone. My only fear is what will happen when we are gone. Her brothers and sisters are mad about her."
"We love her and I couldn't put her in residential care as she wouldn't be happy there"

"Because I love her and we all love her and I miss her when she is away in the workshop during the week"
"I love her that much I wouldn't part with her"
"I feel he is my special child"
"She is my child. I love her. She is so affectionate"
"She is my wife, I love her. It would be different if it were somebody else."
"Because I love my mother"
"I love her and I will miss her when she goes"
"Because I love her and because she needs me"
"I am very attached to the old man. He is one of the family. I got a sense of satisfaction from looking after him."
"I love my mother and all I want is to see her happy"
"Because I love my mother, that's why, and when she dies, I'll die myself too"
"I love my grandmother and I get a sense of fulfilment out of doing it. She's great crack. She's like one of our own (age group)."
"He is very close to me, he's a great companion. I am paying him for his goodness to me when I was young."
"I was always very fond of him. He was the only man in my life."
"She's my flesh and blood. There's a great bond between us."
"She is a sweet old lady who loves meeting people and enjoys company. I like her company too."
"I have cared for my mother and father all these years. I will be lost the day they leave me."

There were similar explanations in regard to the sense of duty such as, *"Well at this stage, a sense of obligation. That's why I keep going. She's my mother. My conscience wouldn't allow me to do otherwise."*

Others stressed the fact that their handicapped child or the elderly cared-for person was "one of the family" and was regarded as such and treated the same as any of the others. However, one quite different and interesting reason emerged, a neighbour who had rented the land of an old lady: *"Grazing, it is an economic arrangement; I get the grazing free, I save her turf and I keep a watchful eye to see that she is alright."*

The rewards of caring began to appear also in these responses, some insisting without prompting that it is really no trouble, others stating of their own accord that they enjoy the task.

The carers were asked a series of questions which might indicate the quality of their relationship with the cared-for persons. The responses are given in Table 8.5.

Table 8.5   Whether Carer Would Describe
                   Cared-For Person As:

%	Carers of Elderly (n=107)		Carers of Handicapped (n=86)		Signifi-cance on Chi Square
	Yes	No	Yes	No	
A very close companion	83.2	16.8	94.2	5.8	0.0338
Very close to carer	86.0	14.0	100.0	0.0	0.0000
Someone carer likes to be with	88.7	11.3	98.8	1.2	0.0125
Someone carer looks forward to returning to	86.7	13.3	98.8	1.2	0.0045
Someone with whom carer gets on well	92.5	7.5	100.0	0.0	0.0260
Someone with whom carer can have a disagreement without falling out	92.6	7.4	96.5	3.5	0.3898
Someone who can often be very demanding	36.2	68.8	54.7	45.3	0.0160
Someone who is difficult to get through to	27.9	72.1	28.6	71.4	1.0000
Someone who is just not happy and cannot be cheered up	16.2	83.8	0.0	100.0	0.0003
Someone who one just could not please	7.6	92.4	3.5	96.5	0.3644
Someone who never shows any signs of thanks or appreciation	7.8	92.2	2.4	97.6	0.1818

The overall reaction is decidedly positive, showing a great
loyalty. However, a substantial minority of the elderly are
described as "often demanding" and "difficult to get through
to" by the carers. Some of the handicapped cared-for are
described as even more demanding. But there is no
gainsaying the strong bond of love and affection which binds
the carers and cared-for. It is slightly stronger for the
handicapped.
    There were "bad moods" on the part of the cared-for: 52.7
per cent for the elderly, 66.7 per cent for the handicapped.
30.9 per cent of the carers of the elderly lost patience
with the cared-for as against 60.2 per cent in the case of
the handicapped. The handicapped occasioned a significantly
greater loss of patience. The bad moods were coped with in
various ways such as ignoring them, coaxing, putting on
music, going for drives and, most of all, the use of silence
until the mood passed off. The carers of the handicapped
felt they had to be firm by not yielding to screams or
scenes.

What annoyed the carers of the handicapped about the cared-for was stubborness, problems with toilet and personal cleanliness, aggressiveness towards the other children, a tendency to repeat questions and to demand attention.
"He refuses to do what I tell him. When he·makes up his mind not to do something, he can be very obstinate."
"He has to be brought to the toilet constantly"
"Her eyes and her nose are always wet. She always wants me there."
"He throws his clothes everywhere"
"She is a great little nagger"
With the elderly it was personality clashes which created problems, but only in a minority of cases. Elderly were sometimes described as "impossible". Their propensity to "say the hurtful word", to be "cranky", to be "stubborn", to "spoil the grandchildren" and a wide range of other complaints were mentioned by a minority of carers.

The majority of both groups of carers felt that they were closer to the cared-for person now than they were at the beginning of the caring experience. Table 8.6 shows the feeling here.

Table 8.6   Whether Carer And Cared-For Are
             Closer Now Than When Caring Began

%	Carers of Elderly	Carers of Handicapped
Closer now	62.2	50.2
Same degree of closeness	31.5	47.6
Less close now	3.6	1.2
Don't know	2.7	0.0

The cared-for persons shared confidences and worries with carers of the elderly in 78.6 per cent of cases· and similarly for the handicapped with 68.4 per cent sharing. Exactly 75 per cent of the elderly entrusted their financial affairs to their carers.

What the carers liked most about the caring task was the affection and appreciation shown by the cared-for person. This was mentioned 48 times in all. Expressions of personal fulfilment and satisfaction were given 29 times. "Seeing the cared-for person happy" was mentioned 29 times. "Personal enjoyment of the task" was mentioned 27 times. The sense of having done one's duty, or fulfilled an obligation was given 8 times. Five stressed that caring was "really no trouble at all".

Some examples of what the carers of the handicapped liked most about their task:
"She's very affectionate and lovable and always says 'thank you'"
"Her affection. She is like a five year old child"

111

"She appreciates everything. She is a very affectionate child."

"He is a pleasure. He is so loving and good-natured."

"Her affection, her company, the little things she does and says, the things that make us laugh together"

"He is an adorable loving creature"

"I suppose I take pride in the fact that I am the most important person in her life"

"I love looking after my child. I love buying her clothes and shoes and have her looking nice."

"I feel I am doing something special"

"She has so much love to give. She is a very sympathetic child."

"I just love caring for him. He likes me to make a fuss of him. He is so affectionate."

"I get a great sense of pride and satisfaction when she achieves something"

"He is all we have left now and I love to see him coming home"

"Doing the best I can for my child, helping her to learn, to cope with life"

"I just like talking to her. She is a pleasure. She is so loving and good-natured."

"Getting all the love back, the satisfaction of it. That's very rewarding."

Similarly with carers of the elderly:

"When he says how thankful he is and how happy he is"

"She is such good company and so appreciative"

"If I can do something to cheer him up it makes me feel good also"

"She is just like a grandmother, like one of the family"

"When I see him happy and comfortable and he always appreciates everything. It makes me happy too."

"He is good-natured and good humoured and no trouble"

"I know I am making life easier for her by doing various jobs for her"

"She is very kind and very appreciative. I am happy when I see her happy."

"She is a very grateful person and appreciates everything I do for her"

"It is my duty to do everything I can for her"

"I like to see him cared for and happy"

"She is very thankful and co-operative"

"I enjoy it"

"To see her warm, clean and content in a loving atmosphere"

"Somebody must care for him. I think it is the least we might give him after a long time in the family."

"I like being with him. I like chatting with him. He is always very cheerful."

"She is a very nice lady and was always very good to me when she had her health"

"He is a quiet man. He never bothered anyone in his life."

*"We are great friends and I love to see him happy. He is
my husband and we care very much for each other. We
enjoy each other's company. I feel a great sense of
fulfilment from doing this task."*
"I find it a great privilege to look after her"
*"I take no notice of it at all. She is no trouble at
all. I feel very good when she says she is happy."*

One or two expressed negative feelings:
"I don't like anything about it"
*"There is nothing in particular I like about it except
that she is my mother"*
"I have no likes or dislikes about it"

These were a tiny minority. The majority were very
positive.

The carers of the handicapped tended to mention the
affection of the cared-for person while the carers of the
elderly stressed the satisfaction that they had from seeing
the old person happy and content. The carers seemed to be
motivated more by feelings than by abstract principles and
so would contradict Dr. Samuel Johnson's [3] opinion on the
superiority of principles over feelings. Recent British
writers like Lewis and Meredith [4] and Ungerson [5] would
tend to support Dr. Johnson, having found that women carers
generally give a sense of duty and obligation as their main
motives. Men, however, tended to emphasise affection and
love.

Coming to what the carers disliked most, the responses
fell into the following main types. Fifty nine of the
carers claimed that there was nothing they particularly
disliked. Twenty six mentioned the fact that they were tied
down a great deal by the caring role, that they had to be
there all the time as the cared-for person demanded constant
attention. Six said that the cared-for person was demanding
both because of his/her personality and in terms of time
needed. Eleven mentioned problems of keeping the cared-for
person clean and tidy and a few of these were specific,
e.g., difficulties regarding toilet. Four carers of
handicapped mentioned having to reprimand and correct as
what they disliked most. Three mentioned losing their
patience, three mentioned tiredness, one frustration, one
loneliness, two the stigma and embarrassment of having a
handicapped child.

One mentioned the physical problem of lifting the
handicapped young person. One mentioned having to give
injections. One mentioned the fact that the elderly showed
no appreciation whatsoever for what was being done and three
mentioned that what they disliked most was when the cared-
for person was suffering and they were unable to do anything
about it.

What is surprising is that even when they were
specifically asked to state something they disliked, 30 per
cent of the carers stated that there was nothing that they

disliked. Only one, and she was the carer in the earlier question who said there was nothing she liked, said in this case that she "disliked everything" about the caring role. The general picture, once again, shows either a loyalty to the cared-for person or genuine feelings that they did not find caring particularly difficult.

Of course, the minority who mentioned that they were tied in, that their care had to be constant, keeps the costs side of the balance sheet before us.

"He cannot be left out of sight. He has to be watched the whole time."

"I always felt a bit embarrassed and a bit out of place having a handicapped child"

"I have to keep constantly at her to keep herself tidy. I feel I am picking on her."

"Keeping an eye on him all the time"

"Having to be available all the time to care for her"

"The fact that he has to be watched constantly"

"She can be aggressive at times. At this stage, I still have to take her out to the W.C. at night. It is upsetting to think that she will not have a normal full life. Keeping an eye on her all the time and worrying about her future."

"Being tied so much. It can be very boring at times."

"Being tied down, the feeling that I will always have somebody dependent on me. That is a worry always."

"The strain of it when I am with him too long"

"Sometimes if I want to do jobs and if there is no one around, I can't do the work as I have to keep an eye on him."

"I am tired changing him"

"Why did it happen to me? I dislike the stigma attached to the condition of handicap."

"Seeing her suffer and not being able to talk with her and explain to her"

"It gets very monotonous and the old lady takes me for granted"

"Looking at my father now that he is blind, when I remember how he used to love to be out working and to read the paper at night"

"Mopping up operations but I am becoming used to it. You need a strong stomach."

"The feeling of being tied and used. The old man's messing at the table, messing up the bathroom and the sleepless nights."

She doesn't appreciate what I do for her"

"Being stuck at home all the time"

"Everything. When I see her condition getting worse it makes me very unhappy."

The carers felt best about their task "when he/she (the cared-for person) is happy". This was mentioned sixty seven times. The happiness of the cared-for person was in itself a reward for the carers. There was a sense of satisfaction at seeing the cared-for person in good humour, in good health and well looked after. The carers of the handicapped were happiest when they saw some improvement in the handicapped, or when they began to do things for themselves, or showed independence or progress. Seventeen mentioned special times when they felt very close to the cared-for person. These included evening time, Christmas time or the time when the cared-for person returned after being away at school or at the workshop. Others said that it was when the handicapped was well-behaved they felt best. Among the elderly sample, some mentioned an improvement in the old person's health or mood as being a morale boost for them also. Five of the carers mentioned signs of appreciation for what they were doing as the source of their greatest satisfaction. One or two were philosophic and regarded it as a job to be done. Two people said that they never felt good about the caring role, one being the person who pronounced negatively twice already. (See Life Histories, Case No. 7). So the carers generally felt happiest when the cared-for persons were responding positively.

"When I see her looking happy and healthy looking"

"When he achieves something new. When I see some improvement, however small, it is a step up and a step in the right direction. I feel very good then."

"When I go to the workshop and see what he is capable of doing and see what all the other handicapped there are capable of doing, I feel I am part of something very different from ordinary workshops and I feel privileged."

"When there is one to one contact with my daughter, when she is sitting on my lap around bed-time. That is when I feel best."

"When I see her so happy and see how much joy little things bring to her"

"When I come back after being away for a while and she hasn't seen anybody for some time and she appears so glad to see me back"

"My job is very rewarding and I feel very good about it all the time. I get great pleasure out of caring for my father and seeing him happy."

"I always like doing it. I never feel different about it."

"I never feel good about it"

The responses to these questions seem to me to be very positive with the exception of a small minority of negative feelings expressed. The vast majority seem to take satisfaction and experience a sense of fulfilment in the caring role. But the few who are dissatisfied or who get little from it are a most important group since they may well be near breaking point. It is these carers who should be identified by community services and given prompt support lest caring collapses and carer and cared-for need hospital or residential care thus in Moroney's [6] sense "rewarding them when they cease to care". Overall, however, 91.8 per cent of the carers of the elderly and 97.6 per cent of the carers of the handicapped said they get a sense of

fulfilment from the task. This must be a very surprising
figure in the light of the literature of caring which
emphasises costs almost to the exclusion of fulfilment or
satisfaction experienced by carers.
   But on the costs side, 20.7 per cent of the carers of the
elderly and 27.4 per cent of the carers of the handicapped
felt that their social life had suffered because of caring.
Of these, 70 per cent said that these effects were "very
serious" or "serious".   There was a strain on their
marriages, attributed to caring, for 8.5 per cent of the
carers of the elderly and for 23.1 per cent of the carers of
the handicapped.   In one case the child's behaviour in
public or when visiting friends so upset the father that it
created tension between the parents. So the mother makes an
excuse rather than risk repeat performances.
   This leads to the question as to whether the carers get
regular breaks or not. It will be seen from Tables 8.7 and
8.8 that the carers of the handicapped leave home very
seldom despite the fact that most of their cared-for go to
schools and workshops.

Table 8.7   How Often Carer Leaves The House

	Carers of Elderly (n = 113)	Carers of Handicapped (n = 86)
%		
Daily	38.0	23.2
Every few days	2.2	2.9
A few times a week	33.7	62.3
Once per week	25.0	11.6

Table 8.8   Breaks For Carers

	Carers of Elderly (n = 112)				Carers of Handicapped (n = 85)			
	Yes	No	Rarely	Never	Yes	No	Rarely	Never
Away on own regularly for a day	62.5	10.7	16.1	10.7	52.9	8.2	27.1	11.8
Away on own for a night	18.6	15.9	12.4	36.3	23.3	11.6	32.6	25.6

   A minority of 27.7 per cent of the carers of the elderly
and 32.5 per cent of the carers of the handicapped said they
would like to get out more often. Their reasons for not
going out varied from lack of transport or lack of money to
not wanting to upset the cared-for person or impose too much
on a trusted helper.
   *"I can't get someone reliable to look after her and it is
   not everybody she will stay with"*

"It's not every place I can bring her. For example, if I bring her to the doctor's surgery she could upset the patients in the waiting-room and might also throw things about the waiting-room itself."

"I just haven't the means to go. Our car is not very road worthy and my husband won't take us."

"I am too busy and I don't have the money"

"It's not easy. It's placing a heavy burden on someone else. I feel I can't go out on account of John."

"I couldn't go out very much as he'd cling to me and start screaming if I were leaving the house without him"

"I would be too worried about my aged mother-in-law to enjoy being out"

"I feel obliged to stay and look after Mary. I wouldn't trust her if I was out too long. Anyway, she would give out to me when I got back."

"I have too much responsibility at home"

"If I went out more often I think it would upset him. He is very dependent on me, so I cannot go out too often."

"We live far away in the mountains here and we don't have a car"

"I know the way he carries on when I go out, tormenting the family as to when I am coming back, so that I can have no enjoyment out of going out"

"I can't go to the pub, where I would like to go, because I have no way of going and no money for the drink. I'd have to ask someone to sit here all night while I'm out."

These replies came from 24.1 per cent of the two samples.

But 47 per cent of the carers of the elderly and 59.3 per cent of carers of the handicapped said that they could only stay away for a few hours without upsetting the cared-for persons. The frequency of holidays away from home is given in Tables 8.9 and 8.10.

Table 8.9   Frequency Of Holidays For Carers

%	Carers of Elderly	Carers of Handicapped
Every year	13.6	13.1
Most years	1.8	4.8
Some years only	10.9	13.1
Never	73.6	69.0

(n = 199)

117

Table 8.10   Length Of Holidays For Carers

%	Carers of Elderly	Carers of Handicapped
A few days only	39.3	12.5
A week	46.4	54.2
Two weeks	14.3	20.8
More	0.0	12.5

(n = 52)

It should be noted that in Ireland the annual holiday is not the institution it is in Britain and the relatively small percentages who take holidays away from home may not be very different for the carers than it is for families generally.

The need to have somebody to look after the cared-for when they are out is one of the greatest problems for carers. In the case of the handicapped, the fathers are the mainstay (64.3 per cent) followed by other family members. Only 1.4 per cent mention neighbours. With the elderly, family members do most also but neighbours assist in 21.6 per cent of cases. Help from neighbours again seems to go much more to carers of the elderly than to those of the handicapped.

The effects, good and bad, of outings for the carers and their charges are reported in Table 8.11.

Table 8.11   Effects Of Outings On Carers And Cared-For

(n = 188)	Elderly		Handicapped	
%	Carers	Cared-for	Carers	Cared-for
Feels better	83.3	27.9	92.4	22.0
Feels much the same	–	63.5	–	74.4
Feels neglected	–	8.6	–	3.6
It varies	16.7	–	7.6	–

The good effects on the carers and the absence of any great ill effects on the cared-for when left at home indicate that more breaks for the carers would be very beneficial. More frequent breaks are one of the important overall recommendations which the carers themselves make and I can readily endorse their view.

The majority of carers had at least one hobby, 79.1 per cent in the case of carers of the elderly and 73.3 per cent in the case of carers of the handicapped. Reading was the most common, mentioned 40 times, knitting and sewing, 30 times, watching television, 21 times, gardening, 15 times.

For smaller numbers there was rug-making, flower arranging, weaving - one woman used her spinning wheel - and crochet was mentioned twice. A few attended greyhound and horse racing, played golf or badminton or went to the pub with friends. Those who had pastimes and hobbies seemed to enjoy them very much.

The carers also reported a considerable amount of emotional stress, tiredness and a sense of being trapped. Serious fears for the future were common among carers of the handicapped. These feelings are shown in Table 8.12.

Table 8.12   Stresses Felt By Carers

n = 194	Carers of Elderly			Carers of Handicapped		
%						
Suffered from:	Yes	No	Not Sure	Yes	No	Not Sure
Loss of sleep	15.5	83.6	0.9	17.9	78.6	3.6
Exhaustion	26.4	71.8	1.8	34.9	60.2	4.8
Emotional stress	25.9	73.1	0.9	45.1	45.1	9.8
Worry about the future	28.7	70.4	0.9	72.9	22.4	4.7
Sense of being trapped	14.0	84.1	1.9	22.0	73.2	4.9

There are serious stresses for a sizable minority in both groups of carers. Particularly serious, in the case of the carers of the handicapped, are emotional strain and fears of the future. These were significantly greater for the carers of the handicapped than for those of the elderly. Similar findings were reported by Bayley [7] and more recently by Richardson and Ritchie [8].

In the case of the carers of the handicapped, the main fear was what would happen to their cared-for when they had passed away or had become too old to continue. The long term future of the child was their greatest worry. This was mentioned 24 times. Next came more short term fears as to what would happen the child after he/she left school, whether a place could be got in a workshop, whether he/she could cope with life and become independent. Doubts were expressed as to whether other members of the family would be willing or able to take over or indeed whether it would be fair to expect them to do so. They had fears about their own health also. A few were philosophic and a few others trusted in God's providence.

"I wonder how will she be cared for when I am gone"
"Who is going to mind him when I am too old?"
"I worry in case anything should happen to his father or myself. I wonder who is going to look after him when I am dead?"
"I wonder where will he go when I die and there is nobody to look after him? I wonder will he be looked after with

love when I am gone?"
"If I don't outlive Grace what is going to happen to her?
If anything happened to her father or myself who would
look after her then?"
(See Life Histories, Case No. 64)
"The biggest worry is Susan being put into a Home when we
can no longer look after her"
"I wonder if he will be able to look out for himself in
life?"
"I wonder if she will be able to look after herself?"
"I wonder if he will be able to cope with life and I hope
that he won't get worse"
"I am always afraid that she will not be independent
enough to cope in life"
"I wonder what will happen to Michael as he gets older?
I wonder if he will be able to work and look after
himself?"
"I worry a great deal about her. I worry about what will
happen when she grows up and becomes a young woman."
"I am not worried for myself but I am very worried for
Jimmy and for his future"
"Since my child has no brothers or sister, will there be
anyone to look after Patrick?"
"I wonder if one of his sisters would look after him when
I am no longer available?"
"My greatest fear is that there won't be anyone to look
after him"
"I take every day as it comes and do not allow fears to
come into my mind. I leave all my worries in God's
hands. He looks after them all."
"I put my trust in God. God has been very good to me so
far. I know He will continue to be."
"I fear that I may not be able to carry on for long more.
I have great fears that Martin might become ill and that
I might have to part with him."
These fears and general uncertainty about the future on the
part of parents were reported as follows by Bayley. [9]
"Anxiety about the future pervaded the life of most if not
all of these families. If they could be given some
knowledge that their subnormal would be looked after in a
way that would satisfy them, a great load would be lifted
from them." (See Life Histories, Case No. 55).
   The carers of the elderly were not as prone to such fears
but some did have worries. Perhaps most of them take for
granted that they will outlive the cared-for persons. Their
answers about the future tended to be philosophic; 22 of the
60 responses were of this kind, "I take every day in
itself", "When the Lord calls my mother I'll be resigned to
it", "As long as I can get about and have my health I am not
afraid of the future". But a number had real fears
concerning the future care of the elderly person.
   "My greatest fear is that of getting stuck with Joanna
   for the rest of my life as she is a very difficult
   person"

"My greatest fear is the fear of being stuck here for the rest of my life"
"My greatest fear is that of having a nervous breakdown"
"If she were to lose her senses and if she became very troublesome, I would then have to put her into a hospital for good and I think that would upset me very much"
"I worry about how I would cope if she became senile and totally dependent on me for everything"
"I have no future"

More than 90 per cent of the carers felt that they were naturally good humoured and less than 2 per cent felt that they were less so now than when they took on the caring task. Only 14.4 per cent of the carers of the elderly and 26.6 per cent of the carers of the handicapped felt that caring had changed them. The changes were not always negative in their view. But Table 8.13 details their perception of a number of the changes.

Table 8.13   Changes Perceived By Carer
                              As A Result Of Caring

%	Carers of Elderly			Carers of Handicapped		
Results of	More	Less	About the same	More	Less	About the same
Irritable	9.0	16.2	74.8	9.6	12.3	78.1
Patient	93.7	5.1	1.1	90.3	9.7	0.0

The perception that caring had made them more patient is an interesting finding. It came up again when the carers were asked how they had benefited from caring and what caring had taught them. 78.9 per cent of the carers of the elderly felt they had benefited personally from the experience while 86.7 per cent of the carers of the handicapped felt similarly. On the question of whether contact with the cared-for persons had taught them anything, 69.4 per cent of the carers of the elderly and 82.7 per cent of carers of the handicapped felt it had. The positive change or benefit mentioned most often was that caring had made them "more patient and understanding". However, we must not forget that in an earlier question as to whether they sometimes lost their patience with the cared-for person, 30 per cent of the carers of the elderly and 60 per cent of the carers of the handicapped said they did. Among the latter, 16.5 per cent had lost their tempers a lot, 44.7 per cent had sometimes lost their tempers with the cared-for persons over the past weeks.
A further intriguing twist is that the male carers were slightly more likely to attribute the virtue of patience to themselves than were the females. And the male carers, without a single exception, regarded themselves as

"naturally good humoured"!

Horowitz [11] has an interesting finding in this context. In her study at the Brookdale Centre on Ageing she found that male carers report less stress in the caring role than female carers. The level of involvement was controlled. Her hypothesis is that men do not become as emotionally involved in the intimacies of caring. It could also be of course, that men are not as open about their feelings as women carers. But the finding raises a very interesting question in the context of which are the better survivors in very demanding caring situations.

Some examples of how the carers in the present study felt they had changed because of their caring role:

"It has made me a more thoughtful person, much less material in my outlook"

"It made me more open to other peoples troubles and less self-centred. It has made me grow for the better and all growth is good. It has given me a chance to live out love, joy and peace in my life."

"I am more outgoing now than I used to be"

"I think it has enriched my life"

On the negative side:

"Sometimes I get worn out from it all"

"My child is a big responsibility and she depresses me at times. I would say I am more nervous now and I suffer a great deal from anxiety. It has made me more anxious and worried sometimes."

"I get fed up and upset at times"

"I can't call my life my own anymore"

"It is tiring. It has made me more serious. I was very light-hearted when I was young."

"It has made me seem much older than what I am"

"It has made me very old but it has not changed my personality"

"It has begun to get me down. I feel cranky and even the other children are now getting on my nerves."

"I feel that I have missed out on a lot of my life and that I look years older than I am"

"I am not as outgoing as I used to be"

"It has made me very bitter and resentful"

"I am a very embittered person. I used to love my own way of life and I no longer have any life of my own."

There was a feeling among some of the carers that they tired more easily now than when they first began their task. A sense of isolation was also reported by some as shown in Table 8.14.

Table 8.14   Tiredness And Other Feelings Among The Carers

n = 182

	Carers of Elderly			Carers of Handicapped		
%	Yes	No	Not Sure	Yes	No	Not Sure
Carers tires more easily now	46.4	50.9	2.7	68.1	27.8	4.2
Sometimes feels very much alone and isolated	16.2	82.9	0.9	23.3	76.7	0.0

The admission to feeling tired more easily could be indicative of a good deal of physical and emotional stress for the carer.

Both loneliness and boredom were reported also. The standard question on loneliness showed a relatively high incidence while a lower degree of boredom was expressed as shown in Table 8.15.

Table 8.15   Loneliness And Boredom Among The Carers

n = 112   Carers of Elderly

%	Yes	No	Often	Sometimes	Rarely/Never
Lonely	24.1	76.9	21.4	60.7	17.9
Bored	22.5	77.5	10.8	11.7	77.5

n = 86   Carers of Handicapped

%	Yes	No	Often	Sometimes	Rarely/Never
Lonely	39.5	60.5	5.7	77.1	19.1
Bored	11.0	89.0	4.1	6.9	89.0

Among the elderly in my previous study the degree of boredom was much greater. [10] The carers of the handicapped tended to report loneliness more often and boredom less than the carers of the elderly. Those who said they felt isolated and alone felt this was chiefly because they were so tied down. Sometimes even when they were out they were anxious about the elderly person. Others saw their isolation as stemming from lack of confidants. Others again lacked a telephone or were living in isolated areas. A deserted wife in a rural area with other children as well as her handicapped son with no telephone, no public transport and living on a Deserted Wife's Allowance, is one example. Others:

"I have to be there all the time, all days"

"She needs constant care and I am not free to go and come when I like"

"I live in an isolated area with very few neighbours. I feel a bit depressed at times. It is a great responsibility and it takes up an awful lot of my time."

I am living in a rural area. We are far away from the town, from the hospitals, from the doctors and so on."

"I am always tied down. When she is out with me I have to keep an eye on her all the time and that means I feel tensed most of the time."

"At times I feel cut off because I have to stay in such a lot"

"I don't discuss my troubles with anybody except my immediate family and close friends. There is no one with whom I can discuss Ciara as there is no information available about her particular disease."

"Because I am here always. I am here from morning till night. I am alone in the house with Pat. No one ever calls. I am responsible for everything that happens in the house."

"At times I feel trapped. I can't have anyone in to talk to. I feel uncomfortable with them because my father-in-law doesn't want them around the place. I just can't stir and when I go out I have to rush back when all the other people are staying on. I feel my friends have lost touch with me as I am not free to go out and join them."

"I wouldn't be living here if I hadn't to look after my mother"

"There is no comfort going anywhere. You are always worried about him. I wish I was miles away from here."

The carers were asked to identify the greatest need of somebody in their position. The five main needs reported were (i) lack of companionship, by which they meant someone in whom the carer could confide and know she was understood, (ii) family support, both emotional and practical - the need for appreciation from other family members, (iii) regular breaks for the carer, (iv) patience as vital to caring, (v) good health for the carer. Help from neighbours, ownership of a motor car, a telephone were mentioned by a few. Four or five mentioned money as their greatest need. Two were anxious to find a job for the cared-for person. Table 8.16 outlines these responses.

124

Table 8.16   What Carers Consider To Be The Greatest
              Need Of Someone In Their Position

	Carers of Elderly	Carers of Handicapped
Greatest need:	Times mentioned	Times mentioned
Companionship/visits/ company	23	22
A break	13	11
Help and support from family	21	10
Help from neighbours	2	5
Patience	3	9
Good health	2	5
Financial help from State	5	1
A job for cared-for person	–	2
Residential care for cared- for person	–	4
Home help	–	2
No need exists	8	1

"Companionship. Someone to talk over and understand the problem."
"Someone to talk to who is interested in Patrick"
"Friends and family. People to talk to and who would take him places because they wanted to, not because they had to."
"Having a break now and then"
"Someone who understands my situation and could give me a break now and then"
"Company. Having someone to talk to."
"The start was the hardest and I often feel that if only I had someone to talk to then, it would have helped me greatly."
"To have someone reliable who would take the child out for periods"
"Plenty of patience and buckets of energy, good health and, above all, a sense of humour"
"To know that you are doing what is best for the old person"
"The little bit of company. It is nice to have somebody pleasant calling in."

When the carers were asked to specify the first thing they would do to support a friend in their situation, they confirmed the priority they gave to moral support and friendship. The responses are shown in Table 8.17.

Table 8.17   The First Thing Carers Would Do To Help
              And Support A Friend In His/Her Situation

Suggested forms of help	Carers of Elderly Times mentioned	Carers of Handicapped Times mentioned
Visit, talk, give moral support	46	37
Mind child/old person for a time	9	19
Give carer a break	17	10
Would help in ways not specified, "anything I could" etc.	23	10
Would help in practical ways with housework, transport, shopping	11	2
Would give financial help	2	2
Would recommend residential care for cared-for person	–	3
Take carer out for a meal occasionally	1	0
Other	4	0
	(n = 117)	(n = 86)

The carers mentioned a number of times that caring had made them more patient, more understanding and less concerned with material things. The great majority felt that they had personally benefited from it. An overall sense of satisfaction and fulfilment from their role was mentioned 66 times. A second response was that caring had made them "more understanding and tolerant" as persons. This was mentioned 27 times. Patience was mentioned 15 times. That they had "become better people" was stated 10 times and "better Christians" 5 times. Nine people said it had caused them to appreciate their own health. All in all this showed that the majority saw their role in a positive light, one which, though difficult, in many cases, had taught them much and had helped them to grow in ways in which they might not otherwise have done.

Carers of the handicapped:

"It has given me a sense of fulfilment. It has given me more understanding for the handicapped."

"It has made me more thoughtful towards others"

"It has made me more thoughtful to older people. I feel for them. It is very important to be nice to people."

"It makes me appreciate my family, the fact that they are allright and in good health. I take great pleasure in the fact that none of my grandchildren are handicapped."

"You don't take half the things for granted. You are sensitive to other peoples feelings and more aware."

"It makes you a lot more tolerant"
"I have become more patient"
"I now have a different understanding of peoples problems"
"It is fulfilling"
"I am happy that I have looked after my handicapped child all these years and I am glad that I never had to put her in a Home."
"It is rewarding. It has made me more patient and understanding."
"It is great to see that she has improved so much"
"It has definitely made me a better person. I feel Brian has paid us back in his own way."
"It has taught me to have more time for others and to realise that there is more to life than good times and a good social life. It has taught me that there are a lot of people with a lot of problems that I wouldn't have known about otherwise."
"It has made me more caring. It brings me down to earth."
"It's hard to explain but it's like a vocation for me"
"I'm not fussy about small things as long as Margaret is alright. She has made my life worthwhile. I am not as selfish as I used to be. I find that I am more considerate towards others. I am no longer as engrossed in myself as I used to be. There is a very close bond between us. I feel very close to her. I often think that if I had no one to care, my life would be aimless."
"Sean's handicap was badly needed in this house. It has made all of us more caring. It has given me a new purpose in life."
"I am not as bothered about material things as I used to be. I know that God is present in him and that I am doing something for the love of God when I am taking care of him. It has made me less selfish and I no longer dwell on my own fears and phobias as I once used."
arers of the elderly:
"It's good for myself to have to consider an old person and their needs. I feel that I will be rewarded in the future life for having looked after my parents in their old age. It has helped me to be grateful for my own good health although I sometimes suffer a little from my chest."
"My mother-in-law has lived a good long life. It is good to hear her talking about her life. I have gained a lot of help from her experience when it comes to looking after my own children. I am very thankful that the rest of the family, especially our children, are healthy. I understand old people better now and how they sometimes feel they are a burden and feel they may not be wanted. I have got more practical as a result of looking after her. Although I am moving on in years myself, I thank God for my own health and that I don't have the pains that my mother-in-law suffers from continually."

"It has been a great education for me. I now appreciate the needs of old people. It has made me more tolerant and more patient with people, old and young. I'd like somebody to do it for me if I ever reach her age. She cheers me up when I am down and out rather than vice versa. It has done a lot for my children. It has made them understand about old age. I believe it helps them and will do so in the future."

"It keeps me busy and happy. I would find the time very long if I didn't have him to look after."

"I enjoy it. I think it's great example too for my children to see me doing it."

"I have done a lot for old people and especially neighbours, and have received no material benefits from it. I have received spiritual benefits I hope and, perhaps, it will do me good when I go to the other side."

"It makes you more understanding of the needs of old people and of the people who are caring for them."

"I feel good to be able to do it myself and not to be under an obligation to anybody else to do it for me"

"It is a great consolation to me to think that my mother was so happy in her last years and I feel I will have luck for looking after her"

"It has made me a stronger person, more sensitive to other people"

"It gives me something to do now that I am retired myself. It fills the day for me this way when I have someone to look after."

"Most people are very happy with what I do, especially my ageing father. I hope I will always continue to do something in the care of the elderly in my family or locality."

It is difficult not to be impressed by the spirit of self sacrifice of the carers. But it is not all one way traffic. They receive a great deal too from the cared-for persons. The carers acknowledge that they have learned a good deal from them including valuable insights into the things which really matter in life. Vanier [12] and Craig [13] have highlighted the ability of the mentally handicapped to recall us to the truth that man's need to love and be loved is more basic than the need for money, material things, pleasure or power. The phrase of St. Francis' prayer, "It is in giving that we receive", comes to mind as does Richard Titmuss's [14] celebration of altruism in *"The Gift Relationship"* even though the exchange here is between relatives and not strangers, as in blood donation.

The carers often expressed a profound spirit of altruism or love when they specified what their caring experience had taught them.

"It is an eye-opener. Otherwise I wouldn't know what handicap was like. You have to experience things like this to understand them."

"That there is more to life than a good time. A lot of people have problems that we know nothing about."

"That no case is hopeless. That where you least expect a return, that's where you will find it. Maeve is now my biggest consolation, though in the beginning, after she was born handicapped, she caused me so much trouble, so much worry, so many sleepless nights. She was a source of great unhappiness then and now she is my greatest source of happiness."

"People should be a lot more content with what they have. It has given me social contact with other parents of handicapped children and this has widened my knowledge greatly. I now appreciate even more the fact that my other children are normal."

"It has taught me a lesson, to thank God for my other normal children. It has taught me that because I have a handicapped child I will never be alone in life. Handicapped children are very loving and it has taught me to understand the problems of other unfortunate people. It has taught me that I wasn't the only one, that handicapped people can lead a normal life in their own way too."

"Even though I am a teacher I had no understanding whatever of children with defects until my own daughter was born"

"That handicapped people are real people with feelings and love and they are God's own children and when I am with him I am very close to God also"

"It has made me more understanding of a handicapped child and more appreciative of my healthy children"

"It has made me patient, understanding and it has made me feel humble"

"It has made all of us much closer as a family"

"It makes you a different type of person. It makes you look at life in a completely different way."

"It has helped me to see God in everyone even in the weakest of His creatures"

In this context it is worth mentioning that the term for mentally handicapped people in the Irish language is "duine le Dia", one of God's people.

These came from the carers of the handicapped. Now some of the responses of the carers of the elderly:

"Her qualities of holiness, patience and concern for other people have taught me to practice these qualities in my own life"

"It has taught me that times passes quickly and we will be old one day and be helpless and it may happen even before we know it"

"It has taught me how dependent old people are on younger people. It has also taught me the dignity of old age."

"It has taught me to be thankful for my own strength and to be able to look after my mother"

"The experience has made me much less selfish. It has helped me realise that there are people in the world less well off than myself."

"She's an influence on me all the time. She has taught

*me everything I know. It would make you ashamed to think
of what old people like her have been able to do in their
struggle through very difficult times in the past"*

*"She has taught me a great deal about crochet, knitting
and so on"*

*"It has made me aware of the fact that we can take our
health too much for granted. We should be grateful for
being healthy."*

*"It has taught me how to love and respect the elderly.
It has taught me to be more understanding, kind and
compassionate towards old people and towards everyone
else as well."*

*"It has taught me that nervous conditions, and especially
depression are very painful ones and that you have to
have great patience with the elderly, especially when
they have nervous disorders"*

*"It has led me to hope that I won't live to be too old
and that my daughter won't have to look after me as long
as I am looking after her grandmother"*

"It has taught me that the world is a cruel place"

*"She has taught me about the Cross. She has shown me how
to accept and carry a cross. Her example encourages me
in my life."*

*"It has taught me that many things happen as we go
through life and we never know what is in store for us
from one day to the next"*

*"Her devotion to her religion and to prayer has helped me
down the years and is an example to me"*

The literature on caring has tended very much to stress
the costs of caring and to neglect to take adequate account
of the rewards. Up to this point, the rewards and
satisfactions of caring would seem to outweigh the costs in
this study. The other study done in Ireland by the National
Council for the Aged [15] (1988) reported a high level of
satisfaction among carers too, although the reward side was
only very slightly examined. But 52 per cent of the carers
"did not mind" looking after an elderly person, 38 per cent
were "very happy" to be doing the job while 10 per cent were
"reluctant carers" and 3.5 per cent were actively "unhappy".
Overall 79 per cent would "do so again" should someone else
become dependent on them. While the negative side was
overstressed in earlier literature the balance began to be
adjusted in recent years by such people as Baldwin and
Glendenning [16] who agreed that the compensations and
rewards of caring are substantial, though they did not go on
to outline them in any detail or give them their due weight
in my opinion. Vincent [17], commenting in 1987 on this
trend, concluded, "Until recently there was a tendency in
the literature to emphasise the costs of caring to
individual women, to the family as a whole and to
siblings... More recent accounts have attempted to look at
the totality of the experience of the carers and they have
looked also at the benefits derived from caring". It looked
as though Abrams' wish was almost to be fulfilled; "We need

to know a great deal more about the rewards". However, the more recent work of Lewis and Meredith (1988) and of Ungerson (1988) and Pitkeatley (1989) even when noting the rewards, play them down or even explain them away. Consequently, the hopes raised by Vincent have not been realised to any great extent at this side of the Atlantic at any rate. The American carers in Norris' [18] biographies are much more positive and closer to the attitudes of those in the present study. But as against this again a Canadian study by Aronson [19] (1990) on a sample of women teachers who care for their mothers makes no mention whatsoever of rewards. Tension, anxiety and guilt are the only emotions reported. Lewis and Meredith [20] concluded that despite the bitterness felt by daughters and the sense of lost opportunities, there was a positive side too. "The fact remains that all but three respondents expressed some positive feelings about having cared despite, in many cases, a heavy burden or long period of care. A majority expressed a sense of achievement that the mothers had not to leave their own home..." Even in cases where the caring had been extremely difficult in all its aspects, all but a few still felt positively about having done the right thing. Though the rewards were reported after the caring had ended they do not extend beyond a satisfied sense of duty on the part of the carers. They do acknowledge however that, "positive feelings about caring are often derived not only from abstract satisfaction at obeying the injunction to care but ... from the companionship, emotional security and appreciation it brings the carer". They stop short of acknowledging that there is any love or joy in the experience even for a minority, despite the fact that it is mothers and daughters who are the subjects whom one would have expected to be very close. In fact, they stress, "One thing is clear, the idea of caring as a simple act of altruism on the part of one family member out of love for another, has little basis in reality". [21]

Ungerson [22] was taken by surprise at finding "a handful of women and, stretching the point somewhat, three of the men who experienced joy in their caring task. During this research I have been struck by two different kinds of carer ... those for whom caring was truly grim, and those for whom it seemed to bestow a certain satisfaction, even in one or two cases, an extraordinary kind of joy. I could not make sense of this at all except in the case of the joyful ones, to think generously in terms of genuine saintliness, or less sanguinely and much more arrogantly in terms of false consciousness". Although this study is a qualitative one, it is worth noting in passing that the two women and three men who comprise Ungerson's five "joyful mysteries" make up 25 per cent of her sample. I am puzzled by the way in which she plays down the expressed satisfaction of the carers.

Some light is thrown on this through a case commented upon by Ungerson. [23] A carer is being interviewed. "I love him (her husband) so much that I won't let him be taken away." When questioned further she replied, "I just think it's my duty. I'm a Lancashire lass; and Lancashire people are like that". Ungerson explains, or more correctly, explains away, "In effect she was indicating the power of ideology. Within a social science frame of reference it would be appropriate to describe Mrs. Fisher's sense of duty as deriving from a set of normative obligations which themselves derive from a set of gender-related norms". Ungerson's [24] own position is stated very clearly at the beginning of her book, "The book that follows is rooted in the women's movement and my own biography, and watered and fed by feminist academic friends and colleagues..." The power of ideology indeed!

The analogy of a balance sheet of costs and rewards may lead us to forget the fact that carers can not always stand back and separate positive and negative feelings. Such feelings may alternate or they may coexist in an internal struggle. Logic can go out the window when strong emotions are stirred. Silverstone [25] describes her personal experience of caring for her mother as a "juggling act". "The powerful feelings and emotions that power family life... are called into play... Love and affection can be intertwined in various degrees with resentment, worry, anxiety, sadness and guilt and extend well beyond the caregiving relationship to the entire family."

The present study is unusual then in the degree of satisfaction and real pleasure reported by carers while at the same time confirming all the social costs reported in the feminist literature. In the idiom of labour and love, the carers,' overall attitude could best be summed up in Shakespeare's [26] words, "The labour we delight in physics pain". One could go further and enter the idiom of self sacrifice with Blake [27]:

"Love seeketh not itself to please,
Nor for itself hath any care,
But for another gives its ease,
And builds a Heaven on Hell's despair"

'NOTES'

1. Abrams, P., 1977, "Community Care: Some Research Problems and Priorities", *Policy and Politics,* Vol. 6 No. 2., p.129.
2. Clifford, D., 1975, *The Public the Client and the Social Services,* Social Studies, Maynooth,
   69 per cent felt loss of face before neighbours compared with 24 per cent before family when it became known that they were receiving benefits.
3. Boswell, J., 1791, *The Life of Samuel Johnson,* Penguin Edition, Penguin Books, p.298.
   Boswell: "I believe natural affection, of which we hear so much, is very small".
   Johnson: "Sir, natural affection is nothing; but affection from principle and established duty is sometimes wonderfully strong".
4. Lewis, J., and Meredith, B., 1988, *Daughters Who Care,* Routledge, London, p.30.
   "On the whole respondents talked more about ties of obligation based primarily on notions of reciprocity than they did about affection, although there is a sense in which for the vast majority the fulfilling of obligations was predicated on affection".
5. Ungerson, C., 1988, *Policy is Personal: Sex, Gender and Care,* Tavistock Publications, London, p.86.
   "..... on the whole men used the language regarded as the language of marriage – that of love – while the women, even in two cases the women who were caring for their husbands, used the language of duty." However, she admits that, "some at least of the carers felt a strong loving basis to the caring they did".
6. Moroney, R.M., 1976, *The Family and the State,* Longman, London, Ch.5.
7. Bayley, M., 1973, *Mental Handicap and Community Care,* Routledge and Kegan Paul, London.
8. Richardon, A., and Ritchie, J., 1986, *Making the Break,* King Edward's Hospital Fund for London. Holden Street Press, London.
9. Bayley, M., 1973, op.cit., p.261.
10. Clifford, D., 1978, *Kerry Diocesan Study on Loneliness,* (unpublished).
    36 per cent of the over 65s reported that they were often bored.
11. Horowitz, A., 1985, *Sons and Daughters as Caregivers to Older People: Differences in Role and Consequences"* The Gerontologist 25, No. 6, p.612-617.
12. Vanier, Jean, 1985, *Man and Woman He Made Them,* Darton Longman and Todd, London, p.172.
    "Very often people look upon l'Arche as if we are completely mad... We consider those whom society devalues as valuable and capable of awakening what is most precious in the human being – the heart, generosity, the dynamism of love. They invite us to

place our intelligence at the service of love. They have the capacity to heal others by calling them to unify within themselves their deep emotions, their capacity for love and their reason. Thus they can become sources of life."

13. Craig, Mary, 1979, *Blessings*, Hodder and Stoughton, Sevenoaks, Kent.
14. Titmuss, R.M., 1970, *The Gift Relationship*, George Allen and Unwin, London.
15. O'Connor J., and Ruddle, H., *The Caring Process: Caring for the Elderly in the Home*, 1988, National Council for the Aged, Dublin.
16. Baldwin, S., and Glendenning, G., 1983, "Employment, Women and their disabled children", in Finch, J., and Groves, D., (eds.), 1983, *A Labour of Love*, Routledge and Kegan Paul, London.
"It would be wrong however to overlook the fact that care of a dependent child has its own compensations, and that many women with severely disabled children derive substantial rewards from their specialised task. These pleasures and satisfactions, rooted in feelings of love and protectiveness, are reinforced by, 'public opinion' and by the ideological values attached to motherhood and the family by contemporary social welfare institutions and practices." (Ch. 3, p.56)
17. Vincent, J., 1987, "Carers Survey", Loughborough University, *(unpublished)*.
18. Norris, J., (ed.) 1988, *Daughters of the Elderly*, Indiana University Press, Indiana.
19. Aronson, J., 1990, "Women's Perspectives on Informal Care of the Elderly: Public Ideology and Personal Experience of Giving and Receiving Care" *Ageing and Society*, March 1990.
20. Lewis, J., and Meredith, B., 1988, op.cit., pp.151-153.
21. Lewis, J., and Meredith, B., 1988, op.cit., p.30.
22. Ungerson, C., 1988, op.cit., pp.144-146.
23. Ungerson, C., 1988, op.cit., p.89.
24. Ungerson, C., 1988, op.cit., p.16.
25. Silverstone, B., in Norris J., (ed.) op.cit.,
26. Shakespeare, W., *Macbeth*, Act 11, Scene 111.
27. Blake, W., "The Clod and the Pebble", *Songs of Experience*.

9 Attitudes to money, work, men versus women and the future

We have reached the final substantive chapter and so inevitably the "bottom line" has to be placed before the reader! In a study of costs and benefits, it might appear relatively simple to compute the financial costs and benefits to the carers but, unfortunately, even this area is very far from clearcut.

Baldwin [1] has recently examined the economic costs of caring for a disabled child in terms of the extra costs incurred and income foregone. She prefaces her comparison between a sample of applicants to the Family Fund, which assists families with a disabled child, and a control group of families from the Family Expenditure Survey (FES) with an interesting outline of the problems involved in this exercise.

Most of the previous studies tended to focus on income rather than on expenditure. Studies on expenditure are usually subjective. Previous studies in this area dealt with adult disabled rather than children. Furthermore, calculations of income foregone "have all the weaknesses of hypothetical estimates based on imperfect knowledge". [2] A final complication is that parents are sometimes reluctant to admit that their handicapped child is a financial burden and may wish to stress the child's normality rather than point up differences. Add to these difficulties the long standing problems of all studies on expenditure with regard to over estimation on some commodities such as food, and under estimation of expenditure on other commodities like drink and cigarettes, and a natural reluctance on the part of many respondents to reveal their true income, and one begins to wonder if economic costs are not just as difficult to pin down as social costs!

However, Baldwin was not deterred by these difficulties from establishing that the care of a disabled child did involve considerable financial costs to the family. "For families in this study the financial impact of the child's condition was considerable and pervasive, affecting not only parents' earnings and expenditure on the disabled child but also expenditure on themselves and other children, the timing of financial decisions and the general management of money". No doubt remains after the evidence produced in this study that severe disablement in a child has a substantial impact on the family's expenditure.

The present study examined the question of extra costs, income foregone and attitudes to State benefits received by the carers. There was a significant difference between the two groups of carers on the question as to whether looking after the cared-for person made life more expensive for the carer. The figures are given in Table 9.1.

Table 9.1   Whether Looking After Cared-For Person
             Made Life More Expensive For Carer

%	Carers of the Elderly	Carers of the Handicapped
YES	27.5	57.5
NO	72.5	42.5

(s = .0000)

When asked to elaborate, the carers of the elderly mentioned possible wages foregone (6 times), extra heating costs (6), special food (5), transport (4), doctors' fees and medicines (3).

The carers of the handicapped listed extra costs for clothes and shoes (21 times), transport (10), medical expenses (7), extra heating (3), special foods required (3), income foregone by cared-for person (2), costs of laundry (1). The handicapped child was thought to be particularly "hard on shoes" and to require "special kinds of clothes". Baldwin's parents also stressed the extra clothing needs and higher clothing costs and similarly with shoes. [3]

Carers of the handicapped reported:

"The main extra cost is transport, taking him to the school bus and collecting him each day"

"He would be more help on the farm if he were normal"

"I had been paying doctors' fees until she was two years of age"

"She requires a lot of shoes and stockings. She has to be taken to the bus and collected each week-end"

"If he wasn't handicapped he would be able to work and keep himself"

"I have to buy tablets and other medication"
"There are special clothes required for handicapped people. I feel that voluntary organizations seek a lot of financial assistance from me through raffles and other functions held to support the handicapped and their workshops and schools"
"Every trip we make to Cork is expensive and we have to go every two weeks. It is seventy five miles each way"
"Because of his illness, diabetes, it becomes quite expensive. Yet, we can just about keep him on his weekly allowance"
"Food - Michael has a very hearty appetite"
Carers of the elderly:
"I need special bed clothes and they do not last very long. There is also the cost of coal and fuel"
"As I live seven miles from her, it can be quite costly on petrol because I go to her house almost every day"
"He has a lot of food fads. He gets notions for different things that I wouldn't normally have in the house. Then he uses a lot of milk and a lot of sugar"
"I have never weighed up the cost, although I suppose there is more heat used and the incontinence pads are expensive"
"I have to pay someone to get an evening meal for my husband and children which I am unable to do myself. My mother also likes a little drop of brandy and brandy is fierce expensive"
"Electricity and heating are very expensive and I have to keep a fire on in her room all through the summer"
"We have a gas fire on all day and, as you know, you cannot get much anymore for £20"
"She likes special foods which I get for her and there are also cosmetics which she likes to have and which I would not like to deprive her of"
The two groups were similarly concerned (62 and 60 per cent) that carers like themselves should receive more help from the State. When questioned on State benefits, a good deal of uncertainty about these benefits and entitlement became evident as Briggs and Oliver [4] also discovered. 37.8 per cent of carers of the elderly and 54.8 per cent of carers of the handicapped in this study said they received State benefits. The difference is probably explained by the fact that the Prescribed Relatives Allowance was a means-tested benefit paid to elderly themselves as a supplement to their pension, £24 per week, while the Domiciliary Care Allowance (£70 per months approximately) is not means-tested in relation to the parents' income. Only in cases where a disabled person has an income, e.g., interest from a compensation award is the benefit means-tested.

In the case of the carers of the elderly, thirteen were receiving the old age pension in their own right, being over 66, seven were in receipt of the Prescribed Relatives Allowance, three received the Widows' Pension and one the Deserted Wives Allowance. Three received Disability Benefit and one has a U.S. retirement pension.

What came through was a fairly high degree of uncertainty (20 per cent and 25 per cent respectively) on the part of carers as to whether they were entitled to the Domiciliary Care Allowance and the Prescribed Relatives Allowance. They were unfamiliar with the official names of these benefits and unsure of where the benefits came from. This did not make our task any easier.

Carers were uncertain too as to whether they were worse off or better off financially as a result of their caring role as shown in Table 9.2.

Table 9.2   Whether Carers Felt They Were Better Off
             Or Worse Off Financially As A Result Of Caring

%	Carers of Elderly	Carers of Handicapped
Worse off	30.1	21.8
Better off	26.9	12.8
Not sure	43.0	65.4

(s = .0100)

Obviously, only a much more detailed independent examination of income and expenditure figures on the lines of Baldwin's study could hope to gain an accurate picture. But attitudes to State benefits came though at the end of the interview when the carers were asked if they would like to add anything or mention anything they felt had been omitted. Among the 48 per cent of carers of the handicapped who gave suggestions, 21 per cent advocated extra financial help. Among the 35 per cent of the carers of the elderly who gave similar suggestions, 28 per cent mentioned increased State benefits.

Carers of the handicapped:

"I think that there should be more financial help from the State. £39 wouldn't take us very far"

"I think that I should be getting money when he comes home on the weekends and long holidays – money for clothes especially"

"The handicapped allowance should be increased as the child grows older and continues to be looked after at home"

"I should be entitled to more financial help as her father is not working due to arthritis which he has for the past ten years"

It must be said that money did not feature as high on the priorities of this group as it did among the carers of the elderly who expressed themselves in a much more forthright manner on this subject.

"I think I should get some little payment from the Health Board or the Department of Health. A home help gets paid

and she only spends so many hours a day with an old person. I am at it all the time. We are always hearing what it costs to keep an old person in a Home. I would be most grateful if you would do something for the likes of me."

"If somebody came to see the situation for themselves, to see if he could get an extra bit of money. It's wrong that a woman can go out to work and get paid as a home help to look after some old person. Whereas the person doing it for their own mother at home gets nothing and its getting harder to manage financially all the time."

"There should be more information for the elderly about their entitlements. So many old people have nobody to look after them and there must be scope for home helps. If the newly married women knew about it, they would be quite glad of a few extra pounds for a few hours per day."

"The money for caring is very poor indeed. I only get £36 per month from the Health Board and Mary gives me £5 out of her pension. but if she were in a Home it would cost the State £200 a week to keep her."

On the other hand, it must be stressed that the majority of the recipients expressed satisfaction with the Domiciliary Care Allowance and the Prescribed Relatives Allowance.

"It covers (the Domiciliary Care Allowance) the cost of the initial expenses for him. It is good enough"

"It is a help to buy things for her. It is good enough at present"

"She manages fine on it"

"I am satisfied with it anyway"

"At this stage of his life it doesn't cost a lot"

"It is a help. Bernard is very young yet. His needs are small"

"I think it is good enough"

"It is all right for me anyhow, but in different situations it may not be adequate, especially if somebody has to hire help"

"Keeping George doesn't cost a lot"

"It is good enough with the way the Country is today with the recession and so on"

"It is enough to keep us going. I can save a little on it"

Now, in relation to the carers of the elderly:

"What I am getting is adequate. I manage fine. We are very comfortable"

"I don't want any money to do what I am doing. It is a pastime"

The main finding here is that there is need for more information on the entitlements of carers as a great degree of uncertainty prevails. There is a minority whose life is a struggle either because of already low income or because of special needs on the part of the cared-for. While dissatisfaction was expressed by a minority and while

increased State benefits appeared among the suggestions of
the carers, there was a greater desire for new or better
social services for both elderly and handicapped - the
perennial dilemma in this area between increased benefits or
services in kind.

Work outside the home

Only 4.7 per cent (4) of the carers of the handicapped
worked outside the home as opposed to 21 per cent of the
carers of the elderly. Bearing in mind that 26 per cent of
the carers of the elderly are male, it will be appreciated
that the participation of female carers in the workforce
full-time or part-time is minimal at 8.6 per cent. Asked if
they worked outside the home before they assumed the caring
role, 27 per cent of the carers of the elderly said they did
as opposed to only 8.4 per cent of the carers of the
handicapped. This brings us into the hypothetical domain
about which Baldwin expressed caution. These responses are
summed up in Table 9.3.

Table 9.3   Attitudes Of Carers To Work Outside The Home

	Carers of Elderly			Carers of Handicapped		
%	Yes	No	Not Sure	Yes	No	Not Sure
Whether carer regretted not working outside the home (n = 168)	14.1	88.9	-	16.5	83.5	-
Whether carer would be seeking work outside the home were it not for caring (n = 165)	13.5	82.0	3.8	20.3	75.9	3.8
Whether it is solely because of caring role that carer is not working outside the home (n = 165)	20.0	77.6	2.4	25.0	73.8	1.3
Whether carer felt that many sacrifice a job to look after an elderly patient or handicapped child (n = 196)	67.3	20.9	11.8	67.4	16.3	16.3

The lack of job opportunities in this area as well as the
other family responsibilities of most of the carers may
explain the relatively low number of would be "takers" of
jobs outside the home. The much larger proportion who
believe that many people sacrifice a job to care for a

relative may represent a lingering stereotype of the single girl who gave up her job to care for the ageing mother, but it may also reveal a desire for work opportunities on the part of many of the carers themselves.

This set of attitudes in relation to working outside the home was investigated further by means of a problem which was posed for the carers. It was posed somewhat differently for men and women.

The women carers were asked:

"Supposing a good friend came to you with this problem. She has a job as a secretary in an office in town but now her mother has got a stroke and needs continual care for the foreseeable future. Should she give up her job and mind her mother or should she seek some other way out? How would you advise her in her dilemma?"

The men were asked:

"Suppose a good friend of yours came for advice. His mother has had a stroke and needs continual care for the foreseeable future. He works in a drapery shop. Should he give up his job and mind his mother or should he seek some other way out? How would you advise your friend in this dilemma?

There were four general responses: one was to advise the friend to give up the job and look after the mother; the second to advise the friend very definitely to keep the job; the third was to advise the friend to seek some other way out rather than giving up the job; the fourth group, the undecided, were unable to advise the friend.

It was most interesting to note the minute attention which carers gave to their answers. It was clear they had thought a lot about this question and they got down to very specific recommendations. They obviously found the question interesting and some of them gave long replies. They identified with the dilemma, to the point of advising as if the friend was actually present. The different responses are outlined in Table 9.4.

Table 9.4   Advice To Friend Re Choice Between Caring For Mother Or Keeping Job

	Women to Women Friend	Men to Men Friend
	(n = 161)	(n = 34)
Would advise friend to give up job and care for mother	47.7	41.1
Would advise friend to keep job	15.5	9.0
Would advise friend to take some other way out rather than give up job	19.3	44.0
Was undecided as to how to advise friend	14.3	5.9

There was an abundance of advice and only one person felt
that she was "in no position to give any advice to anybody".
What is quite interesting is that 47.7 per cent of the women
and 41.1 per cent of the men felt that the care of a mother
was more important than a job. The men tended to advise the
friend to take some other way out rather than give up the
job. Men were less likely to be undecided and they were
more definite in their advice. This advice to seek another
way out was often a very well worked out alternative,
involving the use of home helps, part-time instead of full-
time work, the finding of paid or voluntary help even at the
cost of paying as much to such a home help as the person
earned themselves, if necessary, since a job might not be
easy to get in the event of the mother's death.
Women:

*"If she can afford to give up her job, she should. I
feel she should mind her mother at any cost. I'd tell
her to give up the job and mind her mother. She will
only get the opportunity once and she will never regret
it."*

*"Ideally she should look after her mother. That means
giving up her job. However, she should be financially
helped by the State to compensate her for doing this."*

*"If there is nobody else to look after her mother, I
think she should give up her job. The decision has to be
hers and it's not an easy one."*

*"I would advise her to give up her job and look after her
mother as she might not have her for long and if she
neglected her she would regret it later."*

*"I would tell her that she should leave the job and look
after her mother. She can get another job but she has
only one mother."*

*"I think she should give up her job because her mother
reared her and cared for her when she was young."*

*"I would advise her to give up her job and look after her
mother. It will be rewarding at the end of the day for
her and it may only be for a while."*

*"She should get a home help. How could she give up her
job? I wouldn't advise her to give up her job. They are
so scarce, especially while there are other forms of
help, for example, a hospital. Of course, one can't
throw one's mother out either. But jobs nowadays are so
scarce that you have to grasp them and hold onto them."*

*"She should make very sure before giving up her job
because jobs are scarce and she would be giving up her
independence."*

*"She should hold onto her job. She has her own life to
live. If she were to get somebody to help her to mind
her mother, such as a home help, it would be far better
than giving up her own job."*

*"Her first duty is to home. She should get leave of
absence for about six weeks. If no improvement came in
the mother's condition she should go to the social worker
to discuss the whole question of her care. She shouldn't*

142

give up her work totally but if necessary should get
part-time work, if that is the only option left.
Perhaps, it would be possible for her to acquire the
assistance of a home help and still maintain her job."
"I would be very slow in advising her to give up her job.
She may not get employment at a future date when her task
of caring for her mother is over. She should get a home
help instead."
"I think she should give up her job to mind her mother or
maybe it would be possible for her to work part-time and
get someone in to care for her mother for those hours
when she is at work. I would tell her to make up her own
mind, but if it were financially possible for her to give
up her job, that is one thing. If this were not possible
to do then the rest of the family ought to contribute
their share and this would help her to give up her job
and cope at home. It is certainly a hard decision. From
my own experience, I think that if she were to decide to
give up her job she would find she would be very happy in
looking after her mother."
"It would all depend on the person. Some people are just
not "cut out" for looking after old and sick people. It
is a very serious step to give up a secretary's job. I
would not know how to advise, unless I knew the person
very well. If she's dependent on her job then I suppose
she should try and get somebody in. I wouldn't like her
to neglect her mother but it's very hard to give up a job
as they are so hard to find at the present time. I feel
that she should stay at home but I would be very slow to
tell her that. I would tell her to make up her own mind
but, if financially possible, I would give up my job."
"I think she should give up her job. Her mother should
come first."
"It would depend on her age. If she were a young person
then she should keep her job because she has her own life
to live. If she were married, I think she should give up
her job. If she were single, I think it would be very
unfair to ask her to give up her job. She might perhaps
employ a home help or even consider residential care.
Her mother cared for her when she was a baby. On the
other hand, she can't afford to ruin her life looking
after somebody for a long period of time. She has to
make a life of her own."
"I would advise her to give up her job and mind her
mother. I know a lot of women to-day would not take very
kindly to this advice"!"
These were reactions of the women carers. Now for the
advice given by men:
"If he could afford to give up his job, he should. Old
people should be left in their own homes if at all
possible. I would tell him to give up his job. His
mother won't be always there. He will be rewarded for
it."
"Give up his job and look after his mother. She won't be

always there. Indeed he will miss her when she is gone."
"He should care for his mother and give up his job for a short time. The parents like their own to look after them. It would be most important that he would not allow his mother to be put into a Home. He ought to make every effort to arrange things to avoid this much at least."
"I feel he should not give up his job. But I suppose it would depend on whether he could afford to or not."
"I would tell him to keep his job and to get someone in to look after his mother."
"It depends on the nature of the person. The mother should be placed in a Home. The son should then pay towards her keep there and call to see her regularly. If the mother dies after his giving up his job, then mother and job would be gone."
"Firstly, he should try to get some relative in to mind her. If that fails he should try to get her into a Home. If he were a married man he should take her into his own home. He could land himself in a mess financially if he gave up his job. Then he couldn't look after her anyway. That's only common sense. It would, of course, depend on whether he was single or married."
"It's hard to say. It's hard to give up a job. Jobs are scarce. Perhaps he could get someone in to look after her. It would depend on the kind of person he was. I would advise him to look after her at home if at all possible."
"People differ. Some men are different from others. Some seek help. I would say a home help to live in would be the solution here if that could be arranged."
"It all depends on the man. Some men just couldn't do it. In giving up a job I suppose a lot would depend on his age. It's hard to a young man to give up his job, when jobs are so scarce and he might want to get married. I think he'd be taking a very serious step if he gave up his job. I couldn't see my sons doing it. He should weigh up all the pros and cons. I think he would be better off getting someone in to look after his mother. Anyhow, men are not good at looking after old people."

Women versus men as carers

It has been alleged more than once in the literature of the 1980s that the care of the elderly and the handicapped in the family falls on the shoulders of women, most often housewives, who are prevented from following a career or going out to work because of the caring role. It has been suggested also that they get precious little help from their men folk. The reason for this, it is said, is that the care of the elderly and of children is culturally defined as women's work, so men are not expected to be able or willing to act as principal carers or even to help the women who bear the burden of caring.

The carers were asked whether they considered that men or

144

women are better at caring. The carers of the elderly were asked about elderly cared-for and the carers of the handicapped about handicapped children. The possible answers to the question were that men were better carers, that women were better carers or that both were equally good at caring. The men did not receive a single vote, even from among their own ranks! The opinions are set out in Table 9.5.

Table 9.5   Whether Women Or Men Are Better Carers

%	Carers of Elderly	Carers of Handicapped	Women Carers	Men Carers
Men are better carers	0.0	0.0	0.0	0.0
Women are better carers	59.8	78.6	61.0	56.7
Both are equally good	40.2	21.4	39.0	43.5

(s = 0.008)   (s = 0.846)

The conviction that women are the better carers was supported as strongly by men as it was by women carers. It is agreed that women are generally superior but that sometimes men can be equally good. The reasons given were as follows:

(i)   men have proved to be competent carers, e.g., husbands who can look after their handicapped child or elderly cared-for person just as competently as the carer herself. (mentioned 47 times)
(ii) Women know the art of caring better than men. They have more skills, domestic and nursing. They can cope better with the stresses and strains of caring. (37 times)
(iii) Women are almost always more patient and understanding than men and these are the vital qualities. (25 times)
(iv) Caring is, in fact, a woman's role. They are the ones who actually do most of the caring. (24 times)
      Others went on further to say that caring is the woman's role by nature and by instinct. Here was evidence of a clear role division between men and women. (18 times)
(v)   It depends on the individual not on the sex or gender. What matters is the "caring bent" which is not confined to either sex. Some people have the ability to care for others, some do not. (17 times)
(vi) Men are poor at caring. It is "just not their line". As one carer put it, "men don't have what it takes to look after a normal child let alone a handicapped one". (10 times)

Despite the majority opinion that women are the better carers, there is good support for the notion that men could and sometimes do perform well. However, one detects here an overall cultural norm, accepted by both women and men, that caring is normally the proper task of the woman.

The carers were asked whether they felt that men could be doing more to help with the care of feeble elderly or handicapped children in the home and also whether the task "always falls on a woman with nobody else really doing very much to help". The responses are outlined in Table 9.6.

Table 9.6   Sharing Of The Caring Task
Between Women And Men

(a)	Carers of Elderly			Carers of Handicapped		
	Yes	No	Not Sure	Yes	No	Not Sure
Whether men should be doing more	65.2	19.6	15.2	61.2	18.8	24.0
			(s = 0.6138)			
Whether caring burden always falls on a woman	63.1	24.3	12.6	87.1	3.5	9.4
			(s = 0.0001)			

(b)	Men Carers			Women Carers		
Whether men should be doing more	66.7	13.3	20.0	64.6	22.0	13.4
			(s = 0.4790)			
Whether caring burden always falls on a woman	51.7	24.1	24.3	67.1	24.4	8.5
			(s = 0.0848)			

146

Within an overall framework of agreement it is accepted by both sexes that men should be doing more in caring situations and that the female carers bear the burden of caring without much help from their menfolk or others. This shows substantial support for the thesis of writers such as Finch and Groves [4], Briggs and Oliver [5] and many others. For example, Briggs and Oliver [6] comment on the issue of support from other members of the family, "A common story is of all the other members of the family unit fading away and leaving all the work and responsibility to one person. This leads to enormous bitterness and resentment." Johnson [7] describes a principle of "substitution" which takes place within families. If the spouse of a dependant elder is alive that person usually becomes the principal carer. The spouse is usually female. If there is no spouse an adult daughter is the most likely to be nominated. If there are no women available men take on the task. If both men and women are available women usually provide most of the instrumental assistance with activities of daily living. Men tend to assume a more distant role as financial advisers and decision makers according to Johnson. Men have been described elsewhere as "carers of the last resort" taking on the task only when there is no woman to do so.

A significant finding is the degree to which the carers of the handicapped (87 per cent) feel that the caring task falls on women with nobody else doing very much to help. It seems to contradict earlier suggestions that other family members helped, especially the husbands. But it probably reflects a basic feeling on their part that the help and moral support they receive within the family are peripheral to the actual daily grind of caring which falls on the carers alone. Lewis and Meredith [8] were led to believe that, "Kin and network of friends and neighbours can play a vital role, especially in sustaining the carer's morale, but their contribution to the performance of the caring tasks is strictly limited." But there is very little trace of the bitterness and resentment mentioned by Briggs and Oliver. The two or three wives who complain bitterly about their husbands do so, not because of their failure to help out, but because of their failure to run their farm or business well, thus bringing the family into poverty.

The absence of any great sense of outrage at the inequality which is perceived reminds one of Runciman's [9] similar findings in regard to social class and of Marx's "false consciousness" in those who failed to identify themselves with the class struggle. Ungerson also hinted at "false consciousness" in the context of carers who were happy..

Attitudes to residential care

Residential care is never far from the minds of the carers. In the Diocese of Kerry full-time residential care in large institutions has been, until very recently, the

only alternative to care in the community for the frail
elderly and mentally handicapped children. In the case of
the elderly and their carers we shall see a marked degree of
reluctance towards considering residential homes, public or
private, large or small.

In Britain the Wagner Committee [10] chose the title "A
Positive Choice" for the Report (1988) on residential care.
It drew an reports of satisfaction from a large number of
residents. The Committee wished to promote a fundamental
change in public perception of residential homes so that
elderly people would be better disposed to them. It is a
further though scarcely the final step in banishing the
workhouse stigma. Personal accounts in Norris' [11] carers'
biographies show that the "nursing home" is still a place of
last resort for many elderly and for their carers.

But entry to a residential setting is almost always a
permanent move for an old person except in cases where it
does not work out and the old person has a family willing to
take them home again. The move to a residential setting is,
therefore, an extremely serious step for both cared-for and
carer alike. Both are generally reluctant to take it. It
has an air of finality about it. Temporary residential care
occurs only through hospitals when the elderly person is
ill. There is no other short-term residential care
available. So it is only when caring becomes too difficult
for the carer or, when the carer needs a break, that
residential care is sought. But having said that, it can be
very difficult to get a place in State-run Homes for the
elderly with the result that private nursing homes are a
growing industry. There are now two hundred and thirty six
of them in the Republic of Ireland and thirty of these are
in the Health Board Area of this study. [12]

In the case of the mentally handicapped, a choice was
usually made as soon as the handicap was discovered. The
choice was often an extremely emotional one, coming so soon
after the initial trauma. The problem of schooling at a
later stage could introduce a new decision time. There were
strong feelings on the part of many of the carers on this
issue. Again, the choice has been between the family home
and large residential settings, though in latter years, the
residential home has been adapted to smaller family type
houses. The St. John of God Brothers have two family type
homes in Tralee at some distance from their training centre.
But, as yet, no programme has been initiated in Kerry to
allow moderately or severely handicapped adolescents to
begin to leave their family home or the residential settings
to lead independent lives. Schemes have been in existence
in other parts of Ireland in recent years, under the
direction of the Brothers of Charity, where young adult
handicapped are set up in flats near training centres.

Of course, 23 per cent of the cared-for in this study are
in residential care on a five-day week basis and return home
for weekends and school holidays. Their parents are
accustomed to having their children away from home and, as

will be seen later, these carers have a more positive attitude to residential care. (See Life Histories, Case No. 59). However, they are aware that their children will have to leave the Homes at 18 years of age and so they have fears for the future as described earlier.

The importance of carers "letting go", of "making the break" with their handicapped children as with normal children has been powerfully argued by Richardson and Ritchie. [13] There is an understandable tendency, as the parents grow older, to regard the handicapped as a perpetual child, a helper and a consolation in their old age. This is unlikely to be in the child's/adult's long term interests. It can arise because of parents' natural protectiveness of the weaker child, or because parents like to feel they are needed as they grow older. In this case, the absence of suitable models of accommodation for independent living for mentally handicapped adolescents and adults can act as a further disincentive to parents to "make the break". "Despite the considerable interest in the forms of provision to be made for people with a mental handicap there has been surprisingly little research on the perspective of parents on the move from home ..." [14] A study of elderly parents by Alison Wertheimer [15] suggests that "the strong mutual bond of affection between parents and handicapped fosters an acceptance that the son or daughter will remain at home indefinitely". She concludes that an "abnormal" or atypical social pattern has become normal with these families seeing themselves not as one of a couple but as "a threesome".

This view is confirmed by the results of a North Wales study by Grant et al. [16] which found that parents show a great sense of affection for their sons and daughters and little trace of resentment at their current situation. With respect to the future there was a number, "who found this subject difficult to talk about ... almost taboo. For these people life seemed to be lived on a day to day basis in the vague hope that something magical might turn up". Richardson and Ritchie [17] however, finding that parents preferred to keep their son or daughter at home concluded, that this arises because of "the unacceptability of the options of which they are aware and their lack of knowledge of possible alternatives." There is a good deal of evidence in the present study to support both of these conclusions.

The carers in this study were questioned at different points in the interview on their attitude to placing the cared-for person in such a setting. Early in the interview the question of a crisis involving a choice between home and the possibility of residential care was posed. Such a decision had been experienced by 46.8 per cent of carers of the handicapped and by 13.5 per cent of carers of the elderly. The decision to keep the cared-for person at home was the option chosen by the majority in each group. Only 23 per cent approximately of the carers of the handicapped did, in fact, send their child to a residential home. The sample of elderly could not include people in residential care by the nature of the study and from the nature of provision as there is no temporary care available. The handicapped did include residential care with children attending school and returning home at weekends and for holiday periods.

The thought of residential care is one which is obviously on carers' minds, but while they have nothing in particular against such institutions, they see them as a last resort in their own case. When asked an open question as to what they thought of residential homes for elderly and handicapped children, the majority of the comments were classified as "favourable". But there were some negative comments also shown in Table 9.7.

Table 9.7   What Carers Thought Of Residential Care
             For Elderly And Handicapped Children

Comments %	Carers of Elderly	Carers of Handicapped
Very positive	24.0	36.4
Positive	59.0	46.8
Negative	12.0	15.6
Very negative	5.0	1.3 (n=179)

(s = 0.1300)

There was no significant difference on this question between those whose children were at home all the time and those with children in residential care for five days each week.

In marked contrast was the carers' responses to the question as to how they would feel if they were forced to place their cared-for person in residential care. The replies are given in Table 9.8.

Table 9.8   How The Carers Would Feel If They Were Forced
             To Place Cared-For Persons In Residential Care

%	Carers of Elderly	Carers of Handicapped
Lost	30.8	44.6
Very disappointed	38.5	47.0
Somewhat disappointed	11.5	4.8
Relieved	7.7	2.4
Guilty	11.5	1.2 (n=187)

(s = 0.0045)

The great majority of carers obviously see residential care as the last thing they would choose. To see the cared-

for person confined permanently to an institution signals
break down and failure of their caring role. At least part
of the reason for this reaction can be explained by how the
carers felt the cared-for would react to being placed in a
residential home.
Table 9.9 shows the responses:

Table 9.9   How Carers Believed The Cared-For Person
             Would React To Being Placed In Residential Care

Cared-for person	Carers of Elderly %	Carers of Handicapped %
Would fear it	23.9	14.8
Would resent it	45.0	44.4
Would feel hurt	13.8	18.5
Would not mind	10.1	13.6
Would like it	0.9	1.2
Don't know	6.4	7.4 (n=190)

There was an interesting comparison on this question
between the carers who had their children in residential
care and those whose children were at home all the time.
While there was a significant difference in attitude between
the two groups there was still a good deal of negative
attitudes attributed to the child as shown in Table 9.10.

Table 9.10   How Carers Of Handicapped Believed
                 The Cared-For Person Would
                 React To Being Placed In A Residential Home

Cared-for person	Carers with child in residential care %	Carer whose child lives at home all the time %
Would fear it	6.7	16.9
Would resent it	13.3	52.3
Would feel hurt	26.7	16.9
Would not mind	40.0	7.7
Would like it	6.7	-
Don't know	6.7	6.2
	(n = 15)	(n = 65)

(s = 0.0018)

Only one carer said the child would like the institution.
It seems that the carers and the cared-for are keen to avoid
"relegation" to the "lower division" of residential care as

151

they perceive it.

When asked what they supposed might force them to seek residential care for their cared-for person, the carers said that only a total collapse of their own health and a failure to find another family member to take on the task would force them to seek residential care. If the cared-for person's health or behaviour were to make caring impossible at home this, again, might force the carer to seek residential care. But when they were pressed to say whether they thought that a time would come when they would no longer be able to look after the cared-for person and so would have to seek a place in a residential home, the uncertainty about the future came through as will be seen from Table 9.11.

Table 9.11   Whether A Time Would Come When Carers Would
              Have To Seek A Place In A Residential Home

(n = 187)   Carers of Elderly   Carers of Handicapped

%		Yes	No	Not Sure	Yes	No	Not Sure
Whether carers thought a time would come ... when they would have to seek a place for cared-for person		27.6	47.6	24.8	26.8	41.5	31.7

The high degree of those who were "not sure" included a number who simply could not bring themselves to face the unacceptable. Those with children in residential care had as many fears for the future as the others since they expected that they would have to come out when 18 years of age and find a place in a Workshop or Training Centre if possible.

However, the suggestion of short-term residential care for 2 or 3 weeks to give the carers a break met with a much more positive reaction as will be seen from Table 9.12.

Table 9.12   How Carers Feel About Short-Term
              Residential Care

	Carers of Elderly			Carers of Handicapped		
%	Yes	No	Not Sure	Yes	No	Not Sure
Carers see it as a good idea	56.6	30.1	13.3	69.5	15.9	14.6

152

The majority thought this would be a good idea even though many also felt that the cared-for would either resent it or refuse to go. In this context, the existence of such a facility in their area and an opportunity to see, if not experience it would show its usefulness for both carer and cared-for. No such short-term care exists apart from one or two holiday schemes run by voluntary organizations. Such short-term care might be the bridge which could provide the carer and the cared-for person with the opportunity to see the future and find out that it works, to echo Beatrice Webb on her return from Russia. It would be extremely important that they should have done so before an emergency such as the death of the carer brings the handicapped person to the attention of the social services for the first time as Richardson and Ritchie point out in their conclusion.

These authors have given a new stimulus to thinking through a policy which promises to remove some of the anxiety which parents of the handicapped have about the future. It involves initiatives in housing where the mentally handicapped adolescent or adult can be gradually taught to live as independently as possible. It also involves counselling of parents in the painful process of "letting go". But it does become easier if the parents and cared-for have the opportunity to try it out for short periods before the need for it becomes compelling.

The lack of temporary residential care for the elderly means that carers find difficulty in having a break or taking a holiday. In the past year or two with the cutbacks in the hospital service, the possibility of placing the elderly person in a hospital for a week or ten days no longer exists. Despite the recommendation of the 1968 Inter-Departmental Committee that temporary residential care be provided nothing was done in this area. The 1988 Report on Services for the Elderly [18] recommends Community Hospitals providing:

(a)   assessment and rehabilitation of elderly patients;
(b)   convalescent care;
(c)   respite care to support caring relatives;
(d)   nursing care for terminally ill who can no longer be cared for at home;
(e)   information, advice and support for those caring for elderly in the home.

One hopes that this recommendation is acted on though the present state of the economy and of the Health Service gives little grounds for optimism. Carers would welcome Community Hospitals as indeed they would the new found concern for the carers evident in the Report. Resources are limited but more efficient use should be made of what is spent in the area of Health.

'NOTES'

1. Baldwin, S., 1985, *The Costs of Caring,* Routledge and Kegan Paul, London.
2. Baldwin, S., 1985, op.cit., p.57.
3. Baldwin, S., 1985, op.cit., p.165.
4. Finch, J., and Groves, D., 1980, "Community Care and the Family: a case for equal opportunity", *Journal of Social Policy,* Vol.9 No.4, pp.487-514.
5. Briggs, A., and Oliver, J., 1985, *Caring: Experiences of Looking after Disabled Relatives,* Routledge and Kegan Paul, London.
6. Briggs, A., and Oliver J., 1985, op.cit., p.114.
7. Johnson, C., 1983, "Dyad   Social Relationships and Social Support" *The Gerontologist,* 23, No.4, pp.377-383
8. Lewis, J., and Meredith, B., 1988, *Daughters Who Care,* Routledge, London, p.155.
9. Runciman, W.G., 1966, *Relative Deprivation and Social Justice,* Routledge and Kegan Paul, London.
Runciman studied samples from the different social classes and, applying Rawl's theory of justice, concluded that the sense of inequality did not exist to the extent that the real inequality would have warranted. But the fact that people did not feel relatively deprived did not mean that social justice was being done to them. "It might be objected that there are many manual workers who do not feel any relative deprivation on this account and who have no less self respect or pride in their work than workers in occupations which are more highly regarded by society at large. Are they to be convicted of false consciousness because they are not disposed to resentment or envy? But it will be clear from the sense which the contractual model gives to the notion of false consciousness that it does not require any individual to be roused by feelings of envy. It only means that if a manual worker, however contented, were to feel that manual workers are awarded too little status by comparison with non-manual, this feeling of relative deprivation would be legitimate." (p.330)
10. Wagner, G., 1988, *A Positive Choice,* H.M.S.O.
11. Norris, J., (ed.) 1988, *Daughters of the Elderly,* Indiana University Press, Indiana.
12. Report of Working Party on Services for the Elderly, 1988, *The Years Ahead,* Government Publications Office, Dublin, p.213.
13. Richardson, A., and Ritchie, J., 1986, *Making the Break,* King Edward's Hospital Fund, London.
14. Richardson, A., and Ritchie, J., 1986, op.cit., p.18.
15. Wertheimer, A., 1981, *Living for the Present: Older Parents with a Mentally Handicapped Person living at Home,* Campaign for People with Mental Handicap, p.2.

16. Grant, G., Black, J., Wenger, G.C., and Humphreys, S., 1984, *Progress Summary: Care Networks Project,* Bangor, Department of Social Theory and Institutions, University College of North Wales.
17. Richardson, A., and Ritchie, J., 1986, op.cit.,
18. Report of Working Party on Services for the Elderly, 1988, op.cit., p.8.

10 Conclusion

The study was a comparative one at four different levels. First, the carers of the frail elderly were compared with those of the mentally handicapped. Secondly, the findings in their Irish setting were compared with those of similar studies in Britain. Thirdly, the female carers were compared with their male counterparts. Finally, the concept of Community Care was in the dock throughout, as evidence came to light for and against the charges that it was really family care or care by women. Keeping these different dimensions before the reader made me feel somewhat like a juggler. I hope that this method of presentation did not prove to be too distracting. I shall now summarise what the comparisons have yielded towards a better understanding of the dynamics of caring. In a second section I shall make some policy recommendations for a greater degree of support from all quarters for carers in Ireland.

By not limiting the study to carers of the elderly I followed my own two main areas of interest but I also avoided the danger mentioned by Glendenning [1] of neglecting smaller groups such as the disabled and the handicapped at a time of new-found concern for the elderly and their carers. The carers of the elderly are under the spotlight at the present time but one must recall Titmuss and the early euphoria about Community Care and stress that so far very little indeed has been done, in practice for the carers by statutory social services. But it is nevertheless

156

important to bring carers of all groups forward together. An important reason for this suggestion is the fact that the two groups had more things in common than they had differences. They tended to be women, to be housewives who did not work outside the home. The two groups did not differ significantly in regard to age or social class. There were significant differences in regard to marital status, the carers of the handicapped being for the very most part married and more likely to have other dependants.

The costs, in both cases, were very similar and often very heavy indeed. The feeling of being tied down, the lack of regular breaks and a sense of isolation and loneliness were felt equally by both sets of carers. Depending on the age of the mentally handicapped cared-for person, there could be hope for improvement as with normal children so there was an incentive to make their child more independent. Increased independence brought satisfaction to these carers whereas for carers of the elderly, the prospect generally was one of gradual decline. On the other hand, the real distinguishing feature in this comparison is the uncertainty and fear for the future experienced by the carers of the handicapped. This is a very serious problem for carers who wonder what will happen when they become incapacitated or die. The carers of the elderly do not have this particular difficulty to contend with, although a small minority were troubled about how they would cope when the cared-for person died. (See Life Histories, Case No. 22)

The proportion of women among the carers of the elderly is high compared with British figures such as those in the Equal Opportunities Commission 1984. In this latter the proportion of women was 59 per cent while in this study 78 per cent of carers of the elderly were women as were 97 per cent of the carers of the handicapped. It would seem that where the cared-for person needs a large degree of help, the female carer is the person who does the "daily grind" of personal care and supervision. It would not be true to say, however, that the female carers receive no help or support. The spouses are their main helpers who occasionally substitute for them when they are away or ill. But the more usual help from spouses takes the form of minding and of outdoor activities with the cared-for person. They give moral support also which, even in the absence of more tangible assistance, is still vital to the carers. This important form of support is sometimes underestimated in the literature.

Appreciation from a spouse, in particular, can affirm and reaffirm the carer in the trauma of handicapped birth and in difficult caring situations in both groups. Naturally it would be an even better support for the carers if spouses' help had a definite physical as well as a moral component in all cases.

The division of labour within the family, as evidenced in the study, would situate many of these families within the "neo-traditional family" in Goldthorpe's [2] classification. The husband's help went beyond that of the strict sex division of labour of his "traditional family" but fell far short of the state of affairs within his "thoroughgoing egalitarian family", where both parties are equally likely to be employed and "all family responsibilities are shared as agreed between the spouses on the basis of ability and preference and not on the basis of sex." The husbands in this study are the breadwinners, the wives, for the most part, stay at home and look after all dependants. The husband "helps".

Hannan [3] studied this very question in a similar setting in Ireland and he confirmed that in one third of farm families, husbands helped with housekeeping and child rearing. His term was "modern" family as opposed to "traditional" family. This development was attributed by Hannan to education, the influence of the media, but, above all, to the values of the wife. This conclusion would seem to indicate that female carers can bring about change in their spouses. Jilly Cooper's [4] optimistic prognosis is therefore pertinent to the future of caring. "The male is a domesticated animal which, if treated with firmness and kindness, can be trained to do most things".

Other family members also helped the carers but to a lesser degree than the spouses while relatives outside the home helped less again. Neighbours gave a low degree of physical help to carers but, where they did, it was greatly appreciated. Carers generally did not expect their neighbours to do more than they were doing. In the case of the handicapped, neighbours were reported to give very little help. In the case of the elderly, who had no family or close relatives in the area, neighbours acted as carers. Sometimes, these carer-neighbours became paid home helps to the cared-for and this could be an important pointer to the future of Community Care both for the elderly who have no family/relatives in the area and for those with carers. They came very close to the paid volunteers of British Neighbourhood Schemes since the rate of pay is low. But they could well become a force in community care in Ireland.

What does appear from the findings is that the care of the elderly and handicapped is primarily the domain of the family. Neighbours' help is largely confined to visiting, to providing companionship and pleasurable conversation. Where carers and cared-for are together on their own a lot this can be valuable. Hannan [5] again found that among small farmers this form of friendly exchange was now the main contribution of neighbours in contrast to former times when neighbours worked together in groups, known as the "meitheal", and exchanged horses and machinery. Carers of the handicapped tended to find their companionship more within voluntary groups, especially associations such as the Down's Syndrome Association and the Parents and Friends of the Mentally Handicapped. They were less able than carers of the elderly to name friends of their cared-for persons. But it was important for them that anybody who helped them should do it because they liked the handicapped in their own right.

Community Care then does boil down largely to care within the family but there is a not inconsiderable contribution from relatives outside the home, from friends and from neighbours. But the perception of the community is that caring for dependants is the function of the family so that neighbours are not expected to step in while the family is present. Where there is no family to care, or where family care collapses [6], neighbours feel some duty to assist provided they are not trapped day in day out. Wenger [7] sees the assurance that this will not happen as the key to the success of the Gofal project.

Social policy endorses and reflects this division of caring where the family is expected to look after its dependants and, as Moroney says, the State tends to substitute for the family rather than support it. Very little help is offered. No home helps were given to any of the carers in this study. The public health nurse is the mainstay of the elderly here, coming to visit those in need of nursing care and giving, in some cases, moral support to the carers. The social worker helps a minority of the carers of the handicapped. The role of voluntary bodies is slight, also — they tend to concentrate solely on the elderly who live alone. The recent Report on Services for the Elderly (1988) has, for the first time, focussed attention on the special needs of the carers. The formation of the first Associations of Carers in Dublin and Thurles together with the studies of carers, mentioned earlier, all highlight the need for increased support for carers, provided of course, that "Support for Carers" does not become "the everlasting cottage-garden trailer" of the nineties.

So, on the evidence of this study, at any rate it is true to say that community care as care by the community, is largely care within the family. That said, however, we must not exaggerate; due weight must be given to help and support from outside. Nor is it true to say that the care in the home is all left to women without significant help from anybody. This claim also involves exaggeration. What is indisputable, however, is that women bear the main brunt of caring for both elderly and handicapped and in a larger proportion of cases in Ireland even than in England.

When comparing the two countries, it has to be borne in mind that the findings of the present study might not be sufficiently representative to be generalised to another country, or even to an urban setting such as Dublin. The overwhelming majority were Catholic and many of them devoutly so and this may have a strong bearing on the results. The carers are possibly less materialistic because of this. Abrams [8] was puzzled by the results of his later studies on neighbouring that working class Catholics were more involved in caring than their counterparts. For Abrams as for Hadley and Webb [9], religion was one of the factors which made for active involvement in caring or volunteer work with the frail elderly. Abrams did not see religion as directly causing this but rather as "mediating" it in some, as yet, unexplained manner.

Another reason for not generalising from this study may be that the families here are much more traditional than their counterparts in Britain. At first sight, this would seem to be very much the case. They would almost all fit in to Goldthorpe's 'traditional' model by virtue of the fact that the great majority of the married women do not go out to work but look after the children and elderly dependants. However, the rigid sex division of work in the home which is the second criterion for Goldthorpe's classification is not borne out nearly as fully in the study. Many spouses help. Many of them regularly substitute as carers doing the personal care tasks. And some wives said that their husbands were as good at caregiving as they were themselves. These findings would tend to move up a substantial number of families into the 'neo-traditional' model of Goldthorpe or to the 'modern family' model of Hannan, as described earlier. Married women's low participation in the workforce, 20 per cent in Ireland as compared with 60 per cent in Britain, is due to lack of opportunity more than to traditional values at this point.

There is reasonable hope that husbands will share increasingly in the caring task in the future. Hannan, as we saw earlier, found that education, the media and, above all, the wife's values can influence progress in this direction. The current interest of social scientists stimulated largely by feminists, will give a strong impetus to this movement. Carers' Associations could provide information, and promote friendly rivalry between husbands as carers thus changing attitudes towards caring as "naturally" women's work. But the main agent for change must be the carer herself. She it is who must train her spouse and sons with kindness and firmness to do most things. The churches, schools and the media can help.

The costs to the carers are undisputed but they continue despite these heavy costs. Not only that, but the interviewers predicted at the end that the vast majority were likely to be able and willing to continue with the task.

The reasons why carers continue are complex. They include feelings of duty and obligation, some direct rewards which offset costs and simply an emotional commitment to caring which goes beyond duty and reward. Many express this in terms of affection and love for the cared-for person and it can lead to high levels of self-sacrifice as seen from some of the Life Histories. (See Life History 43)

As well as the influence of feminist ideology in the British literature mentioned earlier, there may be another factor at work which might serve to explain why rewards reported by carers are played down in the literature. This could be the consciousness of researchers that any good news about carers or about the resilience of families in the care of dependants would be seized upon by the Conservative Government and used as an excuse for policies which give such inadequate resources to Community Care and to carers. The social policy researchers, for their part, have no wish to provide ammunition for the Right. On the contrary. They seek to improve community care and, in particular, they wish to improve the lot of carers, women carers. This could, possibly, explain to some extent, why researchers tend to be reward shy. Consequently, the costs are stressed while the rewards are not. These are two of the factors which may help to explain the gap in the British literature – the influence of feminist ideology and the fear of the exploitation of rewards by Government. I mentioned earlier the fact that, in many cases, the carers in the studies had already presented themselves to the social services or to organised groups, which could well indicate that they were in difficulties. In fact, there has been a tendency in the last few years for the Directors of Carers' Associations to present studies from within their own members as, for example, Pitkeathley (1989) and Norris (1988). In this study, the carers were drawn from the "general public" of carers. An analogy might help – to survey how people felt about their present state of health, one could interview a random sample of people going about their daily tasks at home or at work or one could choose a sample in doctors' waiting rooms.

Abrams it was who called for a language of costs and rewards and he stressed that we needed to know a great deal more about the rewards to carers. He proposed that a language be invented which could translate the psychological costs and benefits into cash terms. The problem is that many, if not most, of the carers do not think in these terms, they are not consciously weighing costs versus rewards all the time. Some, incidentally, do not even think of themselves as carers. "I'm a daughter, not a carer" [12], one woman objected. To make social policy depend on this kind of language would be to narrow it and the carers down to a greater reliance on materialistic considerations than seems necessary or appropriate. This calculative approach carries all the dangers of reducing the caring experience to cost benefit analysis derived from Economics. Titmuss put it as follows, "Economists may fragment systems and values; other people do not". This is not to deny the need in social policy to present issues in a materialistic and tight framework. But if you only use the language of cost-benefit in its economic sense you run the risk of losing a lot of understanding of the question. The 'intangible', the spiritual dimension of caring does not count. Perhaps we need a social policy of the "human spirit" in addition to that of "material well-being"?

Like it or not, as a Churchman aware of the danger of sliding into sentimentality or an overly religious view of social life, I can only explain a large part of the dynamics of caring in this study by concluding that the family remains a moral enterprise. The family fosters a set of values in which self-sacrifice can become something other than mere duty for a large proportion of people. The family does this quite naturally still. So the phenomenon of caring, in which social policy has such an interest, has to be explained without devaluing it simply to improve its case by emphasising only costs and disadvantages faced by carers.

Of course, injustices borne by women carers, highlighted in the feminist literature, are ongoing and enduring because the family remains a moral enterprise. That is why the trap springs so successfully on women. But it does not help if, in order to attract support for women carers, one undermines or ignores the willingness with which so many women seem to enter caring relationships. Ireland may be atypical in this respect so that further study may be needed before generalising the results of the present work.

One has, then, the economic approach advocated by Abrams, on the one hand and the self-sacrifice approach of Vanier on the other. The family has something of both. It is under pressure to be both. *"I do what I do out of love but I can't understand why I am not entitled to the Prescribed Relatives Allowance. I was told I could not get it unless my husband was dead! My father-in-law needs constant care so it would be nice to get a little reward from the State as the going can be very hard."* This carer illustrates the case perfectly. There is pressure on the women to be calculative and not to be. An English counterpart of the carer is quoted by Pitkeathley [13], "I do not begrudge looking after my husband as I love him very much, but what I do begrudge is the way the system is run as regards carers. You'd nearly have to go on bended knee for anything you may be entitled to... Think of all we are saving the Health Service and the social services..."

The solution for social policy would seem to be to seek justice for carers while continuing to encourage informal care. This can only be done by creating a supportive framework for the carer. Such an approach would be in the social policy tradition of Titmuss. One can argue that for the State to behave morally it ought to underpin the family as a moral enterprise and as a source of informal care with greatly increased financial and support services. Social policies should support the family with benefits and services as opposed to the right wing policies which impose duties on it, as in Britain in the past ten years. You cannot get moral behaviour from families through this approach. Rather, the way forward is to enter a moral contract with the family. So if one opts for community and family care and argues for a framework of State support for the family as crucial it is because it is cost effective as evidenced by the Kent Community Care Project and other similar projects. Family care frequently prevents and delays the residential alternative and could reverse it in certain cases. The State, for its part, should give the kind of support which ensures that the carer does not collapse. There is real saving here. Moroney [14] strongly advocated such a partnership between State and family. "There is no doubt that State is benefiting. The amount of social care provided by families far exceeds that of the State. It is impossible, furthermore, to assign a monetary value to it and it is inconceivable to speculate the cost involved if the State were to become the primary caring institution... The State is fortunate to have families who care. The corollary to this is that families should also be supported by a caring society."

The clear tradition of Titmuss would lead us further to demand that the State create a moral context within which it should foster the bonds of family and community. You have costs language which is necessary and valid but it is only half the story. You need another language, call it the "language of the heart" to understand the benefits, rewards and self-sacrifice which need to be acknowledged rather than neglected or played down, as they have been in the feminist literature. Finally, I mention once again the fact that many carers reported that caring had enriched them as persons, had united their families and had made them less materialistic in outlook. In other words, the cared-for persons were drawing forth from their carers resources which they would never have discovered had they not been called forth in the caring relationship. This finding confirmed what Vanier and Craig have described. This must be qualified slightly by the fact that a minority felt that caring had damaged them personally and had greatly disrupted their families. (See Life Histories, Case Nos. 25, 29).

SECTION II

In this final section I shall make recommendations for social policy in Ireland. The two aims of policy should be: (a) to reduce the costs to carers; (b) to facilitate and strengthen the rewards. To achieve these aims would be to make caring more stable with consequent benefits to carers, cared-for and the State. I shall first take the carers of the elderly.

A first step would be to include a parallel register of carers to that of the elderly at risk in the community. This could best be assembled at district level by a district liaison public health nurse as proposed in the Report on Services for the Elderly 1988. [15] At the local level the public health nurse could identify the frail elderly and their carers. Local knowledge and house to house visitation would be the way to find this information. Carers, whose age, health or other family responsibilities would indicate the danger of overwork or stress, should be kept "under observation" by the public health nurse. Appropriate help and support should be at hand if problems present themselves to carer or cared-for.

It seems imperative, also, to advocate an increase in the

ratio of public health nurses to population. The Report on the Workload of Public Health Nurses, 1975, [16] recommended a ratio of 1:2,616. The present ratio of 1:3,065 is considerably below target. The corresponding British figure is 1:1,722. The Irish figure hides significant differences between health board regions. Since the public health nurse is the first line of defence of the elderly in the community and the main referral agent as well, it is crucial to the whole policy of Community Care that the service be greatly strengthened as quickly as possible. The alternative to increased numbers might be to involve SRNs in curative nursing or to train nursing assistants or to make clerical assistance available to the public health nurses. The Working Party on Services for the Elderly poses the following question: "when is it more cost effective to care for the elderly at home and when is it more cost effective to care for an elderly person in a long stay hospital or nursing home?" [17] They commissioned research on this issue, two pilot schemes, one rural, one urban, to compare costs. When elderly people in remote areas need continuous nursing care, which neighbours or family are unable to provide, the residential alternative may actually be cheaper. But what of the wishes of the elderly person? Are economics to be decisive? Care in the community is going to cost a great deal of money and for too long anything like adequate resources, in staff and finance, have not been directed to it.

The training of the public health nurse should include modules on carers and on how to support and affirm them. The ability to anticipate and to be ready for the next stage of caring when it comes, whether gradually or suddenly, will be one of the main skills to be imparted to trainee nurses and in turn to carers.

Access to community social workers will also be necessary in cases of severe emotional stress to carers. Public health nurses cannot be expected to be counsellors as` well as everything else, and the services of a community social worker, similar to that available in Northern Ireland, is needed. Social work departments will need to welcome carers among their client groups from now on.

A department of geriatric medicine in all general hospitals could be invaluable for assessment purposes and to raise the status of care for the elderly. The health board area of this study has two general hospitals only one of which has the services of a geriatrician. Distance and travel costs make access very difficult for many potential users of this excellent service. Geriatric departments tend to encourage close liaison between domiciliary, community and extended care facilities and could be a powerful ally of carers of the elderly. They could promote a larger social dimension to the role of the G.P. also. The home help service also needs to be greatly extended and, in particular, the service must be made available to carers in trouble. The problems can result from the illness of the cared-for person or of the carer. Women carers are as much entitled to a home help service as men carers even though the domestication of the male still has a long way to go. (See Life Histories, Case No. 10). The service should be expanded to include night sitting and weekend relief where necessary. There is a pool of potential home helps in the married women in an area where employment, even part-time, is so scarce. And there are all the unemployed men, the overall figure on the register running at approximately 240,000 . We saw that some carers resented the fact that home helps were paid for doing what they were expected to do for nothing! The hourly rate for the home help is £1.50 in the area of this study and the vast majority work part-time. The Carers' Allowance of £45 per week announced in the Budget of 1990 is an important landmark in Irish social policy. There will, admittedly, be a delicate balance to be kept in expanding the home help service, giving carers greater financial recognition and keeping the unpaid services of neighbours in place. Further study in this area would be very interesting particularly as comparative to the Kent Community Care Project and the many others which have replicated it in Britain.

Day Care Centres are another welcome development and they are growing in number and appearing in small towns and villages. They give an important break to carers and cared-for. Transport is a problem and financial help, from Government to voluntary bodies to provide it will be essential if the elderly are to get to and from the centres.

Respite care for the elderly is a growing need as many district hospitals closed over the past few years and most long stay hospitals have, up to now, had very little turn-over. The benefits of respite care accrue to the carer as well as to the cared-for. Consequently, the recommendations of the Report on Services for the Elderly, 1988, [18] that community hospitals be set up to meet this and a number of other needs should be acted upon. The proposal is that existing buildings should be adapted, where possible, and purpose-built facilities provided elsewhere. This idea would give residential care the *flexibility* it so badly needs. As well as "respite care to support relatives", there should be assessment and rehabilitation facilities, convalescent care, day hospital and/or day care centre, and information, advice and support for carers. The need for information and advice for carers should be a priority for health boards and should be provided in the community as distinct from the community hospital. This could be done through Associations of Carers or through other mutual help groups.

The only financial reward to carers at the time the study was conducted was the Prescribed Relatives Allowance, a relatively small supplement of £27.20 per week to the elderly person's weekly pension. This is now superseded by the new Carers' Allowance which is means-tested also but with an extension of eligibility to non-relatives. The

State have begun to acknowledge the service of carers at last. As well as an income, the eligible carers' social insurance (P.R.S.I.) will be allowed so that the carer will have equal pension rights with people in full-time employment.

One of the most important sources of support in the future must be mutual help groups such as Associations of Carers. The first associations for carers of the elderly were set up very recently as stated earlier. These self-help or mutual aid groups have great potential since they can make caring *by* the community more stable. Carers can share their experiences, knowledge and skills. They will recall their worst moments but they will also share the good ones. The State and the Voluntary bodies should give some support to such groups by providing access to buildings, telephones and transport. Such policies need not cost a great deal of money but they could be of major help to carers who would be affirmed and strengthened in their caring role through participation in their own associations.

Carers of the handicapped, to which I now come, have already found good support in their associations, such as the Down's Syndrome Association, the Parents and Friends of the Mentally Handicapped and the Faith and Light (Vanier) groups. State support here, as in the case of the carers of the elderly, would be equally valuable.

The traumatic time, at or after the birth of the handicapped child, should be eased in every way possible. Sensitivity is of the essence on the part of doctors and nurses. Mothers who have gone through the experience themselves could be called in to help. In this study, we heard of a group of mothers who volunteered to assist in this way but were not given any encouragement from the hospital or medical personnel. The "authority of relevance" still comes a poor third to that of knowledge and power!

Assessment should be ongoing and carers should be kept informed of their child's potential as well of its handicap. Since parents are prepared to work so hard for improvements, they should be encouraged to do so, but with kind words of caution also lest they suffer further disappointment later.

Carers of a handicapped child receive an allowance of £70 per month. This would scarcely pay for a normal child. The Economic and Social Research Institute [19] estimate a child under five costs parents an average of £19.60 per week while the figure is £28.30 per week for the 5-14 year old. It would appear that the present rate to the handicapped child needs to be considerably increased to meet the extra costs of the handicapped over the normal child.

The fears which carers have for the future of their cared-for persons should be faced. (See Life Histories, Case No. 64). Putting it off only makes matters worse. Carers should have access to social work counselling which would help them to come to terms with their fears. Social workers could assist in making concrete plans for the care of the mentally handicapped person when the carer is no longer available. These plans could involve transfer to a family member, or to a residential setting. In cases where no relative can be found to take on the task, and sometimes parents are very reluctant to impose it on their other children, counselling will be of little use without some definite housing options. Barbara Wooton would turn in her grave at the thought of social workers who had nothing more to offer carers in this situation than a sympathetic ear and warm words of cold comfort! Sheltered housing has begun to grow up in the vicinity of training centres for the handicapped. Some voluntary organizations and religious orders have set up such residential care where the handicapped are encouraged to live as independently as possible. Only such supervision and help as is deemed absolutely necessary is provided. The training centres include personal care, cooking, laundry and so on in the courses and training provided. Then there are also the l'Arche communities of Jean Vanier, which could be further developed in other areas – there are four or five already. The time to arrange the future is well before a crisis in the carer's health forces an emergency solution. The handicapped person should be given regular experience of the new surroundings, so that carer and cared-for can become accustomed to living apart even for short periods. But if there is to be a future which can be contemplated without fear by the carers, a great deal of buildings will have to be provided for the handicapped throughout Ireland.

The lack of employment for everybody makes employment for mentally handicapped more difficult than ever. They can take part in training schemes with other young people but it is very difficult for them to find a job. (See Life Histories, Case No. 73). This will remain a chronic problem until employment prospects improve for the country as a whole. Sheltered employment must, therefore, remain the norm. But with some imagination, this can and is working profitably in both senses of the word, and some very beautiful artifacts are being produced by the training centres. The St. John of God Training Centre in Tralee has handicapped and outside trainees working side by side in a Government Youth Employment Scheme. The restaurant is patronised by workers from the nearby factories and it runs at a profit. The trainees, some of them old friends from St. Mary of the Angels, recently presented me with a Christmas Crib with porcelain figurines, made at the Centre.

One is impressed at the very low degree of stigma reported by the carers. Apart from children staring and giggling occasionally, there was a very heartening degree of understanding and acceptance of the mentally handicapped among the public at large. The Job's comforter in Case C, p.64, is an exception. Carers of the elderly in this study bore this out – they were very understanding and supportive of the mentally handicapped. If fact, one third of the carers of the handicapped said that people tended to fuss over the handicapped more than they would over their normal children.

The Churches and voluntary bodies should become more sensitive to the needs of carers. Up to now the elderly who lived alone were regarded as the main need group in the community. The Churches can point up the contribution which carers make and enlist support for carers of the elderly. The carers of the handicapped received very few visits from their priests. More support is called for. The prophetic work of Vanier, which has worked its way upward and is reflected in the Pope's addresses on the handicapped, must now work its way downward to priests and lay faithful. The Churches can support and facilitate Carers' Associations and stimulate the voluntary organizations to organise baby sitters or minding services, thus giving carers a break. The Churches can also lend their support to local Care of the Aged Committees for the setting up of Day Care Centres. A number of religious orders have a very strong presence in the area of care of the handicapped and have developed considerable expertise and now carry political clout. Coordination of voluntary and statutory services needs to be improved. The central Christian commandment of love of neighbour must be seen to include carers and involve neighbours to a much greater degree than hitherto.

There has been a recent growth of pressure group politics in Ireland to promote the interests of the handicapped, the elderly and their carers. The danger is that, in order to make the case, all the negative features of handicap, old age and caring will be over emphasised. This will reinforce stereotypes, and in the case of carers, in particular, it will *create* a stereotype. Indeed, the almost exclusive concenetration on the social costs of caring has already gone far in this direction. It would be a pity if this were to happen. Naturally, it would be highly desirable if these groups and their carers were given the necessary State support so that they could devote all their energies to their primary task. It will be a sad day if our carers and their cared-for have no alternative but to carry placards!

I am not the first Irish cleric to speculate on the motives of carers or, to use a modern phrase, to ask, "what makes them tick?". A parish priest, An t-Athair Peadar O Laoghaire [20], wrote early in this century and told a story he had heard in his childhood about the days of the Great Famine of 1846.

"But what about Maire Ruadh. She and Larry had a garden. The blight came on it. I heard her telling how she spent the day, when the stalks were rotting and falling, looking at the garden and she crying, and not knowing in the world where they would get anything to eat. The garden was no good now. When they'd eaten whatever food was in the house, the hunger greatly affected poor Larry. He got rheumatics and wasn't able to rise from his bed. Maire had to go out "gathering" (as they used to call it) seeking alms. That woman used to go out in the morning and she on a black-fast; and she'd go west to Clydagh, over the hills, for four or five miles of a journey. She had some relations there. A small can of milk used to be given to her there and she'd bring that away home with her. She'd put it on the fire until it was curds and whey. Then she'd give the curds to Larry and she herself used to drink the whey. The woman kept this practice up until poor Larry died. I don't know where there was another "lady" who would have done it at the time. The strong faith that was inside her, it was this which obliged her to do the deed."

I wonder, had the carer been asked why she "carried the can", might she not have replied, "He is my husband, and I love him and there is no one else..."

'NOTES'

1. Glendenning, C., 1986, *A Single Door,* Allen and Unwin, London, p.200.
2. Goldthorpe, J.E., 1987, *Family Life in Western Societies,* Cambridge University Press, Cambridge, Ch.9.
3. Hannan, D., and Katsaiouni, L.A., 1977, *Traditional Families?,* Economic and Social Research Institute, Dublin, Ch.3.
4. Cooper, J., 1986, *The Penguin Dictionary of Humorous Quotations,* Penguin Books, London, p.162.
5. Hannan, D., and Katsaiouni, L.A., 1977, op.cit., p.85.
6. Re Life Histories, Case No 75:
   The mother collapsed and went into a coma after breakfast one morning. Danny, her son, placed a pillow under her head, covered her with a rug and went and used one of his three or four words to call a neighbour to come. The mother went in to hospital where she slowly recovered for a time, while the neighbour took Danny in to live with his family. After six months she died and Danny was given a place in a residential home near a workshop.
7. Wenger, G.C., 1984, *The Supportive Network,* George Allen and Unwin, London, p.193.
   "Where family are known to exist in the same community neighbours may hang back or prefer to alert relatives when they are concerned for fear of being seen as interfering."
8. Bulmer, M., 1986, *Neighbours : The Work of Philip Abrams",* Cambridge University Press, Cambridge, p.234.
   "Why, for example, should that norm (altruism) appear to work as a source of informal care so much more strongly among working class Catholics than amongst most other religious groups? Because it is peculiarly a 'community' religion? Because of the peculiar policies of that particular church in relation to birth control? Or because of the relative social segregation of the social milieux in which working class Catholics live? One could list a host of possibilities to explain the differential involvement of particular religious groups in informal care and all of them would point behind the norm of altruism to fairly complicated origins and concomitants of informal care mediated by religious beliefs."
9. Hadley, R., Webb, A.L., and Farrell, C., 1975, *Across the Generations,* George Allen and Unwin, London, p.141. The successful volunteers were more likely to declare some religion than their less successful counterparts.
10. Goldthorpe, J.E., 1987, op.cit., p.140.
11. Report on Working Party on Services for the Elderly, 1988, *The Years Ahead : A Policy for the Elderly,* Government Publications, Dublin, p.34
12. Lewis, J., and Meredith, B., 1988, *Daughters Who Care,* Routledge, London, p.21.

13. Pitkeathley, J., 1989, *It's My Duty Isn't It?* Souvenir Press, London and Canada.
14. Moroney, R.M., 1976, *The Family and the State,* Longman, London, pp.138-139.
15. Report on Working Party on Services for the Elderly, 1988, op.cit., p.44.
16. Report on the Workload of Public Health Nurses, 1975, Report of a Working Party, Government Publications, Dublin.
17. Report of Working Party on Services for the Elderly, 1988, op.cit., p.183.
18. Report of Working Party on Services for the Elderly, 1988, op.cit., p.134.
19. Conniffe, D., and Keogh, G., 1988, *Equivalence Scales and Costs of Children,* The Economic and Social Research Institute, Dublin, p.xii
20. O Laoghaire, P., 1915, *My Story,* translated by O Ceirin, C., 1987, Oxford University Press, p.31.

Bibliography

Abrams, P., 1977, "Community Care : Some Research Problems
and Priorities", *Policy and Politics,* Vol. 6 No.2

Abrams, P., Abrams, S., Humphrey, R., and Snaith, R., 1981,
Action for Care : A Review of Good Neighbour Schemes,
Berkhamstead, Herts., The Volunteer Centre.

Allen, G., 1985, *Family Life,* Basil Blackwell Ltd., Oxford.

Anderson, W., et al., 1974, *Geriatric Medicine,* Academic
Press, London.

Arnesberg, C.A., and Kimball, S.J., 1940, *Family and
Community in Ireland,* Harvard University Press.

Baldwin, S., 1985, *The Costs of Caring : Families with
Disabled Children,* Routledge and Kegan Paul, London.

Bayley, M., 1973, *Mental Handicap and Community Care,*
Routledge and Kegan Paul, London.

Bone, M., Spam., B., and Martin, F.M., 1972, *Plans and
Provisions for the Mentally Handicapped,* George Allen and
Unwin, London.

Boswell, J., 1791, *The Life of Samuel Johnson,* Penguin
Edition, Penguin Books.

Bowlby, J., *Child Care and the Growth of Love,*
Hammondsworth, Penguin Books.

Briggs, A., and Oliver, J., 1985, *Caring : Experiences of
looking after Disabled Relatives,* Routledge and Kegan
Paul, London.

Bulmer, M., 1986, *Neighbours : The Work of Philip Abrams,*
Cambridge University Press, Cambridge.

172

Burke, H., 1987, *The People and the Poor Law in 19th Century Ireland,* W.E.B. (Women's Education Bureau), England.

Census of Population, 1981, Vol. 2, Central Statistics Office, Dublin.

Challis, D., and Davies, B., 1980, "A New Approach to Community Care for the Elderly", *British Journal of Social Work,* Vol.10 No.1

Charlesworth, A., Wilkin, D., and Dune, A., 1982, *Carers and Service : A comparison of men and women caring for dependent elderly,* Equal Opportunities Commission.

Clarke, B., 1974, *Enough Room for Joy,* Darton, Longman and Todd, London.

Clifford, D., 1975, *The Public, the Client and the Social Services,* Social Studies, Maynooth.

Clifford, D., 1975 (a), "Stigma and the Perception of Social Security Services", *Policy and Politics,* Vol.3 No.3

Clifford, D., 1975 (b), "The Poor in Town and Country", *Social Studies,* Vol.4 No.1

Clifford, D., 1977, *The Kerry Diocesan Study on Loneliness* (Unpublished).

Clifford, D., 1979, "How Lonely the Aged?", *Intercom,* Vol.10 No.10, Catholic Communications Institute, Dublin.

Clifford, D., 1980, "Old age hath yet his honour and his toil", *The Furrow,* Vol.31 No.9

Clifford, D., 1983, (a), "This is my ball and you can play with it", *The Furrow,* Vol.34 No.7.

Clifford, D., 1983 (b), "And ready to greet him when he comes again?", Attitudes of the elderly to death, *The Furrow,* Vol.34 No.11

Clifford, D., 1986, "The First Friday Communion Call", *The Furrow,* Vol.37 No.11

Clifford, D., 1989, "Dear People...The Carers and the Church" *The Furrow,* Vol.40 No.10

Conniffe, D., and Keogh, G., 1988, *Equivalence Scales and Costs of Children,* The Economic and Social Research Institute, Dublin.

Convery, J., 1987, *Choices in Community Care : Day Centres for the Elderly in the Eastern Health Board,* National Council for the Aged, Dublin.

Craig, M., 1979, *Blessings,* Hodder and Stoughton, Sevenoaks, Kent.

Curry, J., 1980, *The Irish Social Services,* Institute of Public Administration, Dublin.

Dalley, G., 1988, *Ideologies of Caring : Rethinking Community and Collectivism,* MacMillan Education, London.

Daly, M., and O'Connor, J., 1984, *The World of the Elderly: The Rural Experience,* National Council for the Aged, Dublin.

Davies, B., and Challis, D., 1987 (a), *Matching Resources to Needs in Community Care,* Gower, London.

Davies, B., and Challis, D., 1987 (b), *Case Management in Community Care,* Gower, London.

Equal Opportunities Commission, 1980, *The Experience of Caring for Elderly and Handicapped Dependents,* A survey report.

Equal Opportunities Commission, 1982, *Who Cares for the Carers? Opportunities for those caring for the elderly and handicapped*, A survey report.

Equal Opportunities Commission, 1984, *Carers and Service: A companion of men and women caring for dependent elderly people*, A survey report.

Finch, J., and Groves, D., 1980, "Community Care and the Family : A Case of Equal Opportunity", *Journal of Social Policy*, Vol.9 No.2.

Finch, J., and Groves, D., 1983, (eds.), *A Labour of Love*, Routledge and Kegan Paul, London.

Gilligan, C., 1982, *In a Different Voice : Psychological Theory and Women's Development*, Harvard University Press, Cambridge, Mass.

Glendenning, C., 1986, *A Single Door*, Allen and Unwin, London.

Goffman, E., 1961, *Asylums*, Anchor Books, Doubleday and Co., New York.

Goldberg, E.M., and Hatch, S., *A New Look at the Personal Social Services*, Policy Studies Institute, London.

Goldthorpe, J.E., 1987, *Family Life in Western Societies*, Cambridge University Press, Cambridge.

Hadley, R., and McGrath, 1980, *Going Local : Neighbourhood Social Services*, National Council for Voluntary Organizations, London.

Hadley, R., Webb, A., and Farrell, C., 1975, *Across the Generations*, George Allen and Unwin, London.

Hannan, C., 1975, *Parents and Mentally Handicapped Children*, Penguin Books, England.

Hannan, D., and Katsaiouni, L.A., 1977, *Traditional Families? From Culturally Prescribed to Negotiated Roles in Farm Families*, The Economic and Social Research Institute, Dublin.

Hannan, D.F., 1979, *Displacement and Development : Class, Kinship and Social Change in Irish Rural Communities*, The Economic and Social Research Institute, Dublin.

Health Services and their Future Development, 1966, Government Publications, Dublin.

Hensey, B., 1972, *The Health Services of Ireland*, 2nd edition, The Institute of Public Administration, Dublin.

Hunt, A., 1978, *The elderly at home : a study of people aged sixty five and over living in the community in 1976*, Social Survey Division, O.P.C.S.

Johnson, M., 1981, *Ageing Needs and Nutrition*, Interview Document, Policy Studies Institute, London.

Johnson, M., 1982, "Observations on the Enterprise of Ageing", *Ageing and Society*, Vol.2, Cambridge University Press.

Kelly, B., and McGinley, P., eds., 1990, *Mental Handicap: Challenge to the Church*, Lisieux Hall, Chorley, Lancashire, England.

Kivett, V.R., "Discriminators of loneliness among rural

elderly : implications for intervention", *The
Gerontologist,* Vol.19 No.1.
Lapierre, D., 1986, *The City of Joy,* Century, London.
Land, H., 1978, "Who cares for the family?", *Journal of
Social Policy,* Vol.7 Part 3.
Lewis, J., and Meredith, B., 1988, *Daughters Who Care,*
Routledge, London.
Lewis, O., *The Children of Sanchez: Autobiography of a
Mexican Family,* 1961, Penguin Books.
Litwak, E., 1985, *Helping the Elderly,* The Guildford Press,
New York.
Lonsdale, S., Webb, A.L., and Briggs, T., (eds.), 1980,
Teamwork in the Personal Social Services, Croom Helm.
McCenkey, R., 1987, *Who Cares?,* Souvenir Press, London.
Moroney, R.M., 1976, *The Family and the State :
Considerations for Social Policy,* Logman, London.
Moroney, R.M., 1980, *"Families, Social Services and Social
Policy",* U.S. Department of Health and Human Service,
Washington.
Morris, P., 1969, *Put Away,* Routledge and Kegan Paul,
London.
National Council for the Aged, *Home from Home? A Report on
Boarding Out Schemes for Older People in Ireland,* Glendale
Press, Dublin.
National Council for the Aged, *Housing of the Elderly in
Ireland,* Glendale Press, Dublin.
National Council for the Aged, 1982, *Day Hospital Care,*
National Council for the Aged, Dublin.
National Council for the Aged, 1985, *Institutional Care of
the Elderly in Ireland,* Glendale Press, Dublin.
National Economic and Social Council, 1981, *Major Issues in
Planning Services for Mentally and Physically Handicapped
Persons,* Government Publications, Dublin.
Nissel, M., and Bonnerjea, L., 1982, *Family Care of the
Handicapped Elderly: Who Pays?,* Policy Studies Institute,
No. 602, London.
Nolan, C., 1981, *Damburst of Dreams,* Pan Books, London.
Nolan, C., 1987, *Under the Eye of the Clock,* Weidenfeld and
Nicholson, London.
Norris, J., (ed.), 1988, *Daughters of the Elderly, Building
Partnerships in Caring,* Indiana University Press, Indiana.
O'Connor, J., Smythe, E., and Whelan, B., 1988, Caring for
the Elderly, Part I, *A Study of Carers at Home and in the
Community,* National Council for the Aged.
O'Connor, J., and Ruddle, H., 1988, *The Caring Process:
Part II, A Study of Carers in the Home.* National Council
for the Aged.
O'Connor, S., *Community Care Services An Overview: 1987,*
National Economic and Social Council, Dublin.
O Laoghaire, P., 1915, *My Story,* translated by O Ceirín, S.,
1987, Oxford University Press.
Page, R.M., 1984, *Stigma,* Routledge and Kegan Paul, London.
Pitkeathley, J., 1989, *It's My Duty, Isn't It? The Plight
of Carers in Our Society,* Souvenir Press, London.

Power, B., 1979, *Old and Alone in Ireland,* St. Vincent de
     Paul Society, Dublin.
Power, B., 1987, *Attitudes of Young People to Ageing and
     Elderly,* National Council for the Aged, Dublin.
Pulling, J., 1987, *The Caring Trap,* Fontana Books, England.
Pyke, M., 1980, *Long Life,* J.M. Dent and Sons Ltd., London.
*Religious Beliefs Practice and Moral Attitudes : A
     comparison of two Irish Surveys 1974 - 1984,* 1986,
     Research and Development Unit, Maynooth, Ireland.
Report of the Commission of Inquiry on Mental Handicap,
     1965, Government Publications, Dublin.
Report of Commission on Mental Illness, 1966, Government
     Publications, Dublin.
Report of Commission for Social Welfare, 1986, Government
     Publications, Dublin.
Report of Inter-Departmental Committee, 1968, *The Care of
     the Aged,* Government Publications, Dublin.
Report of the Working Party on Services for the Elderly,
     1988, *The Years Ahead : A Policy for the Elderly,*
     Government Publications, Dublin.
Report on the Workload of Public Health Nurses, 1975, Report
     of a Working Party, Government Publications, Dublin.
Richardson, A., and Ritchie, J., 1986, *Making the Break,*
     King Edward's Hospital, London.
Robb, B., 1967, *Sans Everything,* Nelson, London.
Rossiter, C., and Wicks, M., 1982, *Crisis or Challenge :
     Family Care, Elderly People and Social Policy,* Study
     Commission for the Family, London.
Runciman, W.G., 1966, *Relative Deprivation and Social
     Justice,* Routledge and Kegan Paul, London.
Sainsbury, S., 1970, *Registered as Disabled,* George Bell and
     Sons, London.
Sainsbury, S., 1974, *Measuring Disability,* George Bell and
     Sons, London.
Shakespeare, W., *Macbeth,* Act 11, Scene 111.
Shanas, E., Townsend, P., Wedderburn, D., Friis, H., Milhij,
     P., Stehouwer, J., 1968, *Old People in Three Industrial
     Societies,* Routledge and Kegan Paul, London.
Skeel, M., 1982, *The Third Age,* Darton, Longman and Todd,
     London.
Southern Health Board, 1987, "Care of the Elderly in the
     North Lee and South Lee Community Care Areas", (Report of
     a Working Party for Health Board Staff).
Spink, K., 1990, *Jean Vanier and l'Arche: A Communion of
     Love,* Darton, Longman and Todd, London.
*Survey of Religious Practice Attitudes and Beliefs in the
     Republic of Ireland, A,* 1976, Research and Development
     Unit, Maynooth, Ireland.
Thomas, D., 1982, *The Experience of Handicap,* Methuen,
     London.
Tinker, A., 1981, *The Elderly in Modern Society,* Longman,
     London.
Titmuss, R.M., 1958, *Essays on the Welfare State,* Unwin
     University Books, London.

Titmuss, R.M., 1968, *Commitment to Welfare,* George Allen and Unwin, London.
Titmuss, R.M., 1970, *The Gift Relationship,* George Allen and Unwin, London.
Tizard, J., 1968, *Community Services for the Mentally Handicapped,* Oxford University Press.
Towards a Better Health Care, 1970, McKinsey and Co., Dublin.
Townsend, P., 1957, *The Family Life of Old People,* Routledge and Kegan Paul, London.
Townsend, P., 1962, *The Last Refuge,* Routledge and Kegan Paul, London.
Townsend, P., and Wedderburn, D., 1965, *The Aged in the Welfare State,* George Bell and Sons, London.
Tunstall, J., 1966, *Old and Alone,* Routledge and Kegan Paul, London.
Ungerson, C., 1987, *Policy is Personal,* Tavistock Publications, London.
Vanier, J., 1979, *Community and Growth,* Darton, Longman and Todd (Translation), London. Also 2nd edition 1989.
Vanier, J., (ed.), 1982, *The Challenge of l'Arche,* Darton, Longman and Todd, London.
Vanier, J., 1984, *Man and Woman He Made Them,* Darton, Longman and Todd, London.
Vincent, J., 1988, "Carers Survey", *(Unpublished Paper,* Loughborough University).
Walker, A., (ed.), 1982, *Community Care : The Family, the State and Social Policy,* Basil Blackwell and Martin Robertson, Oxford.
Webb, A.L., and Wistow, G., 1987, *Social Work, Social Care and Social Planning : The Personal Social Services,* Longman, London and New York.
Wenger, G.C., 1981, "The Elderly in the Community : family contacts, social integration and community involvement", *Working Paper No.18, Social Services in Rural Areas Research Project,* University of North Wales, Bangor.
Wenger, G.C., 1984, *The Supportive Network,* George Allen and Unwin, London.
Wenger, G.C., 1985, "Loneliness : A pattern of measurement", *(Unpublished Paper).*
Wenger, G.C., 1990, "Elderly Carers : the Need for Appropriate Intervention", *Ageing and Society,* Vol.10 Pt.2
Wertheimer, A., 1981, *Living for the Present : Older Parents with a Mentally Handicapped Person living at Home,* Campaign for People with Mental Handicap.
Whelan, B.J., and Vaughan, R.N., 1982, *The Economic and Social Circumstances of the Elderly in Ireland,* The Economic and Social Research Institute, Dublin.
Woodruff, D.S., and Birren, J.E., 1975, *Aging: Scientific Perspectives and Social Issues,* D. Van Nostrand, New York.
Young, M., and Wilmott, P., 1986, *Family and Kinship in East London,* with new Introduction by Young and Wilmott, Peregrine Books, London.

Appendix 1
Life histories

As explained in Chapter 4, I included a section on the history of caring in the interview. It was not a full life history but a personal account of how the carers first came to take on the task and of their experience until the time of the interview.

The aim was to induce the carers to tell their story in their own words, the interviewer merely prompting them occasionally and keeping them on course where necessary.

The resulting accounts could form a report on their own and Malcolm Johnson would maintain that they would present a truer picture of the reality experienced by the carers than the responses to the formal questions in the remainder of the interview.

The personal accounts give an excellent background to the study as a whole. Some individual biographies were deeply moving and gave a deeper insight into the joys and sorrows of caring than the formal questions could have achieved on their own. It would appear, also, that the opportunity to tell their story in their own way for a while helped the carers to speak more freely throughout the remainder of the interviews. It should be emphasised that these accounts were taken at the beginning of the interview before any questions had been asked.

The life histories then are a backdrop to the study as a whole and I place them in the appendix section. This allows me to present more than one third of the total number which ensures, on the one hand, that the cases are broadly

representative, and on the other hand the more interesting
accounts are included.
   The names and some incidental details have been changed
throughout to preserve the identities of the carers.
I made an analysis of the accounts under a number of
headings and Tables 1.0 and 1.1. set out the frequencies
with which various issues were mentioned in the spontaneous
telling of the carers.

Table 1.0   Life Histories : Patterns For Carers Of Elderly

	YES	NO
	%	%
Carer always lived with old person	46	54
When old person became feeble, was naturally cast in the role of carer	65	37
Crisis arose in old person's life which forced carer to live with old person or vice-versa	35	65
Carer returned from abroad to look after the old person	7	93
Carer gave up permanent job to care for old person	6	94
Carer praises Public Health Nurse	3	97
Carer praises her husband for the help he gives	11	89
Carer anxious whether she/he can continue with the task	11	89
Carer finding the task increasingly difficult and complaining about it	11	89
Carer expresses intention of continuing caring as long as possible	76	24
Carer expresses negative attitudes to sending old person to institution	13	87

Table 1.1   Life History: Patterns For Carers of Handicapped

	Yes	No
	%	%
Carer found out gradually child was handicapped	67	33
Carer taken completely by surprise by the actual announcement	51	49
Carer shocked and stunned when told	58	42
Carer unwilling at first to accept child	12	88
Carer angry at the way she was told	14	86
Carer still angry with medical people because of the manner in which she was told	12	88
Carer tends to blame herself	6	94

                                              cont...

	Yes	No
	%	%
Carer tends to blame Almighty God	1	99
Carer saw handicapped child as a punishment	2	98
Carer mentions husband as taking it better than herself	6	94
Carer angry with the help medical people gave after the birth	15	85
Carer mentions husband as a great source of support at the time	3	97
Carer speaks of experience as the worst in her life	34	66
Carer has levelled off now	86	14
Carer has grown to love the child	70	30
Carer sees child as enriching the whole family	35	65
Carer sees child as damaging to the family	2	98
Carer worries about what will happen to the child when she is gone	12	88

CASE NO. 1

Lucy Cotter, 53, single, looks after her mother, Maryanne, 87.

"I took my mother's old age when it came. I felt no great emotional strain when my mother became old. Our family is a very close one. It might be different if I was all on my own, but Geraldine my sister, is with me and she is very good. John, my brother, his wife and family just live one hundred yards over the road. He is a farmer. They come up a lot to visit us. My nieces and nephews are very good in relating to my mother. They enjoy each other's company. I suppose when my mother became house-bound I felt a little tied down, tied to the house. But as I have a car I can go shopping and go to town whenever I need to. I think when she will die, though she is 87 years of age, I will miss her a great deal. She was very good to us when we were growing up. My sister and I have been happy to look after her. So when my caring task will come to an end there will be a void in our lives. Geraldine and myself are not the types that go out a lot. We like to stay at home knitting, reading or watching television. So her presence does not intrude a great deal in our lives. It has been a great joy for us to look after her."

CASE NO. 2

Annie O'Sullivan, 36, is married with three children aged 9, 6 and 4. Her husband is a farmer. She looks after her mother, 66.

"I am an only child and I was always very close to my parents. My father died several years ago and I cared for him until he died. When I got married and moved into this new house, I visited my mother regularly and then three years ago I felt that my mother was lonely and depressed and I asked her if she would like to live with us and she agreed and I think she was delighted. I always made up my mind that I being an only child would have to look after my parents, so I don't resent it in any way. My mother in not bed-ridden. She is not a burden at present. The only problem is that she suffers from depression. But she goes to the Clinic and they help her overcome it even if only temporarily. I think it is my duty to look after my mother. She was always very good to me. I don't know if I would feel the same if I had to look after my mother-in-law."

CASE NO. 3

Bridget Coakley, 50, is married with three children aged 13, 11 and 9. Her husband is a farmer. She looks after her mother who is 90.

"My mother and father were publicans. I worked in the pub after leaving school. My father died eighteen years ago when my mother was nearly seventy and still quite capable. I married and I still worked in the pub but not full-time. However, when my mother got a stroke fourteen years ago and though she recovered, I have been looking after her ever since. I am completely tied down. I have a ticket for the All-Ireland Football Final and I can't go! I have two sisters, but though they both come to see her one day a week, that's it. Anyway, though she abuses me, would you believe she can still give me a clatter across the head, we fight, still 'tis me she wants. She can be very annoying. She feels she is still in charge of the pub and she comes out to the bar and empties the till. She is very fastidious about her appearance and must have a change of underwear and jumper every second day and rubs Oil of Ulay into her face before going to bed. Sometimes, I feel she'll bury me, I feel so worn out. Still, there's no way I'd put her into a home while I am able to carry on. My brother lives nearby too and he's her pet. He leaves all the bossing to me. I have to manage her when she becomes difficult. I have tried to get my sisters to come more often and even spend the night but they always have an excuse."

CASE NO. 4

Maura Casey, 36, is married with two children. She looks after her mother-in-law, 78.

"I was in England before I got married. I came home and I married into this house fourteen years ago. At that time, both my parents-in-law were alive and active. They were able to look after themselves that time and were able to the first nine or ten years. Then, my mother-in-law became a diabetic ten years ago, but she was able to cope well enough until four years ago. Then she went blind and is on insulin. I had to administer the insulin every morning and do urine tests four times a day. She improved and recovered some sight. This pleased me.

My father-in-law had high blood pressure, but was able to do most things for himself. Then three years ago, he got a stroke. He was no trouble really but he had to be looked after for five weeks before he died. My mother-in-law is always in the house and I can't leave the house. I can't go out or, if so, only for a short period. I would not feel happy if she were on her own. I would be more worried if I was out than she would, in case anything happened to her. The public health nurse came once to show me how to give the insulin injection after she had come out from hospital. The nurse never came back, but then she had probably done her job in relation to this case. I have never sent for her as I felt that I did not need her. My husband has a workshop here in the back of the house and he is always near at hand to help if any emergency occurs. We have a telephone.

I was married for twelve years before we had the first child - we now have two and this has given me great happiness and also has pleased my mother-in-law greatly. "

CASE NO. 5

Voureen O'Neill, 40, is a housewife with four children aged 17, 15, 12 and 8. She looks after her mother-in-law, 85.

"Ulick and I got married nineteen years ago. When I came into the house after marriage, I did not think of the task of looking after my parents-in-law. I thought that they would be able to look after themselves always. My father-in-law was alive then. I did not realise that it would be so difficult to look after them.

Twelve years ago, my father-in-law died suddenly of a stroke. Initially she missed him but she came to terms quite well and quickly. About that particular time her arthritis became very painful. She then had a hip operation and must have the other one done this year.

From the beginning I resented the fact that I was the one who was shouldered with the responsibility of caring for her. Why was I the one when she had three daughters of her own? Each of them could have taken her to their homes, if not for good, at least for long periods of time. My husband understood how I felt and supported me in my views.

We built a room for her onto the house about two years ago. This was good, both for her and for myself. It

made each of us fairly independent of each other and I and Ulick could look after her. I do the cooking for her and take her her meals.
In my task of caring for her, I never felt really tied. Ulick my husband, is a great support. Our children who are now growing up, look after her quite a lot too and they get on very well together."

CASE NO. 6

Catherine McCarthy, 19, has just finished school and has not yet found a job. She looks after her grandmother, 89, and lives in her own house near the family home.
"Rita, my sister, used to look after my grandmother. She was attending the Comprehensive School during the day and she looked after our grandmother at night, staying with her. When she left school and got a job in Dublin, Angela and myself took turns in going down to stay with her and look after her. Angela did the Leaving Cert. last year and left home as well to go to University. I now find myself caring for my grandmother.
I did the Leaving Certificate two years ago and completed a Secretarial Course last year. I am presently unemployed and looking for a job. I find that I have the time for caring for my grandmother. I stay in my own home during the day helping around the house and then go down to her house and stay the night with her. The task of caring is something I grew into. My sisters before me did it so it was natural that I should continue to do it when my turn came. I enjoy it very much. Although she is a great age, 89 years of age, she is still very healthy and very humorous. She can be very funny at times, although she can be very annoyed as well at other times.
I think that old and young people get on very well together. I am 19 and she is 89, yet we can discuss and talk about anything under the sun.
If I do get a job and have to go away from her, I am going to miss doing what I am presently doing. However, I know that she will be well looked after by my father and mother who only live a few hundred yards from her. Perhaps, in time, she might have to move in and live with them in their house."

CASE NO. 7

Emily Cleary, 82, looks after sister Anne, 74.
"I came back to Ireland in October 1979. I had never intended to stay here for good even though my brother David, and my sister Anne, used to write to me and ask me to come. I spent nearly fifty years in Canada altogether. I was 21 years of age when I left Ireland

and I hadn't much education so I worked with families and then I spent 25 years with a drug company. I was very happy in Canada. I had my own apartment and good neighbours although I kept very much to myself all my life. When I came back here in 1979, I didn't really intend to stay here for good. My brother, David was alive then and there was stock on the farm and a neighbour worked here every day and my sister Anne used to do the housekeeping. Things were bearable then. I wasn't here long before things began to go wrong. I was crippled with arthritis and spent a year in bed. I couldn't even touch the floor with my toe. I was barely up and hobbling when Anne was taken sick with arthritis and spent some time in hospital. My brother, David, died in 1985 and that was the beginning of the end for me. Roles were reversed in the house and Anne left everything to me. I have to do all the chores as best I can with little or no help from her. I have no interest in anything. I regret ever having come back. My doctor in Canada advised me against coming back. He said the damp climate wouldn't agree with me. I have nothing to offer now and life has nothing to offer me anymore. Look at us here, isolated without even a phone. If anything happened to us in the night, were finished. We are both invalids, both of us having walking aids. I have to pay a taxi to take me to town every Friday to get the shopping. We can't go to Mass, so the priest brings us both Holy Communion on the first Friday. I have nothing to live for, nothing to look forward to. I am just a 'has-been'."

CASE NO. 8

Claire Daly, 61, looks after Lynda, 91, a neighbour.

"Lynda has lived next door to me for years now. We were good neighbours to each other and even before I started giving her meals, I would do little things for her. Then she got sick a couple of years ago. She was in hospital and one of the nuns wasn't too happy about her being on her own. They wanted her to go into residential care. Lynda was disgusted. She wouldn't hear of it and so she asked me if I would help her out. She had nobody else to turn to. She has been a widow for years and has no children. She is from Northern Ireland and, as far as I know, doesn't have any relatives around here.
So I did what was my Christian duty by her and I had no regret whatsoever. It is as easy to get her a bit of food ready when I am getting it ready for my own family anyhow. Nurse Carey who lives nearby is a good neighbour too and comes to see her morning and evening. I would describe Lynda as a very independent woman and though I clean the house for her and get her meals, she likes to

go around and do her own bits of dusting and manage her own ornaments. My son, Thomas, tends to her front and back garden. She is a British citizen so she gets no help from this State but she gives me a little something for myself."

CASE NO. 9

Simon Walsh, 72, retired, looks after Teresa his wife, 74. He has a daughter married nearby and his son, Seamus who has a nervous problem lives in the house with them.

"I married Teresa, 45 years ago when we were both young, good-looking and full of life. We loved dancing and going to football matches and Teresa was a great tennis player. We hadn't much money as I was unemployed and joined the Army from 1938 and was away for five years in the Curragh. Then I got a job after I came back and life was good. We had seven children, but two died as babies and Seamus had a nervous breakdown twelve years ago. He was almost trained as a plumber and he has never worked since. He has been a constant worry to me. Teresa is crippled with arthritis and only walks with a walking aid. Then, three years ago, she became senile and is now like a child. She keeps looking for her father and mother and I bring her over to the graveyard and show her their grave. She's happy for a while but in a couple of nights she starts all over again and we are off to the cemetery again. Though I have a daughter married near me, I am the person Teresa wants. Anyhow, she has a husband and young family. I retired from work seven years ago and since then, I am always with her. We sleep down stairs as she couldn't climb the stairs, but as we have no bathroom or toilet downstairs, she has to use the commode which I empty. But, through it all, I see her as the lovely young girl I married in 1940. I am glad that I am spared to look after her and I hope I can continue to do so. I take her for a drive every day and she loves this. My son, Seamus helps me a bit. He is very moody. He has an Invalidity Pension and so he is not dependent on me financially and he looks after himself sometimes. I am afraid that if anything happens to me Teresa will be put into a home, but as she is senile it won't affect her as much as the normal person. This is a small consolation for me."

CASE NO. 10

James Lucey, 71, looks after his brother, Daniel, 76, and another brother who lives with them in the house.

"My two brothers and our sister, Kate lived here in this little house all our lives. We all worked, except Kate as labourers and we were very happy. Although we hadn't

much money, Kate looked after the three of us and kept
the house shining and gave us lovely meals. Then six
years ago, Kate gave the dinner and before we had it
finished, she got a massive heart attack and was dead in
a short time. We got an awful fright, and to tell you
the truth, we never got over it. But we carried on as
best we could, though we aren't making such a good job of
it. I am the youngest and I do what I can to help the
rest of them. I try to keep the place fairly tidy but
the worst job is the ironing. I manage the washing all
right by steeping the clothes and by using hot water and
powder, but my ironing is a dead loss. The cooking is
tough too but we aren't too fussy. The five dogs deal
with the real bad efforts! I tried to get my brothers
not to keep big sums of money in the house but they
wouldn't listen to me and last spring, these two fellas
came to the door selling quilts. They brought in two big
quilts and opened them up to show them to us. When we
said we didn't want them they kept persuading us and
bringing down the price. When they went away, we found
that the bedroom was ransacked and that the £1,200 that
was hidden in the mattress was gone. So, I take their
money to the Post Office now but they miss it. It was a
great comfort to them to know that they had that
security. I don't know if we can keep going. I suppose
it all depends on how my health will hold out, but we all
miss our sister and wonder why God didn't take one of us
instead."

CASE NO. 11

Paul Leahy 55, a farmer, looks after his father 82.
"I took care of my mother for years. Her eyesight was
very bad, and when she died in 1977 my father was just as
bad and I have cared for him since. I do everything for
him. He sits by the fire all day. I am out from 9.30
a.m. until 12.00 noon and he is able to get around slowly
but his eyes are very bad now. He had an operation for a
bladder complaint and he has a urine bag for two years
now. It is a life saver for him and I take care of it
well now as I am used to it. I was always very close to
my mother and father and anything I wanted they helped me
along with it. When my mother died, it was a relief as
she was suffering and she was almost blind too. It was
hard looking at her but I am sure she is in Heaven. My
father and I have always had a good relationship so it's
only natural that I should do what I am doing."

CASE NO. 12

Anne Fleming, 22, looks after an elderly couple, both in
their eighties. The more fragile of the two is Annie, 81.

*"I was asked to take on this position of responsibility
by their daughter, because she wanted them to remain in
their own home. I see it as a responsible task although
I am no relation to them. It is a challenge because I am
dealing with other people and I am also anxious to devote
myself to the simple things in life. My motive for
taking on the job is out of a sense of caring for people.
I had some experience in a residential home for the
elderly in Dublin and then I answered an advertisement in
the paper. The old couple's daughter is a lecturer in
Dublin and she was looking for a paid Home Help to mind
her parents. I took on the job but my interest is not in
money. It is looking after old people which I see as a
vocation in my case. I am now two months looking after
them and I like this country area very much. I think
that we should be looking after old people out of a sense
of responsibility, love and charity, not just as a duty
or as a job. I see my job of caring for these old people
as arising from a genuine concern for the old."*

CASE NO. 13

Bridget Anne Treacy, 33, lives with her husband and five
children a short distance away from Nora, her husband's
aunt.
*"I came to live here when I married eight or nine years
ago. At that time, Nora lived five miles away but I
didn't really get to know her until she came to live
here. When she first came to live here, Nora's daughter-
in-law was caring for her, but they were having their
tiffs and Nora began to call on me. Then twelve months
ago they had a real falling out and she began to call on
me more and more, so that it was really a full-time job
for me. Someone like a social worker or a nurse had
forms and I filled them out and I was getting £15 a
month. I worked right up to the week my last baby was
born and then I had to stop going down for a while, so I
don't get the money any more. Still nobody bothers going
to her house and she depends on me, so I have to keep
calling on her. You see, without me, she has no one to
bother with her. To tell you the truth, she is not a
very nice person. Her own daughter came home from
America and only stayed a few days as she couldn't stick
it. Her sons don't go near her either. They can't stand
the way she talks about people. I don't like it either
but I go down there because I feel sorry for her, though
if I can go down, why can't they? She went into a Home
once but came out again. She suffers from terrible
depression and the doctor says its her age. She does
nothing all day. She doesn't even watch television.
It's her own fault that the neighbours don't call. The
people around her are very nice, but she talks about them
so they don't go near her. My husband is her nephew and*

187

that's how I came in contact with her first. I really
don't know how long more I will be able to keep going.
Yet, I do feel sorry for her. She is so much alone. But
I feel sorry for myself too. Why should I be the one the
burden is on and she is not the only old person around
here? There are many other old people around here who
never have a visitor. Wouldn't it be great if something
could be done so that at least they could have someone to
call once a day?"

CASE NO. 14

Patricia Meehan, 39, is married with five young children.
Her husband is a labourer. She looks after her father-in-
law, Murt, 83.
"I went to England to work for a couple of years. When I
came back, I came down South to visit my sister who had
married a Kerryman and lived in the next parish. As I am
from Donegal, I didn't know anyone from here, but I love
the people around here and I met Thomas. We fell in love
and got married and came to live with his parents Murt
and Rena. As that was fourteen years ago they were both
fairly young and they made me very welcome. We got on
very well with them from the start and they were very
helpful to me.
My mother-in-law was a great help to me when I had my
children. We never thought of getting a house of our own
even if we could afford it. Over the years, naturally,
they have become very feeble, and while my mother-in-law
is very active, my father-in-law is crippled with
arthritis, is totally blind and has diabetes. I love
them as if they were my own parents and I look after
them, especially my father-in-law, and I hope, with God's
help, that I can continue to do so. They are quite happy
and comfortable here and when people say, "would you not
try to get him into some Home", I get very annoyed. The
children love them and they love the children and, please
God, they will be here with us until they die."

CASE NO. 15

Nancy Collins is 61, single and looks after an old lady who
is 87 and no relation. They met at the Community Centre
where a lunch for elderly people is arranged each day.
"Bridie used to come to the Community Centre for her
lunch and I met her there. She invited me to her house
and I used to call regularly afterwards. Her nephew, Ger
was alive then and we'd all have great crack. He was
very good to her and he used to call a couple of times
each day. It was a loss to her when he died. She used
to have a lot of friends calling then. I feel badly that
the Home Help only spends an hour every day with her. I

don't think that's enough. I feel badly about it so I spend all afternoon with her. I heat up the lunch she gets from the meals-on-wheels service or maybe I do a nice bit for her myself. She has got very feeble in late years. Her appetite is not as good as it used to be. I call because I am a friend. It's somewhere for me to go out of here for a few hours every day."

CASE NO. 16

Maurice Cantillon, 55, a farmer, helps to care for Deborah, 75, a neighbour.

"When Deborah's husband died, she came back to her own home to live with her brother on the farm next to ours. He died about five years ago, the year she came to him and she was left alone in the place. The farm is willed to a cousin of hers but he rarely calls to see her. She has no close relations living anywhere near here. She is a very old woman, but we try to take no notice and keep calling on her as she needs someone to look after her. She has fallen out with a lot of her neighbours. Her sister wanted her to go into an old folks home, but she wouldn't hear of it. Another neighbour, who is a Garda, also calls to her and keeps a vigil on her place in case robbers might call there at night. Either my son or myself milk the cow for her in the morning and in the evening and we also do any farm work that's in need of being done. But she never pays us or appreciates what we do for her in the least. Our greatest worry is that she takes a few drinks when she goes to town and often brings a bottle to drink at home. I am afraid that she will fall or that the house will go on fire when she is in this state."

CASE NO. 17

John O'Carroll, 74, looks after his wife, Margaret, 65. Two sons, one 28 and the other 31 live with them.

"We were married thirty seven or thirty eight years ago and we have two sons who have no jobs only drawing the dole. We had a very bad old house, but about six years ago we got the County Council house we are now living in and it is a great improvement. My wife is a terror for the worry as long as I know her. About seven years ago she got very bad with the nerves and depression and she had to spend some time in hospital. Since she came out, she is on very strong tablets and I'd say only for them we couldn't stand her. She gets very bad with depression and when she's down and out she doesn't bother about anything. I have the Old Age Pension but we don't get anything else like the free electricity or coal because of those two useless sons who are living with us. I don't go out much because she misses me herself, but then where would I go? I'd love to go to the Village one or two nights a week and drink a few pints of Guinness with the lads, but I have no way of going and the Guinness is too dear. And I suppose I couldn't leave herself and she couldn't take a drink on account of the tablets. We are together now for going on forty years and I suppose I might as well stick it out and I suppose we might as well stick it out together. But I can tell you, 'tis a tough old life."

CASE NO. 18

Betty Hayes is 70 and she looks after her brother, Mattie, who is 68.

"I first emigrated to the United States when my mother died. I built up a nice life-style there. I had an apartment and a nice job with a good salary. The one day a telegram arrived to tell me to go home that Mattie my brother, had got a stroke and was very bad. The doctor thought Mattie wouldn't live at all. He was in hospital for a while and then I brought him home. I said to myself I'd stay for a year to help him to get on his feet again. I'm still here! If I weren't here Mattie wouldn't be here. He'd have to be in a Home. I have no home, no income, nothing in this country except two suitcases. I could live like a lady in the United States with my own apartment and my job. I could, of course, walk out but it would do me no good. I'd be worried about Mattie. He needs full-time care. All I have is what I get from the United States Social Security. Sometimes it comes monthly and then at other times, its maybe five or six weeks. I have used up all my savings. There in the summer, when things were very bad, I went to the Information Centre in town to see if I could get any financial help for minding Mattie, but they told me I couldn't. Then I applied for the pension and I was rejected because they said I had a little too much in my United States pension. But I love Mattie and I couldn't turn my back on him now. Since he got the stroke, his memory is gone and he doesn't talk much and you have to be there all the time. He'd never think of eating or of asking for anything to eat unless you put it in front of him. So I feel I must stay on."

CASE NO. 19

Jack Spillane, 37, is married with four young children. He looks after Nora, a neighbour, 72.

"In 1969 I bought the next farm to Nora. I winter cattle there and so during the winter I call to the cattle twice every day. I visit Nora every time I go to see the cattle. While I am not very close to her personally, I still feel responsible for her because there's nobody else. The only access to where she lives is access through a strand and so her comings and goings are limited by the coming and going of the tide each day. She goes to town every four or five weeks, but she has to be back before the tide comes in. Sometimes she is stuck at home for long periods and then she becomes very lonely. You have to be very careful of how you put things to her though, as she can feel very slighted for the least little thing. She's not sick or feeble or anything like that. It's simply that she's living in a very inaccessible locality with no neighbours around and those that are there, are old bachelors, nearly as old as herself. Since I go to see the cattle there every day, I feel obliged to visit Nora too, and feel badly that any of her own relations never come near her. I think it's sad too. Nora had a life of her own and probably would have got married and so on, only that she came back home to mind her own parents before they died. I am hoping and so are her friends in town that she would apply for one of the old people's cottages near the town which the County Council are building there. Otherwise, I am afraid that the loneliness of her house is going to get her down eventually."

CASE NO. 20

Donnacha Foran, 74, looks after his sister Anne, 73 and his nephew Donal.

"I am taking care of my sister for a long time. She is a very nervous person and is in bed most of the time. She gets very depressed. I have two of them in bed every day. My nephew lives with me and he also suffers from nerves, so I have to look after him and I do a little bit of farming to keep me occupied. The home help visits me once a week and takes my clothes and their clothes to the laundry and it helps a lot. I have another nephew who lives close by and he takes me out twice a week to the pub. He is good to me and calls every evening. I keep going on fairly well, thank God, considering that my sister is so depressed. However life has to go on. I have given up hard work on the farm since I became over 70. I used to love going with the horse and cart in the days gone by. My sister was once away in hospital. I felt sad then but was very glad when she came back. I manage to come out of every crisis, but getting out of the house is a very important break for me."

191

CASE NO. 21

Jimmy Crean, 60, and his two bachelor brothers look after their mother, 93.

"My mother had been in good health until about ten years ago when she was 83 years of age. Up to that time she did everything in the house, got our meals, did the washing, but then gradually she became feeble and her sight went. Her memory is very poor also. She tends to forget and keeps repeating the same things over and over. She is able to get up every day for a time but someone of us always stays in the house with her as we would be afraid that she might fall and would not be able to get up herself or might break her hip. The three of us live here in the house with her and we all help to care for her. I do not consider it difficult."

CASE NO. 22

Nellie Griffin, 56, single, looks after her mother, Catherine, 90.

"I never worked outside the home, so I was always helping my mother, but it is only in the last five years that I am doing more and more for her. She is now 90 and she can still do an awful lot for herself. The only difficulty she has is with dressing herself. I like to polish the kitchen tiles and I am terrified that she will slip on them and break her hip or something like that. I also have to watch her with the stairs. Her health is good but she suffers from a hiatus hernia, so I put two blocks under her bed and raised her pillows so that she has more comfort. I am very happy with my life. I wouldn't change anything if I had it to live over again. I like being in the house and I am not sorry that I did not have a job outside. I have no regrets. I love my garden. The flowers are going off now but you should have seen them two months ago. Mother sits in the garden when the days are fine. Other than that she stays indoors. Like myself, she doesn't care much to go out anywhere. She has a slight touch of arthritis in her right hand now and her grip is not as good as it was, so I don't like to see her near the fire. When we have a disagreement it is usually over the price of things. When something is too dear, she gives out to me over it and this annoys me a bit. But, of course, it is my duty to look after my mother and I am glad to do it. I consider myself very lucky to have my mother with me so long and if anything happens to her, I would not like to live much longer myself. You see, that is my purpose in life, caring for my mother and I am happy and content to do it."

CASE NO. 23

Jim Barrett, 52, looks after his mother, Marie, 81. He also looks after his father 92, who does not live in the same house.

"I am caring for my mother and father all my life. I stayed at home on the farm. All the family left home one by one and went to England and America. I have one sister, a nurse up the country who comes home in the summer. We look forward very much to her visits. I built a new house five years ago. I had the money so I said to myself, 'I will make life comfortable for my parents in their old age and for myself when my own time comes'. My father is a little old-fashioned and refused to sleep in the new house. My mother fought with him about staying in the old house, but it was no good so we leave very well alone. He comes in during the day. He's a little stubborn. I never married myself and I suppose I never will now, but I am very happy the way I am. It's a pleasure caring for my mother and father. Long may they live. They are very healthy apart from a heavy cold now and then. I have never felt tied down. They are always looking forward to the boys coming home or my sister coming from Galway. They usually come from the States every two years and it's something to look forward to and it keeps up all our spirits."

CASE NO. 24

Cathy Leen, 56, is married and has three grown up children. She looks after her brother-in-law, Jerry, 63, an invalid.

"When I married David twenty-two years ago, Jerry was in the house. He was an invalid from birth. My father-in-law, mother-in-law, David my husband, his brother and his sisters looked after him up until then. At that time, I could easily have placed him in a residential home. His own family did not expect me to carry out the task of caring for him. However, I decided that I would try myself to look after him. I found it very difficult in the beginning especially the first few years, the fact that he was totally dependent upon me all the time put a lot of pressure on me. Also at this time, the oldest child was born. The fact of becoming a mother and looking after him added great strain. Anyway, once he got used to me and I got more accustomed to him, things got a bit better. My confidence grew and in time I realised I had the ability to look after him. As the years went by, and the children got older, it has become much easier. Of course, without David my husband, I couldn't carry out all that I do. It is really the two of us that care for him. I would say that Jerry's presence has brought the family closer together. Jerry has a Disability Allowance but that does not go far

nowadays in buying things that he needs between the
electricity and the special bed clothes that he needs as
well as other things. It can be very expensive. I feel
very strongly that some form of State assistance should
be granted to people in our situation. I get a great
sense of satisfaction from looking after Jerry".

CASE NO. 25

Daisy O'Neill, 34, is married with three young children.
She looks after her father-in-law, Donal, 77.
"I am a native of Co. Clare. I married about twelve
years ago. My husband, Pat got the farm from his ageing
parents. I knew when I was getting married that his
parents would be in the house. I did not mind and I kept
an open mind on the situation. But I am afraid from the
first moment things were not working out. I think it was
the old story of a new woman coming into a house and
putting her own stamp on it. Early in the marriage,
Pat's father gave over the place and they seem to have
slipped back from being involved after that. We did not
relegate them to a subordinate position but they seem to
have withdrawn into themselves after he signed over the
place and they took no active part in things anymore.
That was unfortunate.
My relationship with my parents-in-law was one of
constant quarrelling with odd remissions. Some years
ago, my mother-in-law became ill and died. Her husband
missed her a lot. I am afraid that the tension between
my parents-in-law and myself affected the happiness of
our marriage for a time. His resentment got me down and
obviously, my husband was torn between loyalty to me and
to his parents. During these years, I had a miscarriage
and a still born baby. All this had a devastating effect
on me. There were times I did not know how I could cope
with it all. However, here I am today with the situation
greatly improved. I have great faith in God and I pray a
lot. My husband has a cousin, a nun, and she has come
often and she has given us great support. I have come to
terms with my father-in-law's mood swings. We are
blessed now with three children and expecting our fourth.

CASE NO. 26

Joe Burke, 56, looks after Dave, 63, no relation.
"Dave O'Donnell strayed in here about thirty years ago
after he had come out of the Mental Hospital. He is here
since. He had nowhere else to go. Nobody wanted him so
I took him in. Do you see that old caravan out there in
the yard? He lived in that for twenty five years. It
was the local Parish Priest who got after the County
Council to build that mobile home over there for him. He

lives there alone and he is as happy as Larry. He didn't
have as much as a box of matches when he wandered in
here. My daughter gives him the bit of food and when he
goes out of here, it will be in a coffin. I wouldn't put
him into a Home nor would my children. Do you see that
big cross over there by the wall? I brought that all the
way from Dublin and when I am put under, that cross will
be put over me and when Dave's turn comes he will be
buried beside me. I often ask him for a hand around the
farm, mind you, and do you know what he says to me? "I
haven't time", and maybe he'd be after spending an hour
looking up at the sky. That man would sleep the round of
the clock. I often wonder if there was a competition for
sleeping he'd win it hands down! I am not a religious
man and I haven't much time for the clergy, but if more
people would take people in off the street, it would be a
better country. I bought an old house a couple of years
ago and I have plans to turn it into a place where old
people around here could spend time during the day for
company and maybe have a hot meal and then go back to
their own homes at night. I knew a man once who spent
forty years in a Home. I was asking him different
questions about it and he kept his head down all the
time. When I said, 'Would you like to come back to your
own home', he raised his head for the first time and
said, 'yes'. That made a deep impression on me."

CASE NO. 27
Ursula O'Regan, 36, is single and midly mentally
handicapped. She looks after her uncle, William, 83.
"When I was small my uncle took me in here. I have been
here since and I keep going every day doing the best I
can."

CASE NO. 28

Helen Begley, 47, married with four children, looks after
her mother-in-law, 86, who lives close by.
"When I married, we built a new house next door to the
old farm house. She preferred to continue to live in her
old farm house and did not move into the new house with
us. She's very active and independent and able to look
after herself. She had a bit of a heart attack a few
years ago, but seems to have recovered fairly fully. I
take her her dinner every day and she gets the other
meals herself. Up till now there hasn't been any work
involved in caring for her. Her daughter comes in to
sleep in the house with her every night."

195

CASE NO. 29

Sheila Conway, 44, married with two children, looks after her mother, 86.
"About three years ago, my father died. Then my mother came to live with us. Until then she had been living twenty miles from here with my father and he looked after her. I had no choice but to take her when he died as she could not cope on her own. She is practically blind. The only other choice I had at that time was to send her to an Old Folk's Home and I certainly did not want that. It is hard on her to adjust to her new home and new friends here. She misses her old home and her old nighbours. I find it very hard caring full-time for her as she is very cranky and often goes into a bad mood. She expects everything to be done for her and she doesn't appreciate what we do for her. Our freedom has been curtailed since she came to live with us. All the family can't go out together anymore for a day and at times, if I go out for a few hours, she goes into a sulky mood. I have only one brother and he is in Dublin, so I have no other close family members to help me out. My husband is very good and understanding and gives whatever help he can."

CASE NO.30

Rosaleen Twomey, 45, married with six children and looks after both her parents.
"I am an only child and my parents have both lived with me all my life. My father is 90 and my mother is 85. My father and mother enjoyed good health until they reached the age of 85. My father went blind with glaucoma and my mother has become senile. Minding my father is a fairly full-time job and minding both parents can be very hard at times, but I do it because I like doing it."

CASE NO. 31

Terence O'Connor, 49, single, a farmer, looks after his mother, Bessy, 81.
"I was the only member of the family who didn't get married. Two of my brothers lived in Loughborough in England for a while, but they came home and live not too far away now. So, I lived here with my mother and father and did a little bit of farming and went to work for odd days for other farmers as a labourer. My father died about six years ago. My mother was fine until about two years ago when she broke her hip. She was in hospital and had a number of operations. She has to take great care of herself since and won't leave the house at all now as she's always afraid that she'd fall again. Her

kidneys have also given trouble and she has swollen feet a great deal of the time. I'm the one who is single and at home. She's my mother and looked after me when I was a child, so it's my turn now. I don't mind though and I don't regard it as any great trouble at all."

CASE NO. 32

Gerard Lacey, 45, married with three children, helps to look after his first cousin, Kathleen, 68.

"Kathleen has been handicapped for as long as I can remember. I think she must have got polio or something when she was young. My mother is her aunt and my father and myself were always back and forth across the road to her place doing jobs for her. About six years ago, I returned with my family from Wales. My father still continued to look after her. Then, five years ago, my father died suddenly and it seemed natural that I had to follow in his footsteps. She has two other first cousins living about half a mile away, but they wouldn't have been able to care for her as it was mainly heavy physical tasks that were involved, especially the turf for the fire. She has a thing about turf. She is never satisfied until her turf is home whether it's convenient for me or not. I get the grazing of her few acres from her. She has nieces and nephews in America and if she contacted them in the morning to help and to take over her land, I wouldn't mind at all. She's her own boss as far as her land is concerned. She is able to do all her own jobs inside the house. She has visits from the social worker and from the St. Vincent de Paul Society and she goes to Fatima on pilgrimage and she goes to the seaside for old folks' and sick people's holidays. She does worry about her turf though and that's my main concern as far as Kathleen's care is concerned."

CASE NO. 33

Julia Cronin, 42, is married with four children and looks after her mother-in-law, Ella, 77.

"I married Jim six years ago. My mother-in-law was in the house. We could not have got on better. She was 71 then. Her health was good. Since then, her health has failed a little. She has a weak stomach and she's on tablets for her heart. Her illness had no negative effect on me. I was glad that I was, and still am, able to help her. She can do a lot of things for herself. For example, she can still make a cup of tea. Jim and I have four children and looking after my mother-in-law does not in any way interfere with bringing up our children or looking after them. In fact, she is a great help to them. She talks to them and they get on very well with her in the kitchen where she can mind them and keep them from the fire. She is a religious person and prays for us all. She has brought me and all the family closer to God and to one another. She is a unifying force in the family. I admit that I am a very busy person but I enjoy every minute of it. I don't regret that she's in the house. I hope to continue looking after her with the help of God."

CASE NO. 34

Ailish Duffy, a Home Help looks after Thomas Houlihan, 87.
"I had been caring for my own father at home for many years. When he died last year, I realised that I would have to get a job. I saw an ad. in the paper and having come and got an interview, I got the job. I see it simply as a job. I don't know how long I will stay here. It depends on how I get on. I have been working here now for seven months and I'll do my best and see how things work out."

CASE NO. 35

Jim Carey, 41, unemployed, separated, looks after his mother, 84.
"About eight years ago I came back from England on holidays. My father was dead at that time and all the other members of the family had married and moved out. When I came home, I didn't intend to stay at home, but there was no one else here at home with my mother, so I stayed with her. At that time I got a job as a factory worker, but became redundant after three years. My mother's health was good at that stage and she was able to look after herself and cook the meals. Gradually however, her sight got poorer and poorer. I worked for another two years, but now I am unemployed for about the last three years. Because of her poor sight, my mother needs a lot of care. Our next door neighbour cooks the dinner for her every day. It would be great if she could get a home help. Our only income is my mother's Old Age Pension and my dole and it's hard to run a house on those two small allowances."

CASE NO. 36

Kitty Devane, 33, lives with her parents-in-law, her husband and five young children. She looks after her father-in-law, 80.

"When I married Paddy in 1977, I came into the farmhouse where his mother and father lived and still live. At that time, both of them were in very good health. My mother-in-law is still quite healthy. After two years of our marriage, Paddy inherited the farm from his father. I feel that was the time when a change came in my father-in-law's life. Until then, he was the one who made the decisions and felt responsible for the running of the farm. Now, he seems to have felt out of things and began to suffer mentally and physically. Mentally, he suffers from delusions and depression. At one stage, he got pneumonia and every spring he goes down with bad colds. He also developed a heart condition. When this change began to take place, I got upset and worried. It was all very new to me then. Our two older children were born at the time and this seemed to have been a great responsibility to me. I felt that if his condition got worse, I would not be able to cope with him at home. But the support of my husband and my mother-in-law helped me to cope with his condition. His mental instability upset me. His wife was the object of the mental persecution he went through. He gave out a lot to her and there was no basis or foundation to this. This phase seemed to pass. Now he is very forgetful and confused. I even tell him something and in five minutes he has forgotten it. Over the years, I have got very attached to him and I am enjoying looking after him."

CASE NO. 37

Lily Walsh, 31, is married with two young children. Her husband is a foreman with a contractor. She looks after Anne Lambe, 76, as a paid Home Help.

"The lady next door was looking after Anne Lambe for some time, but her own health failed and there was nobody to look after her. Three neighbours were approached but they refused. I said I would give it a try and I am still looking after her. Anne has been widowed for many years. She moved in to live with her brother and sister-in-law but they didn't hit it off, and when these bungalows were built about six years ago, she got one of them. She has a son and a daughter married in Liverpool and they come home to see her every year. She is very independent and loves her little house and is quite happy in it. But she loves to feel I am near, that she can either call me herself or send a child across to me if she wants me. As I live almost directly across the road, I don't find it too hard, but I am expecting another baby

in January and I hope I can continue with it then. Anne
has got used to me now and I have learned to "time" her
and it is hard for an old person to adjust to a new
person. But she would do anything rather than go into an
Old Peoples' Home. On the other hand, it is a job. I
was asked to do it. I agreed to do it and I receive £56
a month from the Health Board as a Home Help in this
case."

CASE NO. 38

Una Groves, 63, is married with a grown up family. She
looks after her husband, John, 79.
"About ten years ago, my husband had an eye operation in
England where he was at the time. His eye could not be
saved however. Then, about four years ago, his second
eye started to give trouble. He attended a doctor in
Dublin, but the doctor's couldn't operate in case he
might lose what little sight he had. Now, he's almost
totally blind except for a slight glimmer. He gets very
depressed sometimes and very irritable. It must be very
hard to be blind. Sometimes, I get very irritable too
and then I get sorry because I think he can't help it.
He's very independent around the house here. He knows
where everything is. He can put on his clothes and feeds
himself and so on. Everything he can do for himself, he
does. I'd never manage only for my son and daughter-in-
law who live less than a mile away. They run the farm
and call here to me twice a day. My daughter-in-law
brings the children over after school every day and that
gives my husband great consolation. It takes him out of
himself. They also bring him down to their own home
every week and that's a great help to him and to me as
well. I don't take any notice at all of it. I was
brought up that way, to care for the sick and the old, so
I don't think much about it. I just take every day as it
comes."

CASE NO. 39

Hannah Roche, 77, looks after her husband, Jim, 79.
"My husband, Jim, was always a very active man. He
worked very hard like the rest of his generation during
his lifetime. He mowed acres and acres of hay with a
scythe when he was young. He was a farmer. He cut a lot
of turf as well. In his youth, he used to compete in
races at sports. He was a great runner and competed in
sports all over the countryside. About fifteen years
ago, he began to get stiff and arthritis set in. As time
went by, it got worse and about nine or ten years ago,
the situation got so bad that he became confined to the
house. Then, he was able to do very little for himself.

He began to lose interest in things. This began to put a lot of strain on me. I spent a lot of time looking after him. It took me a while to get used to it. Now that he was unable to go out and do his usual work and do the jobs he was accustomed to, he began to suffer from mood swings and became very irritable. He was hard to "time". This added to the severe pain of the arthritis and made life miserable for him and also, to a certain extent, for me. Naturally, I felt very much for him. It upset me very much to see him suffering. However, as time went on, I grew accustomed to the situation. The medication he takes eases the pain somewhat. Also, I have great faith in God and Our Lady. I pray a lot. I am also blessed with a very good family. Michael our son, is single. He lives about a hundred yards from us and does everything for us. Sheila and Mary our daughters, are married and living a few miles away. They come over very often. I have a son, John, in Bristol. He writes a lot and comes every two or three years. Although we have a heavy cross with Jim being struck down with arthritis, I thank God for having given me the strength to keep going."

CASE NO. 40

Nellie Murphy, 48, a widow with five children, looks after her mother-in-law, 79.

"About ten years ago, my mother-in-law lost her independence. She developed arthritis and uses a stick. She is a very heavy woman. When she first got ill she had to go back to the hospital. But she was only there a few weeks when she was anxious to come home again. She stayed here then for a while but soon wanted to go back to her own house. Then, she had to have treatment in the Mental Hospital as she thought we were trying to poison her. She was very good for a while after that, but since, she doesn't seem to know where she wants to go, hospital, here or her own home. That will all have to stop as it has become very aggravating. She is more than welcome to stay here as we have room here now, but I can't stand any more of this chopping and changing. I don't mind looking after her really. I think people have a duty to their mother-in-law. After all, she was very closely related to my husband and she is my children's grandmother. I think if I didn't look after her, I'd have it on my conscience. You often find that people who don't look after their mothers or mothers-in-law often suffer from guilt after the parent or parent-in-law dies. She has no other relation around here. She has three daughters and two sons in England, but they are no good to her. I felt it unfair at first that I should have to do it when they were there. We contacted them and they

*were all ringing to find out how she was and they all
said they'd contribute money, but nothing ever came of
it. We realised then that we'd have to do it ourselves.
Her neighbours are very good to her but they only can do
so much. My husband died last year. Herself and him
didn't really get on very well. He used to be trying to
talk sense to her, but, of course, she didn't like that.
He was a very good man and very good to her, and like in
a lot of cases, she preferred a son in England who never
did anything for her. I have pity for her though, and I
think she is sorry now that she didn't get on better with
my husband when he was alive."*

There were two cases in which the interviewer found that the
cared-for person had gone to a long-stay hospital or a Home
for the elderly. In these cases, the interviewer went on
with the interview, but they were not coded or counted.
However, they may be of interest, with regard to the
circumstances which led to the carer's decision to seek
residential care.

CASE NO. 41

Kathleen Cleary, 39, single, a Civil Servant, was looking
after her mother, 72, until a few weeks before the
interview.

*"My mother was brought up in a pub and when her father
and mother died, she took over the place. My father was
a farmer and when they got married my father moved into
the house over the pub. They had five children. I
became a Civil Servant. Nine years ago, my father
decided to give the farm to one brother and the pub to
the other. So I suppose my mother didn't fancy living
with a daughter-in-law, so my father and herself bought a
house across the way where they retired. My mother was
only 61 and she missed the bar and the company terribly.
She became moody and silent. Then she got hardening of
the arteries and began to get senile about two years ago.
She had to be minded, so my father stayed with her until
I came from work each evening. Then, a month ago, she
slipped in the kitchen and broke her hip. It is not
knitting properly and so she is now a complete invalid
and has gone completely senile. We had no choice but to
take her to a Home for the elderly when she left the
hospital. But she seems happy there as she doesn't know
any better. But if she wasn't senile there's no way
she'd go into a Home. I suffer from high blood pressure
myself and I am on tablets at the moment so I am afraid
that looking after my mother and working was not on,
though I know I was criticised by my neighbours."*

CASE NO. 42

Ned O'Hara, 39, was looking after his aunt, Betty, 82, until some weeks before the interview, when her house was burned.

"My Auntie, Betty lived here until she was about forty. Then, she went to London, where she worked in a hospital. Then she got a very bad bout of hepatitis and she never recovered fully from this. She returned to Ireland twelve years ago. She lived alone here in the estate. She never really enjoyed good health after her return. She sat down too soon. She stopped moving out long before she needed to. She could have remained active much longer. But she maintained an interest in life and she kept up her appearance. She would do her face up and look well. She was fond of reading, she read the papers mostly. She was very keen on the royal family and she kept up with these in the papers and magazines. Then about 3 months ago, she left the gas oven on. The house went on fire and she received several burns so she spent six weeks in hospital. She was lucky to escape. She was most anxious to be independent and could not go back to her home for the present but went to the Old Folk's Home. It's just almost a mile from here. She has numerous visitors there and is glad to see them. She was always talking about her pains and aches. But since she went into the Home, she has no complaint except that they get up so early in the morning, 7.00 a.m.! I have been working to get the roof on her house recently. At the back of her mind, I think she intends to return home when she is well enough to do so. She didn't like visitors at home because she said they came at times which suited themselves, not at times which suited her, so she closed her door to visitors for the last few years. I myself enjoyed going up there evenings to see her. I met many people on the street as I went up and chatted with them, heard the news and brought the news to her. She was always keen to hear what was happening in the parish. I think that in a few months she will certainly be doing her best to come back and I will have her house ready for her, if she is well enough to do so.

Between the time we chose our sample and the time the interviewers were selected, trained and got to the homes of th elderly, twelve of the elderly had died. We had instructed the interviewers that, in such cases, the interview would still be of interest, provided that the carer felt up to the interview. The result is that we have seven interviews with carers who had recently lost their cared-for person. These also provide some very interesting information.

CASE NO. 43

Josie Kelly, 49, single, looked after her mother, Anna, who was 80.

"I was working away from Ireland for many years. I worked in England and in the United States. Then about sixteen years ago, I came home on holiday from the U.S. and I figured that, as I was the only unmarried daughter, it would be best for me to get a job in Dublin, just to be near my parents in case they needed me. There were nine of us in all in the family, but, by this time, Mam and Dad were alone in the house. I visited them at week-ends and whenever I was needed. But they never asked me to stay. My father died ten years ago and my mother seemed to go down hill from that time on. When my father was dying of emphysema, I came home for good to help my mother. My mother suffered from bronchial asthma, so then she got shingles and finally diabetes. We lived together, just the two of us, for ten years before she died on the 5th June, 1985, and those were the happiest years of my life. We didn't even have a television set and there weren't enough hours in the day for us. It was only in the last four years of her life that she needed full-time care and it was in the last seven months that she became an invalid. Then I got a wheelchair for her and was able to wheel her out down the road when it was fine. She got a stroke and was confined to bed for the last week. Yes, I gave up my job, but I would willingly do it all over again. It was a pleasure to do things for her. She never spoke ill of anybody and she never wanted to put me out. If she wet her nightdress, she would hide it from me so that I wouldn't have to change it. "I'll be the death of you, Josie", she used to say to me. If only I could have her back! I would willingly do it all over again. I have no job now and I am all alone at 49. But I hope to get something shortly because it would be a waste of life for me to stay here doing nothing. Surely, there is someone else who needs someone like me to care for them."

CASE NO. 44

James Horgan, 80, was minding his wife, Joan, 78, until she died in February 1985.

"She was a kind of invalid for years. Her hips were very bad. You could hear the bones creaking. She walked with a frame and I was always afraid she would fall. The doctor wanted to put her into hospital, but she wouldn't hear of it. She wanted to die in her own bed and be 'waked' in her own bed like her ancestors before her. I would never have forced her. I did the best I could for her as she was always a good kind woman. My daughter came a few times a week to help me. All my neighbours

were good too. She was a great woman for praying. I
often woke up at 2.00 in the morning and I would say to
her, "Are you talking to me?" "Will you stay quiet and
let me say my prayers", she would reply. Do you know
who was very good to her too? Fr. Tom Kelliher. He is
dead now too, God rest him. He brought the Bishop to see
her when he visited the parish and the Bishop was looking
out the window at the view right here from the top of the
hill. When he left, I said to her, "Faith, Joan, he
won't have a view like that in his Palace". Oh, I tell
you she was a holy woman! That television would be cut
off short the minute she thought there was something not
nice on it. She died in February and, as sick as she
was, I would have preferred if she had lived on. When
she was here I was always on the go, bringing her a drop
of water or something else and that kept me going. But,
most of all, I had her company. I tell you I miss her
sorely. 'Tis a fright to be on your own. The day drags
on and on. I have two sons, but I never know where they
spend the day or when they will be in. There is no one
like your own life's partner. She was always good to me
in life and I was inspired above all at the way I was
able to keep going at the end. It was a good thing that
she kept up the tradition of her ancestors and died in
her own bed and was 'waked' in her own home just as she
wanted it. "

CASE NO. 45

Eddie O'Shea, 63, looked after his mother, 90, who died some
weeks before the interview.
"I left Ireland in 1958 for England and came back in
August 1978 for good. I loved England. My mother was
always writing to me to come home. So when I came home
on holidays in 1978, my father signed the place over to
me. My sister didn't marry until she was 29. I always
thought that she would be the one to look after my
mother, but then she left, and I knew it was up to me. I
was sorry to leave England. I loved the place and there
was plenty of work there. My father died in May 1976 and
I bought out the house. I made improvements, put in hot
water and a bathroom. I think it is very important to be
clean. I had worked with the disabled in England so I
knew what old people needed. I cut the legs off the bath
and put in a low toilet, so I had the place ready for my
mother when she began to fail in health. She was agile
up to about 88 years of age and then she began to go off.
She didn't get a stroke or anything. I suppose it was
old age. The public health nurse was a great help.
There were things she could do that I, being a man,
couldn't do. You see, she was losing control of herself.
She hated hospitals. I remember I had to go to hospital
myself for three weeks and she went to my sister then. I

wasn't in the door home when she was hot on my heels back
into the house. I knew what she liked. When my sister
would come around to the house and make tea, she would no
sooner be gone out the door when my mother would say to
me, "Make a proper cup of tea there, Eddie." I loved
making her meals. She was very comfortable. I put in a
wall heater for her and would put hot water bottles in
her bed because her circulation was bad. When my father
died I put in a television. She said, "Don't bring that
thing into the house", and I declare to God, after a
while, she knew every programme and when it was going to
be on. She'd say, "Turn up the television, Eddie, Garda
Patrol is on". She died on the 21st February, aged 90,
and I'm on my own again now. I won't go back to England
anymore."

CASE NO. 46

Eleanor Tobin, 35, and engaged to be married, looked after
her mother who had died shortly before the interview.
   "My mother had polio when she was three years of age and,
as a result of that, one of her legs was crippled and she
used a crutch. Still, she and my father were very happy
and they had two daughters and one son. My brother, Joe,
worked in the building trade and I had a job in the Old
peoples home. So even when my father died, we were
fairly independent. My mother was able to do the
housework, the washing and a bit of gardening. Then four
years ago, her health got bad and I decided to give up my
job and look after her. Now that she is dead, I am very
happy that I did so. We were very close and she loved
having me around. I tried to get a little allowance for
looking after her, but, though I went to the doctor, the
Health Board and the County Council, I wouldn't get it.
I don't know why because I did everything for her. I
wouldn't get the dole because I wasn't available for
work, so I managed as best I could on my mother's pension
and what my brother, Joe gave me. My mother had every
bit of comfort that I could give her and I have no
regrets at all. I am engaged to be married, but would
not get married while my mother needed me. My fiancee
and myself are going to be married in October and I hope
that we'll be as happy as my parents were and that I will
be lucky to have a daughter to look after me as I have
looked after my mother."

CASE NO. 47

Kathleen O'Meara, 51, married with five children, was
looking after her father, James, until he died a few months
before the interview.
   "I am married twenty six years and my father lived with

us all the time. *Since I can remember, he was suffering with arthritis. He always had difficulty in tying his shoes, but he worked on the farm when he could and he fell in with the family in every way. He was a mild man, not given to complaining, so it was easy to get along with him. I was the only child so the relationship was there and I feel that it is half the battle when the bond is there. There was a patch when I had it hard. When the children were young, they would get on his nerves. They'd be playing around the kitchen and he'd want peace and quiet. You know how it is with old people. As I said, I was an only child so he wasn't used to a lot of children in the house. He would reprimand them and they would just ignore him and I would want to keep the peace. I knew the children had to play. He would complain them to me and they would complain about him to me. So you see, I was torn between all of them. These times were very difficult for me and I felt uptight and I must admit that, at times like that, I wished that he wasn't in the house. That's as far as it went. I would never have put him into a Home and he hated hospitals too. He would never have liked to end his days there. When he was getting feeble towards the end, the children were very good to him. He is dead three months now and we miss him. If I hadn't cared for him I would have missed out on a lot. One thing I must say about him is that he never minded to see me go out. In fact, he liked to see me go out, not like more who would be cribbing all the time. He was easy to please in that way."*

CASE NO. 48

Maura Fleming, 57, looked after her father-in-law, 97, who died six months before the interview.
When I married here in 1961, both Mr. and Mrs. Fleming were living here and both quite active. After she died, I had to take over the responsibility of caring for him. He was no trouble. He could do most things for himself. We all miss him now that he is gone and I have lovely memories of him. He was great company for me here in the house. He was lovely to have around and so was my mother-in-law. They were a lovely couple."

CASE NO. 49

Ester Dillon, 37, married with two children, looked after her mother-in-law who died at the age of 75.
"This was my mother-in-law's old home, where she lived with her husband and reared her family. When I married her son, I came to live here and it was only natural that my mother-in-law should come to live with us. There was no question of a granny flat or anything like that. We

207

all lived together and had our meals together. That was
ten years ago and even though she was only 65 years then,
she wasn't too well, at least she pretended she wasn't
and I took over the work. She had diabetes for years and
just wouldn't do what she was told. She would eat sweets
behind our back and would put sugar in her tea. She was
very lazy and I would even have to wash her face. I was
very fond of her though but she acted childishly and
wouldn't go to bed happy unless she had a row with my
husband every night. She slept a lot in the chair. In
fact, I think she was rather lazy. She loved to come
with us in the car shopping or even going on holidays.
She always collected her pension herself. That made her
feel good. Although she was a bit contrary we all loved
her and we miss her a lot. The children are heartbroken
after her and my son's asthma flared up badly after her
death. She died very suddenly and very quietly sitting
in the chair. It was lovely that she finished up in her
own house and in her own chair."

CARERS OF THE MENTALLY HANDICAPPED

CASE NO. 50

Peggy Sugrue, 48, has a son, Sean, 5. She lives with her
husband and seven other children.
"When Sean was born the nurses felt there was something
wrong with him. The doctor told me to take him to a
specialist. But he told me that he thought the child was
normal and to bring him back after six weeks. At that
meeting he told me again he thought the child was normal.
I had my suspicions all the time as I felt he wasn't
quite normal, but, of course, I didn't want to hear it
confirmed. He was nine months when I realised that he
wasn't as he should be. I already had seven children and
knew what to expect from a normal child.
The district nurse confirmed that he was handicapped when
he was one and a half years old. The doctors never told
me anything. The social worker called and said if I took
him to a residential home they would do theraphy on him.
I took him a few times to a speech therapist. When we
started thinking about school I didn't want him to go
into any residential home. I was hoping that I could
keep him at home and get him into a day-school. We went
to the day school to find out if they would take him.
They did and he started school there last September. But
the transport is a problem as we have to bring him five
miles to where he gets the bus and then we have to
collect him each evening. Getting to realise that he was
handicapped was a slow, painful process, but I was able

to accept it better that way than if I had been told
outright at the start. I got used to it gradually. I
was very down and out about it first but that wore off
after a while."

CASE NO. 51

Jane McKenna, 50, has a daughter, Ciara, 9. Her husband is
a farmer and she has five other children.
"Ciara was very small when she was born, 4lb. 4oz. only.
She was in an incubator for two days after the birth.
When she was six days old, I brought her home and she was
slow to drink and she got a lot of sickness when she was
a baby. She put on very little weight and when she was
five months old, I took her to a child specialist. He
told me she was Down's Syndrome. It was the biggest
shock of my life. It was an awful feeling for my husband
and myself. We had to come home and tell the other
members the bad news. But, we said we would do what was
best for her. When she was nine months old, after a long
discussion with the doctor, we decided to send her to a
residential home, but we would not leave her there. When
she was four years, she stayed in a home for a few weeks
of the holidays, then when she was six we sent her to a
special day school. We had a lot of difficulty in
getting the transport for her. She comes home every
night. She is very happy in the school and she loves it.
Her speech is also improved and she has learned to do
puzzles. She has also improved at using a knife and fork
at meals. I felt very sore that I left the maternity
hospital when she was born and that I was not told that
she was handicapped. She was five months old when I was
told. I did not know where to turn for help at that
time. Now, we have a Down's Syndrome Association.
Mothers should be told about this association before they
leave hospital in cases where children have this
handicap."

CASE NO. 52

Niamh O'Sullivan, 47, is married with three children.
Sinead is 8 years old.
"When she was about six months, I realised there was
something amiss. First, I noticed that she had no
balance to sit up. She was one year and nine months when
she walked and was slow talking and slow at everything.
She was over three years of age when we took her to a
specialist and he ordered us to take her for tests. It
was my own local doctor who told me the results. He said
that she was moderately handicapped. When I heard this I
was stuck to the ground. When I told my husband, he was
dumbfounded. For many nights, I cried myself to sleep

and woke up crying in the morning. *Eventually, we got used to the idea. She was almost six years of age when she started school and is very happy at the play school and is progressing well. She comes home every night and we have all settled down now."*

CASE NO. 53

Muiris Lawlor is 64 years of age. He is a widower and his daughter, Susan, is 19. His son, 23, lives with him also.

"When Susan was about four years, we noticed that she was a bit slow but thought she might pick up. She went to the national school until she was six years. She wasn't doing any good there and the school doctor recommended that she go to a Special School. Then she went to the Special School for the mildly handicapped for one year. At that time a school for moderates opened and she was thought to be more suited there. She goes and comes each day. She attended that school until last year and after discussions with the teachers it was decided that a Workshop would be the next step. This was arranged so she goes to the Workshop each day now. My wife died just twelve months ago and, naturally, if she were here, it is she you would be interviewing and not me."

CASE NO. 54

Margaret Bohan, 51, lives with her husband and three daughters. Lynda, aged 8, is her foster child.

"I had two short-term foster children and after some years they were sent back to their parents. So then I rang the Social Services to see if there was any other child that needed fostering. They told me about Lynda who is handicapped. She was about to be sent to a residential home. The nurses then brought her to me. There has never been any contact with her parents as her mother rejected her at birth. We have never regretted taking her in. She is one of the family now."

CASE NO. 55

Mary Dunne, 43, has a daughter Anita, 8½. Her husband and two sons are the other members of the family.

"Anita was two hours old when they told me she was handicapped. My first reaction was to put her into a home immediately. But that only lasted for half a day. I had a great fear after that that she would die because she had a murmur in her heart. I prayed that God would give me the health and strength to look after her and keep her alive. I had blood pressure brought on by anxiety and the doctor tells me it is caused by the fear

I have that if anything happened to me, Anita would end up in an institution. I cannot bear that thought."

CASE NO. 56

Lizzy Rohan, 36, has three children. Her daughter, Stella, is 11.

"Stella was perfect when she was born. It was very sad what happened to her. I was in town one day and it was very hot. She was four and a half months old at the time. I left her in the car in the carry-cot while I was doing my shopping. I must have been away for two hours or more and there was no window open in the car. When I came back she was almost blue. She was rushed to hospital where she nearly died, then they told me that she would be retarded. I couldn't sleep at night. I prayed and prayed. Then we could do nothing about it. We had her in the Home for a couple of years and the nurses there asked parents who felt they could bring them home to do so. We brought her home two years ago and she has settled down very well here. I sometimes wonder if it was the fact that I left her in the car was the cause of her handicap. But we are very happy with her now and we wouldn't part with her for the world."

CASE NO. 57

Nellie Kane, 54, is married to a farmer. They have fourteen grown chldren, three of whom are still living at home. Oliver is 17.

"I can remember the day well when I first thought there might be something wrong with Olly. He was about three years of age, not toilet trained and always clinging to me. I sat him down at the table and he was crying and Thomas, my son, who is a teacher said, "Do you know, mother, I think Olly, might be retarded". From that moment on, I knew. I sat down and cried my heart out and from then on, I accepted it. Looking back, I must have been suspicious for a long time. I thought he had a short neck when he was born and I said it to my husband but he said, "Nonsense, woman". Olly was a very quiet child too when he was a baby. He has a congenital heart condition and a kidney infection which I discovered myself. He didn't walk until he was two years old and he didn't sit up until he was one. But I put all that down to his heart condition. I asked my doctor about him and he told me nothing. By this time, I had all the other children and my day was a long hard one. I didn't have time to think. I took him to be assessed by a psychologist who told me that he was somewhere between moderately and mildly handicapped. I had him assessed again a second time and I was told much the same. When

211

he was five, a friend who is a nun wrote to me and told me she had a place for Olly in a residential home. The psychologist had told me that if I could keep him at home with my large family it would be very good for him. The Sister had felt sorry for me because I had a large family, but I decided that I would do what was the best for Olly and that meant keeping him at home.

Then, a few years later, I was at a meeting one night and that changed my life. It was a meeting of the Parents and Friends of the Mentally Handicapped and they suggested the setting up of a Day School. Everybody thought it was a good idea. They got to work on it. He was six then and he was in the Day School by the time he was seven. He is now seventeen and he will be leaving that school and he will be going to the Workshop in September. He is better than I even dreamed he could be. There is nothing he cannot do around the house and I am delighted I made the right decision to keep him at home."

CASE NO. 58

Josie Crean, 29, is a housewife. Her husband is a farmer and they have two children aged 8 and 3. Her son, Anthony is 5 years old.

"The one thing that I regret is that I wasn't told there was something wrong with Anthony when I was in the hospital. He was about five months old when I suspected that there was something wrong. The strange thing, once I was told about it, I accepted it straight away. My own doctor told me all about Down's Syndrome and I had no hesitation in accepting Anthony just as he was. I feel special, like just as if I was chosen, you know, singled out. He is a special child, a gift from God. When he was twelve months old, my doctor told me that the best thing I could do was to have another child as the chance that I would have another handicapped child was very slight. When he was two, Muriel was born and I found out that the doctor's advice was right, because as Muriel began to do things, Anthony began to imitate her. When she began to eat with her fingers, he began to use his. Please God, nothing will ever make me put him into a residential home. As long as I have my health I will look after him."

CASE NO. 59

Gretta Coffey is 55. Her daughter, Bernie, is 15. She lives with her husband and two other children.

"When Bernie was born, I was suspicious from the very beginning that something was wrong. Nobody told me. I was told by the doctor to come back in a few weeks with Bernie and he passed this off by saying, "They take more

care of babies than of the mothers now". Still, that
feeling was there. She was only a few weeks when she got
very sick. She had a chest problem. I thought she was
going to die. In fact, on our way to the hospital, my
husband and I were discussing where we were going to bury
her. When our local doctor looked at her on arrival, I
heard him say, "My God, what can I do with her?" He held
her up to the light and looked at her very closely. He
had got his information already, of course, but he never
said anything to me. I was called to the clinic then and
the bottom fell out of my world. I felt I was in a dark
tunnel with no light at the end. My husband couldn't go
to the clinic with me that day and I had to take the blow
all on my own. My daughter was handicapped. She wasn't
very old when I got hepatitis myself and had to spend
three months in hospital. It was a combination of
hepatitis and depression caused by the fact of Bernie's
handicap. There were terrible days then. Some days,
perhaps, I wouldn't have any visitors as it was very far
from home. It was so lonely and depressing. But I think
what kept me going was reading. Bernie was at home for
part of the time. My mother-in-law looked after her.
She was in hospital a great deal too and you might say
that the nurses reared her for the first few months. One
good thing about my stay in the hospital was that it
opened my eyes. There was one nurse there who was very
good and who used to talk to me a great deal about
handicapped children. All of this talking helped me
greatly and I felt better. We got on fine then though
she was still being bottle-fed at the age of three. I
didn't have the time or the patience to encourage her to
spoon feed. At three, she got a very bad attack of
chestiness and we had to go to a hospital again. I
thought she would die again this time. My husband's
sister was a nurse in this hospital at the time and this
helped us greatly. We were so grateful that Bernie got
well again after this bout. My sister-in-law and the
curate here and a few other relations got together and
persuaded us that she would be better off at the Home.
My parish priest, on the other hand, was against this
idea. That put pressure on us. But what really decided
me was her illness. I felt she would be better looked
after if she were somewhere she could have ready access
to a doctor. In the beginning, I found it very hard. We
used to visit her every three weeks and every time, I
just cried and cried. One evening I didn't cry and I
mentioned this to one of the nurses, that I mustn't be a
good mother to leave my child without crying. She said,
"Why should you cry?" I realised she was right. Crying
wasn't going to help the situation!
All that hassle has passed now. She comes and goes in
the bus every week-end. Though, mind you, I find that if
we bring her back ourselves we all get upset again.
Otherwise, she is getting on very well there. In the

beginning, I felt bad about sending Bernie to the Home.
I felt that God had sent her to me and that I was letting
God down by not caring for her myself.   Now I am happy
because I feel she has got every chance.   Her speech is
not wonderful, but at least now I know she has one of the
best speech therapists available, so I have no guilt.   I
am convinced it is harder to leave them go than to keep
them at home.   When you keep a child at home, you have
peace of mind.   They are under your eye and you know
what's happening.   But when you send them them away,
while you know you are giving them a great chance, you
worry in case they will be lonely or sick.   I have
adjusted a good deal to all that now.   I cried, too, when
I saw Mary, her sister, going out dancing.   I knew Bernie
could never go with her to discos.   I am over that hurdle
now too.   Now, I am more worried about Mary, with the way
the world is going.   At least, Bernie, will always be
protected."

CASE NO. 60

John Daly, 62, a widower, has two sons and a daughter.   His
daughter Debbie is 18 years old.
"When my wife died eleven years ago, I took on the
responsiblility of looking after Debbie, when she came
home every week-end from the Workshop.   I look forward to
her coming now as she is no trouble and can be better
than the other two sometimes.   She was about twelve
months old when we found out she was handicapped.   We
kept her at home until she was five and then she went to
the Home.   She got great training there and can do
anything around the house."

CASE NO. 61

Rita O'Connor, 64, is married with one daughter, Noranne,
10.
"When I found that Noranne was handicapped, I experienced
a great trauma, a frightening experience.   I had no one
to turn to in the beginning.   My husband was very much
afraid of the situation too.   I cried a lot in those
early days.   In the hospital where Noranne was born, I
got great support from a nun who had a brother who was
handicapped.   On coming home, I did not go outside the
door for three weeks.   I felt a sense of shame in front
of the neighbours.   Then Christmas was coming and I had
to go out.   In the beginning a friend asked me if I would
have preferred if Noranne had died at birth and I
answered that I would.   But as time passed I began to
grow to accept the situation more, I became delighted
with Noranne.   In the beginning, the district nurse was
very helpful to me too.   At present, I find the situation

quite normal. I live a normal life and so does Noranne.
She lives as normally as she can, given the situation.
She rises in the morning, attends the day-school, going
back and forth by bus, comes home and spends the evening
with the family."

CASE NO. 62

Carmel Browne, 39, is married with two sons and her
daughter, Lucy, 8 years.
"She was four days old when the doctor told me Lucy was
Down's Syndrome. I lost my head and screamed and
shouted. I have never really come to grips with it over
the eight years. I never can, deep down. She was easy
to rear, a great sleeper. She was slow to sit up and
walk though. At a year and eight months, she finally
walked. My husband accepted it much better than I did.
She is not a difficult child. She is bright and is doing
well at school, but I can't get rid of that terrible
feeling about her being handicapped. I don't think I
will ever get over it, even though she is not badly
handicapped."

CASE NO. 63

Angela Heffernan, 57, has five children. The youngest,
Geraldine is 12.
"When Geraldine was born, she was twelve pounds and very
purple and puffed. The nurse delivered her in the
Hospital, and they told me she wasn't well. I could see
that for myself, that she was handicapped. I was
shocked. I told the doctor to take her away. I didn't
want her and, strange to say, to-day, I wouldn't part
with her for the world and the boys are mad about her.
What an awful shock for any woman! You could walk
yourself to the sea and throw yourself in at that moment.
But now when I see even young girls having handicapped
babies, it's difficult to understand. But I find the
meetings of the parents very good. You will always see
cases that are worse than your own."

CASE NO. 64

Helen O'Dea is 40. She has four children, aged 15 to 9,
including Grace who is 13.
"I was suspicious from the start that there was something
wrong with Grace. When she was three months we took her
to a doctor and he said she was fine. When she was four
months, we took her to The Children's Hospital in Dublin.
They did tests and said they thought she was spastic.
When she was ten months old, it was confirmed and she was

*severely handicapped. It was terrible being told this
final diagnosis. Then we took her to a Spastic Clinic
for physiotherapy every week but that didn't do her very
much good. When she was one year and nine months old, we
took her to America, and we worked on a programme for two
years with re-assessment every three months. She
improved a lot on that programme and it also gave us a
better understanding of her. It was during that time
that she became a person for me and from then on, she was
treated as another member of the family. She is
completely immobile and everything has to be done for her
but she is very happy and very quiet. My only problem is
if I don't outlive Grace, what is going to happen to her.
At this time, in this area, the only place for mentally
handicapped children with her degree of disability is the
Psychiatric Home. This, of course, would be terrible to
contemplate."*

CASE NO. 65

Lucy Brick, 43, is married and with three children. Her
daughter, Colette is 7.

*"Six weeks after she was born, I was told that Colette
was mentally handicapped. Her birth was very slow and
complicated. I was very upset when I heard she was
handicapped and cried and cried for days. I almost had a
breakdown at that time, but I had to accept the situation
and we decided that we would do everything we could for
her. The public health nurse called a lot to me and was
a great support. Then I got in touch with other mothers
and it was consoling that some of these had worse cases
than mine. Thank God, she can walk, can understand some
things. But she was very troublesome when she was
growing up and she would throw toys at the television or
at the window. She was also very bold but a lot of this
has worn off. She often locked herself into the bathroom
and we had to break down the door. But, thank God, she
is much better now. It's grand to get the break when
she's at school."*

CASE NO. 66

Anne Devane, 30, is married with three young children. She
looks after her husband's brother, Dick who is 23.

*"Three years and three months ago, I started looking
after Dick when his father died. His mother had died
sometime before and the father had looked after him for
those years. But then when the father died, not one of
the other members of the family were willing to take him
into their own homes. We are glad to have him and it's a
good thing for our own children too, I think, that he is
here. Dick was a resident at a home for ten years before*

his parents took him out to live with them. They didn't
have a bathroom so his father used to bring him to our
house for a bath every week. Then when the father died
and the other members, and there are ten of them, all
refused to have Dick, we felt that we ought to take him.
He is no trouble really except for the things which I
have to do for him. I am a Londoner myself and and met
my husband there and we moved home some years ago to live
here."

CASE NO. 67

Mary Muldoon, 58, lives with her husband and her son,
Cormac, 23.
"Cormack was about two years old before I noticed there
was anything wrong. I remember saying to my mother that
he was very slow. Eventually, I took him to a specialist
who told me that he was retarded. The bottom fell out of
my world. It was an awful shock for me and more
especially for my husband. But what could we do, only
accept it. He was the only one we had. He brings us
great joy now even though he is handicapped and we love
him very much. I suppose it would be worse if we had no
child. I am delighted with his present job in the
Workshop and I thank God for it".

CASE NO. 68

Nora Healy, 37, lives with her husband, daughter and son,
James, who is 10.
"When James was born he was in an incubator and was very
sick. He had to be fed through a tube. He was in
hospital for a few weeks. They told me there that he
would be a slow learner. They wanted to keep him and
send him to a Home in Cork, but we couldn't leave him.
We would die without him. So we brought him home and he
was fine. When he started to walk at about one year and
ten months, we noticed that he was dragging one leg
pretty badly. The doctor told me that he had weak
muscles in his thigh. I started bringing him to the
Clinic and he goes there regularly for physiotherapy. I
do the therapy at home myself as well twice every day.
We have to straighten the leg and lift it to see if we
can strengthen the muscles. He has to call to see a
specialist this December and I hope that they'll do
something for him. I'd like it if they did fix his leg
before he gets too much older. He went to the local
national school for a year but didn't make much progress.
The teacher hadn't time to give him the special attention
that he needed. So he is now in a school for moderately
handicapped. I'd prefer if he could go to the Special
School for mildly handicapped. I think he's too good for

*the 'moderate' school and he's picking up a lot of bad
habits from the other children there. They told me there
that he'd find it too difficult in the school for 'milds'
just now and to give him another year. He has a great
friendly way with him and if anyone comes in he has his
hand out to welcome them and invites them to come in. I
have great pity for him and I worry about him. But what
can a person do? I'd never leave him into a Home and
we'll do the best we can for him here."*

CASE NO. 69

Sheila Cronin, 55, lives with her husband and twelve
children. Stephen is 15.

*"I blame myself really. I had enough children, eleven
before Stephen. I should have been satisfied. I'll
never forget it when he was born in the local hospital.
All I kept hearing was, "He won't live', "He won't walk",
"He will always be sickly". He was brought to Cork for
tests. I was called up there by the specialist. It is a
sixty mile journey. What did he tell me do you think?
"He won't live, he won't walk, he won't talk". I told
him if he had nothing new to tell me, he should have
spared me the journey! Then Stephen was taken to
hospital for a while. After six weeks or so, I got word
to bring him home from there. I'll never forget the
state the child was in when I collected him at the
hospital. The first think I noticed was that he had
diarrhoea and they had no nappy on him. I remember I had
a white cardigan on me and I used that as a nappy for
him. It was a disgrace. I took him home that time and I
swore he'd never go to hospital again. We was very
sickly from then on and often got croup. I tried to cope
as best I could myself and only called the doctor as a
last resort. My youngest was only two at that stage, so
I suppose I was kept going. Of course, my older
daughters were at home at that stage and they helped. My
oldest girl took a great interest in him. When he
stopped being sickly and began to get strong, I realised
that Stephen was going to live irrespective of what the
doctors told me. When he was about six, I heard about
the Home and was advised by people to send him there. I
did so. He gets on very well there and comes home every
week-end and comes home for his holidays at Christmas,
Easter and Summer. We are all very fond of him and I
suppose I spoil him really. I do sometimes have a
feeling of being tied down by Stephen when he's at home,
but he's a lovely little boy and I don't mind."*

CASE NO. 70

Margaret McCrohan, 60, is married and her sister lives with the family. Conor is 14.

"*I have to say that I have come to terms with it at this stage. I was very disappointed at first and very puzzled. Everyone else knew before I knew. Conor was born in the local hospital and a lady in the town told me afterwards that she knew the morning he was born that he was a 'mongol'. That hurt me deeply. Mind you, something did strike me about his eyes very shortly after he was born but I put it out of my mind again. It was the local district nurse who dropped the bombshell. She came regularly after I brought him home from hospital. She used to always come at the wrong time, when the lads were coming home from school and I would be up in a heap. I was wondering why she should be coming so often. Then she told me he was Down's Syndrome. She didn't explain anything about the condition to me but gave me examples of other children in the locality, one who attacked his parents and one who went around peeping in windows at night. I was left with the impression that I had a sex maniac or somebody very dangerous on my hands. I was frightened. She advised me to put him away. I was in a terrible state. Do you know I had to force myself to feed him when he cried. My husband lost weight and I myself lost a great deal of weight too.*

But by degrees I met people who explained what Down's Syndrome was. In the meantime, I was working away with him at home. He walked at one year and ten months. I got him toilet-trained at an early age too. Then I sent him to the local national school, but there were a lot of young children in Baby Infants and the teacher hadn't time to give him sufficient attention so Conor began to soil his pants, something he had never done before. I then decided to send him to the residential home, but I brought him home every week-end as it broke my heart to leave him behind me there. My husband didn't want him to leave the house at all. He told me that I could teach him as much as they could there. I'm sure I could too, but as the nuns pointed out when I used to bring him up there on a daily basis initially for speech therapy and so on, it's in the child's social development that the residential school scores. I found it very hard to part with him in the beginning. I'm used to it now though. He's great now and, as I've said, I've come to terms with it. He can cycle. Yesterday, for the first time, he put a sentence together. That gives me great satisfaction."

CASE NO. 71

Kay Carmody is 46. Her husband is a farmer and she has ten children aged 19 to 6. Richard is 6.

"Looking back, the only thing I noticed when I was expecting Richard was that I was very dizzy in the mornings. Otherwise, I was in the best of health. He was the only baby in the hospital at the time he was born. The nurse told me he never cried when he was born and he wasn't taking his bottle from them. Then the doctor told me he had jaundice and they were sending him to Cork for tests. He was there for six weeks. I have a sister a nurse in that hospital and she used to phone me and tell me how he was. I was to bring him home for Christmas, then it was discovered that he had a hole in his heart, so he had to go on special medication at this stage. I was getting suspicious and when I went to collect him in January they told me he was Down's Syndrome with complications of the heart and they didn't know how long he would live. There and then I decided to do the best I could for him. My mother-in-law had been in the house with us and she had just died and it seemed to me that this child had been given in her place almost. It seemed that I was destined to be caring for someone. He is six now and is off all the medication and I had him in Cork recently and they told me that I needn't bring him back for two years and that seems to me to be a good sign. I would love now to have him at school. He is six and I feel he would be better off with strangers his own age. His father however doesn't want to part with him and has refused to do so up to now. But now that he is six, I think that it would be good for him."

CASE NO. 72

Ann Fahy, 42, is married with three daughters and her mother, 75, lives with her. Josephine is 18.

"Josephine was born in England and at nine months I realised that she wasn't sitting up and doing the things other children at her age were doing. I took her to a specialist and he didn't accept that she was handicapped as she looked quite normal and was putting on weight. She was born six weeks prematurely and only weighed 3 lbs. 2½ ozs. and was in an incubator for eleven weeks. She was 5 lbs. 2 ozs. when I took her home from hospital. On my own instinct, I took her to another specialist and had tests done and it was confirmed that she had cerebral palsy and I was told she would never walk or never talk. It was an awful shock to me when it was confirmed that she was handicapped, even though I had suspicions that something was wrong. My husband was a great support and only for his help I couldn't have got through. Gradually, we began to accept it and got used to it. It meant a lot of time was spent in hospitals, taking her for speech therapy, for physioteraphy and a lot of time involved each day in doing exercises with her. It meant getting up a couple of times each night to turn her in the bed. She got convulsions also and this meant that I couldn't leave her with anyone else, so I was looking after her twenty four hours every day. We didn't have any social life when she was small. When she was four years she went to a handicapped school in England, being collected and brought back each day. That was a great break for me as I was free to go shopping and so on during the day-time. She was six and a half years old when we came back to Ireland. I was unable to get her into a day school here and then we heard of a five-day school in Cork, but it didn't suit her. So I took her back out of there. She got a kidney infection there. She stayed three months there. Then she went to a Special School in Limerick, where we collected her and brought her back each day. That school became a national school so she was at home for a while and then we got her going to the special school. She was there for six years until she was 18 years and now we are hoping she will be placed in the Workshop for the handicapped. There have been some very difficult times."

CASE NO. 73

Martina Dowling, 56, is married with five children. Timmy is 22.

"Timmy was born in the U.S. Children are not allowed to go to school there until they are five. We left to come home and live in Ireland when Timmy was just that age, with the result that he was well over five when he first went to school here. I think that is what happened to him. He was in with children younger than him and he was frustrated. I don't like the term handicapped at all. Timmy is not handicapped, he is slow. He did his Group Cert. you know. I had him assessed in Cork and they told me he needed remedial teaching because he was slow. Timmy is very sharp and he is better off with strangers. He did a Training Course and they put him into a workshop and that was the worst thing that could happen to him. They were much worse than him there. He didn't fit in. Timmy is a borderline case. A firm took him in some time ago. He was doing very well, but they started to leave people off and Timmy had to go. There would have been a strike if he had been kept on, but he has references and good ones. If only someone would give Timmy a break! He won't get up for his father in the mornings, but he will get up no bother next week when he will be going to Dublin. Timmy would be a good worker if only someone would take him on. He was with a local newspaper but, when his six months were up, they took someone else on. He was very disappointed. He can be very stubborn. His father worries a lot about him. A job would mean so much to Timmy and to all of us".

CASE NO. 74

Sally Baker, 55, a widow with two children, 23 and 18. Her son Luke is 25.

"I was very small when I was carrying Luke. The doctor questioned me if I had my dates right. I already had a still-birth. It was two weeks overdue, so my doctor wouldn't take any chance this time. He took me into hospital. I got various injections and labour was induced and Luke was born. He was 4½lbs. He was very bad for eating and they fed him through a tube. Then they decided that they'd keep him a while longer and train him to a bottle. I used to visit him every time I went to town shopping. On one such occasion, I met one of the nurses. She as as good as any doctor and she told me that he had greatly improved and that he'd raise his little head when he'd see me. He did just that, and do you know, I thought I saw something in his eyes that day. But, of course, I wouldn't believe it. If anything was wrong with Luke wouldn't the doctors and nurses have told me? He came home after a few weeks. At night, after the others would go to bed, my husband and myself would sit by the fire and we'd be looking at him. Both of us felt that something was wrong but neither of us wanted to be the first to say it.
When he was nine months old, I took him for his first injections. I was told then that he would be slow, that what normal children could do in three months, Luke mightn't do for twelve months. Down's Syndrome was mentioned. I couldn't bear it. I cried and cried that day. We taught him to walk along by the chairs. We repeated simple words for him and he'd say them after us but he'd never say them off his own bat. We persevered with the toilet training and eventually we succeeded. There was never any question of sending him anywhere because the doctor had mentioned the first day he told me about Luke's handicap that he'd be better off in an institution and I had shuddered. It sent shivers through me. Then there was a Mission and the priest visited our house. He told us to make up our minds and send Luke to where he would have some schooling, otherwise, we'd be doing the child an injustice. We didn't want that at all and we took the priest's advice. We wrote to a number of places.
So we decided to take him to a Home in Dublin. I'll never forget that train journey. We were miserable. The first sight we saw when we got there didn't cheer us up at all - old men sitting in chairs in the grounds shaking themselves and nodding their heads. Then the Matron was stiff out too. She told us the best thing to do was to leave him there and go home. I'll always remember that picture of him at the top of the stairs. He looked so helpless and so sad. We rang every week to see how he was getting on. They would say he was fine. At

*Christmas we guessed that all was not well. He came home
the following Easter and still didn't want to go back.
He didn't like it there and we were upset because of
that. He spent another year there however. He had to.
There was no place else. Then word came from the Home
here that they had a place for him and we were very glad.
When we took him to the local Home we used to see mothers
and fathers crying when they left their children there.
We couldn't understand them at all. We were so happy to
have Luke accepted so near home, we had gone through so
much in Dublin. When he finished his time, he went to
the Workshop twenty miles away, come home at weekends.
He found it strange in there at first because he stayed
five nights, coming home at the week-ends. But he was
happy that some of his former friends were now working
there with him. So we got in touch with the Parents and
Friends regarding the possibility of getting him a place
in the local workshop. We were delighted when the phone
call came to tell us that he could come. All the family
discussed it beforehand. But before we decided, we
considered the full implications of what it would mean to
have him at home here all the time. We came to the
conclusion that since he was here three nights a week as
it was, the extra four nights would make no difference.
It's easier that way. When he was going away for the
week, he needed a case of stuff going.
Now, it's like any other child going off to school and
coming home each evening. He's delighted that he can
come home every night to his own bed. He does his own
little jobs around the house and he helps with looking
after my mother. He's no trouble at all. I suppose
really I'm more tied down with my mother than I am with
Luke, as she is 88. I am lucky though that all my family
are around me. My daughter is next door. I mind her
children if she wants to go out and she comes here to
look after Luke and my mother when I want her to. I
suppose to me Luke is like having a young child around
the house all the time. Luke is just different. He
needs a little extra care. My mother needs much more
care since she is 88 and I have to do most things for
her, but there is no question of putting her into a Home.
I'm an only daughter and my mother and myself have always
been very close."*

CASE NO. 75

Nelly Foley, 71, is a widow and her only child, Danny is 31.
*"My first child was still-born and I had two miscarriages
after that so Danny was my last and only surviving child.
My husband and I were delighted. We thought he was
perfect and it wasn't until he was two years old that the
local doctor told me that he was retarded. As a baby he
was constantly sick. I think I had the doctor with him*

for every tooth and when he was six months old he came
down with pneumonia. I thought he was finished that
time. I had so many ups and downs with him that I was
just glad he was alive. That is how I felt. I think I
must have accepted it straight away when the doctor told
me he was retarded, but his father didn't. He was both
disappointed and worried. He worried over what would
become of Danny in the beginning and thought it would be
better to put him into a Home. I wouldn't hear of it.
Danny was mine, sent to me from God, and if it was to be
my Cross, I would carry it as best I could. So I kept
him and reared him with gentleness. The more gentle you
are with these children the better they will become as
they thrive on praise. I am well rewarded for it. He
stayed at home until he was 27 as there was no way of
sending him to a school and he was with me at all times
during those years. Then when the Workshop opened ten
miles away, they persuaded me to let him go there and he
goes there now every day and comes home each evening.
They had a Hallowe'en party there and they got apples and
nuts and each of them got a packet of wine gums, and he
came home that night and took the packet of wine gums out
of his pocket unopened and handed them to me. It gave
him more happiness to give them to me than to eat them
himself."

CASE NO. 76

Cecilia Finnegan, 48, lives with her husband and six
children. Maeve is 8.
"At my age, I did not want another baby. I had five
other small children and that was enough. My father,
aged 82, was here in the house too at that time. He was
incapacitated and had to be lifted in and out of bed. I
had to go to hospital for a rest in the last month of my
pregnancy. When she was born I asked about her. When
they told me she was physically and mentally handicapped
I was shattered. I had been struck at my weakest spot.
I was dumbfounded. I was very angry and lashed out at
the doctors and the nurses and at anybody else within
earshot. She wouldn't feed and you couldn't hold her.
Her arms and legs just flapped about. How was I going to
face home to five young children, to a bed-ridden father
and to a house without running water? Before I was due
to be discharged, I explained this to the Matron and
pointed out to her what a bad feeder Maeve was and so on
and the hospital agreed to keep her and they did so for
six weeks. It was awful then. I don't know how I
survived, but I did. I am as tough as nails now.
Nothing would move me. I had lost hope and interest in
everything then.
Donal, the next youngest, was a year and a half when
Maeve arrived. I used to have to strap him into his

chair while I was feeding her. The feed could take up to two hours. He was neglected, the poor child, and shows the effects of it to-day. Now he picks on Maeve, teasing her, pulling her hair.
Those first years she reminded me of a dead rabbit. You'd hold her in your arms and her legs and arms would just flop around the place. It was very hard to feed her. I felt isolated. The first time the district nurse came, do you know what she said to me? "Well, what can you expect, at your age?" So we didn't hit it off very well that day! Then on her next visit she said, "There's no improvement here at all", when she looked at Maeve. I was very hurt at that because I thought there was great progress. My sister knew the Matron in a residential home and when Maeve was only a few weeks old, she brought me to visit her. She offered to take in Maeve at that stage, but I said I'd have a go at home first. I was able to keep going because her offer acted as a kind of prop to me, and wasn't she changed to England, and that was the end to that. The local doctor was good too, and on a few occasions when she saw I couldn't cope with Maeve, she took her into Hospital for me. About four or five years ago, the social worker called around and gave me great hope again that Maeve could find a place in the Home. She went there when she was seven.
It struck me at my weakest point when Maeve was born. I had a horror of handicapped children always. A friend who worked with me had a handicapped child. I never went to see her. I could not face her. And now here I was myself with one, but I have got over that now, mostly anyhow. I feel I should be doing a lot more for Maeve, but there's no money here for the extra amenities. I often say to my children, "I only wish ye were as little trouble as Maeve". She more than repays any love I give her and is a great consolation. She comes home for weekends now and for the holidays three times a year. The district nurse called recently to see if I would bring her to Lourdes. I told her that I didn't want any miracle. She wouldn't be my Maeve at all then. But if I was a deeply religious person, I would probably consider the whole thing as a guarantee of sainthood! The experience has taught me that no case is hopeless – where you'll least expect a return, that's where you'll find it. Maeve is my biggest consolation now, whereas in the beginning she caused me so much trouble and worry."

Appendix 2
The questionnaire

(Instructions for interviewer are in italics and in brackets)

A . <u>GENERAL DATA:</u>

1. Name of Principal Caring Person (carer): _____

2. Address: _____ .

3. Age of carer: _____
4. Sex of carer: Male 1   Female 2   *(Ring appropriate*
                                          number)

5. *Although we have agreed that you are the Principal carer, is there anyone whom you would consider to be almost on an equal footing with you?*
                    Yes 1   No 2

6. *If YES, please state who it is:* _____

7. *Occupation of carer:* _____
    State whether -   Fulltime 1   Part-time 2
8. *Has carer others who are dependent on him/her?*
                    Yes 1   No 1

9. *If YES, list them fully:* _____

10. *Does carer live in same house with cared-for person?*
                  Yes 1   At night only   3
                  No   2   During daytime only 4

11. *If living in same house, who else lives in the house?*

    _____

12. *Marital status of carer:*
                  Married 1   Widowed   3
                  Single   2   Separated 4

13. *Cared-for person:*
        Frail old person 1   Mentally handicapped 2

14. *Name of cared-for person:* _____
    (Note: Use cared-for Person's Christian name from here on.)

15. Age of cared-for person: _____

16. Sex of cared-for person: Male 1   Female 2

17. Relationship to carer: _____

18. Marital Status of cared-for person:
               Married 1   Widowed   3
               Single   2   Separated 4

19. Previous occupation of cared-for person: _____

20. Who else lives in household with cared-for person?

    _____

21. Do any relatives of cared-for person live closely (within 1 mile)?
                  Yes 1   No 2

22. If YES, who are these relatives?
    Son   (...)   Daughter (...)   Brother (...)   Sister (...)
    Niece (...)   Nephew   (...)   1st Cousin (...)
    Parent (...)   Other (...)   -   Specify _____

23. Do any relatives of carer's who are not related to cared-for person live closely (within 1 mile)?
                  Yes 1   No 2

24. Any such relatives of carer or cared-for person live within the following distances?

	Carer		Cared-for Person	
within 2 miles?	Yes 1	No 2	Yes 1	No 2
within 3 miles?	Yes 1	No 2	Yes 1	No 2
within 4 miles?	Yes 1	No 2	Yes 1	No 2
within 10 miles?	Yes 1	No 2	Yes 1	No 2
within 70 miles?	Yes 1	No 2	Yes 1	No 2

25. Has cared-for person sisters/brothers elsewhere in Ireland?
                    Yes 1   No 2

25(a) Has cared-for person sisters/brothers abroad?
                    Yes 1   No 2

26. Any friend or helper of carer or cared-for person who might be
    regarded as of special support?
        Carer   Cared-for Person
      Yes 1   No 2   Yes 1   No 2

27. If YES, explain and state how far this person lives from carer or
    cared-for person? _____

28. Has carer any relatives living elsewhere in Ireland?
                    Yes 1   No 2

    Has any relatives living abroad?
                    Yes 1   No 2

29. Is carer responsible for looking after anyone else besides cared-
    for person and those listed in Q.8., e.g. neighbour/friend?
                    Yes 1   No 2

30. If YES, please state who else is looked after: _____
    _____

B. **RELEVANT BIOGRAPHICAL SECTION:**   HISTORY OF CARING TASK

31. Can you recall how you first came to assume the task of caring for
    the cared-for person?

    *(Prompt if necessary - Could you cast your mind back to the
    beginnings of caring, of coming to terms with this task you now
    carry out. Allow the carer to go back and tell the "story" in
    his/her own way. Empathy as the tale unfolds, occasional comments
    to keep the narrative moving and on course. Carefully note the
    main details, look out for motives expressed, sense of duty felt by
    carer, fears or other emotions expressed at the initial stages.
    Guilt or blame may come through. But the carer tells the story in
    his/her own way and interviewer listens sympathetically, notes the
    main stages of the story and the feeling with which it is told.
    Note what the parent felt at the discovery that the child was
    handicapped. Also what the carer felt when it became clear that
    fulltime care of the elderly person was now thrust upon her/him.
    Try and keep this section to 20 minutes or so. (Three pages were
    kept blank for the biographies)*
    *Interviewer should check at the end of the story that the following
    facts are established, if possible. If they are not, the
    interviewer should ask questions to establish these facts.)*

a) Were there others who might have taken on the task when you did?
                    Yes 1   No 2

b)   If YES, who were the other/others? _____

c)   How were you the one to whom the task of caring was entrusted?
     _____

d)   Did carer feel that it was *unfair* to him/her in any way that this
     task was placed on him/her?
                    Yes 1   No 2

e)   Length of time carer has carried out this task of caring:
                    Number of years ....

f)   Was there a crisis point where a decision had to be taken between
     caring for the cared-for person at home or seeking residential
     care?
                    Yes 1   No 2
     If YES, please elaborate: _____

g)   Who made the decision to keep the cared-for person at home?
     _____

h)   Who else participated in making the decision?
     _____

i)   Was this before or after or at the very time carer took on the
     caring role?
                    Before 1   At the very time 2
                    After   3   Not sure   4

j)   Did carer feel a special sense of duty to assume this task?
                    Yes 1   No 2   Not sure 3

k)   If YES, please elaborate: _____

l)   In your own childhood, did your parents look after any elderly
     person in the home such as a grandparent/handicapped adult or
     child?
        Grandparent   Handicapped Adult   Handicapped Child
        Yes 1   No 2   Yes 1   No 2   Yes 1   No 2

m)   For what main reason do you think you go on caring for the cared-
     for person day inday out? _____
     _____

C

(Ask all Carers of Frail Elderly)

32. Can we now talk about the sort of help that the cared-for person
     needs. Perhaps it is easier for me to go through a list of things.
     They might not all be relevant to you.

Does cared-for person have any difficulty in:

	On own No. diff.	With super- vision	Only with help	Carer	Others Name Relation- ship	How Often	Code WHO
				W H O H E L P S			
Having an all over wash or bathing self	1	2	3				
Washing hands/face	1	2	3				
Putting on shoes and stockings	1	2	3				
Doing up buttons/zips	1	2	3				
Dressing self other than above	1	2	3				
Getting to and using WC	1	2	3				
Getting in and out of bed	1	2	3				
Feeding self	1	2	3				
Shaving (men) Brushing/combing hair (women)	1	2	3				
Cutting own toenails	1	2	3				
Getting up and down-stairs	1	2	3				
Getting around house	1	2	3				
Getting out of doors on own	1	2	3				
Taking drugs/medication	1	2	3				
Other difficulties (specify)	1	2	3				

33. In terms of arranging care to meet (personal care) needs, what presents you with the most difficulty? _____

34. Have you found ways of solving these difficulties?
_____

35. To what extent would you say cared-for person is housebound?

	YES	NO
Bed/Chair Bound	1	2
Permanently housebound	1	2
Able to be left for short periods	1	2
Tends to wander if left alone	1	2
No real risk if left for several hours	1	2

(Ask carers of elderly only)

36. So far we have touched on mainly personal tasks but what about housework, shopping etc.?
    Who does? *(Go through list)*

	Carer	Others Name relationship	How often*	Code WHO*
Cleaning house				
Cooking				
Washing dishes				
Laundry				
Making fires				
Bringing in fuel				
Gardening				
Household repairs				
Household decoration				
Shopping				
Collecting pension				
Budgeting				

CODE: WHO *

Cared-for person only	1
Carer only	2
Carer and cared-for person	3
Cared-for person and others	4
Carer and others	5
Others in household	6
Others outside household	7

CODE: WHO OFTEN *

Daily	1
Several times weekly	2
About weekly	3
Less than weekly	4
Less than monthly	5

37. Do any of these tasks present you with special difficulties?
    (Record Verbatim)

_____

38. Have you found ways of solving them?
    (Record Verbatim)

_____

39. *(Ask carers of Handicapped Child only)*
    (S = cared-for person in this case)
    (R = carer)

    IMPAIRMENT AND DISABILITY
    I wonder if we could talk a bit about the things S can do and those where there are still difficulties.
    (Interviewer: Refer to notes as appropriate)

    What about continence?

(a) Wetting (nights)	1 Freq.	2 Occ.	3 Never
(b) Soiling (nights)	1 Freq.	2 Occ.	3 Never
(c) Wetting (days)	1 Freq.	2 Occ.	3 Never
(d) Soiling (days)	1 Freq.	2 Occ.	3 Never

_____

231

Mobility and self-care?

(e) Walk with help   1 Not at all   2 Not Upstairs   3 Up stairs
                                                 elsewhere

(f) Walk by self   1 Not at all   2 Not upstairs   3 Up stairs
                                                   and
                                                   elsewhere

(g) Feed self   1 Not at all   2 With help   3 Without
                                                   help

(h) Wash self   1 Not at all   2 With help   3 Without
                                                   help

(i) Dress self   1 Not at all   2 With help   3 Without
                                                   help

Vision, hearing and speech?

(j) Vision   1 Blind or almost   2 Poor   3 Normal
(k) Hearing   1 Deaf or almost   2 Poor   3 Normal
(l) Speech   1 Never a word   2 Odd words only
                    3 Sentences normal   4 Can talk but doesn't

---

Reading, writing, counting?

(m) Reads   1 Nothing   2 A little   3 Newspapers and/or books
(n) Writes   1 Nothing   2 A little   3 Own correspondence
(o) Counts   1 Nothing   2 A little   3 Understands money
                                                   values

Speech

If this person talks in sentences, is speech:

CODE: 1   Difficult to understand even by close acquaintances,
               impossible for strangers?

         2   Easily understood by close acquaintances, difficult for
               strangers?

         3   Clear enough to be understood by anyone?

         4   Does not talk in sentences?

Behaviour

(a) Hits or attacks others   1 Marked   2 Lesser   3 No
(b) Tears up pages, magazines, cloth-
     ing, damages furniture   1 Marked   2 Lesser   3 No
(c) Extremely overactive. Paces up
     and down restlessly. Does not
     sit down for a minute   1 Marked   2 Lesser   3 No
(d) Constantly seeking attention –
     will not leave adults   1 Marked   2 Lesser   3 No

(e) Continually injuring self
   physically, e.g., head banging;
   picking at sores; beating eyes   1 Marked   2 Lesser   3 No

---

Other handicaps or illnesses
(a) Epilepsy: Frequency: 1 One or more major seizures per month
                        2 Occasional seizures   3 No seizures

(b) Chronic physical disorders/illnesses (specify below)
        1 Yes   2 No

....

In general how would you describe S state of health?
        Good or excellent   Alright for age
        Fair   Poor

---

40.   Of all these things, which prevents you with most difficulty?

---

41.   Have you found ways of solving these difficulties?

---

42.   I wonder if I could ask how S copes with a range of different
tasks around the house and who helps?

Does S have difficulty in	Can do on own or with difficulty	Under super-vision	Only with help	WHO HELPS S	
				Who Helps?* R; Anyone else (Name)	How Often?*
Having an all over wash or bathing self	1	2	3		
Washing hands/face	1	2	3		
Putting on shoes and stockings	1	2	3		
Doing up buttons/zips	1	2	3		
Dressing self other than above	1	2	3		
Getting to and using WC	1	2	3		
Getting in and out of bed	1	2	3		
Feeding self	1	2	3		
Shaving (men) Brushing/combing hair (women)	1	2	3		
Cutting own toenails	1	2	3		
Getting up and down-stairs	1	2	3		

Getting around house	1	2	3
Getting out of doors on own	1	2	3

* CODES: <u>Who Helps?</u>

		<u>How Often?</u>	
No help given (not needed)	1	Daily	1
No help given (needed)	2	Several times daily	2
R only	3	About weekly	3
R and HH members	4	Less than weekly	4
R and others outside HH	5	Less than monthly	5
Others only	6		

(Interviewer: *List named helpers and their relationship to S*)

<u>Helper</u>	<u>Relationship to S</u>

43. In terms of organising these household tasks are you presented with any special difficulties?

44. Have you found ways of solving these difficulties

45. During the last week has S been:

	A lot/ mostly	Some- times	Hardly at all/never
Restless	1	2	3
Irritable	1	2	3
Aggressive	1	2	3
Obstinate	1	2	3
Affectionate	1	2	3
Appreciative	1	2	3
Forgetful	1	2	3
Impatient	1	2	3
Cheerful	1	2	3
Repeating requests again and again	1	2	3

Can you give some examples?

46. During the last week have you:

	A lot/ mostly	Some- times	Hardly at all/never
Lost your temper with S	1	2	3
Had to restrain S	1	2	3
Been frightened of S	1	2	3
Been embarrassed by S	1	2	3
Found it difficult to leave S	1	2	3

Can you give some examples?

---

47. Are there any problems of incontinence?
       Yes 1   No 2

48. If there are, how do you manage?

D. HELP FROM OTHERS WITHIN HOUSEHOLD:

    (If there is nobody else in the household, go to E. below)

49. Do other family members help - such as spouse, children, brothers
    or sisters living within the household?

            Yes 1   No Answer   3
            No   2   Not Applicable 4

50. Does carer's spouse help?
            Yes 1   No 2   No Answer 3

51. If YES, explain what he/she does _____

52. Would you note spouse's help as:
        Essential 1   Very Important 2   Important 3
        Not Very Important 4   Non-existent 5

53. What do other family members who live in household do?
    (List who does what among children, brothers/sisters, or others
                within the household)

---

54. Would you describe the contribution of this group as:
        Essential 1   Very Important 2
        Important 3   Not Important   4

235

E. HELP FROM OUTSIDE THE HOUSEHOLD:

55. Do family members living <u>outside</u> household help in any way?
        Yes 1   No 2   No Answer 3

56. If YES, please tell me what they do _____

57. Would you note their contribution as:
        Essential 1   Very Important 2
        Important 3   Not Important 4

58. If NOT, do you feel they ought to help more?
        Yes 1   No 2

59. If YES, please elaborate: _____

60. Do neighbours give some help in caring?
        Yes 1   No 2

61. How many neighbours are involved? ....

62. What exactly do they do to help? _____

63. *(Read this list fully before allowing interviewee to reply)*

                        Financial   1
        Help with household chores   2   *(Note: More than one*
      Friendship and moral support   3   *answer possible here)*
      Looking after cared-for person
            for periods   4
            Other (specify)   5

64. Would you rate the help of neighbours as:
        Essential 1   Very Important 2   Important 3
        Not Very Important 4   Non-existent 5

65. Is there something your neighbours could be doing for you, but do not do?
        Yes 1   No 2

66. If YES, please explain _____

67. Do any voluntary bodies come to your aid?
        Yes 1   No 2   Not Sure 3

68. If YES, which organizations? _____

69. What do they do for you and your cared-for person?
_____

70. How would you rate the help given to you by these organizations?
        Essential 1   Very Important 2
        Important 3   Not Important 4

71. Do you receive help from professional people?

        Yes 1   No 2

72. Name the professionals who help: _____

73. Do the following come to visit cared-for person?

Doctor	Yes 1	No 2
Public Health Nurse	Yes 1	No 2
Social Worker	Yes 1	No 2
Priest	Yes 1	No 2

74. Does cared-for person have a home help?

        Yes 1   No 2

75. How often do the following visit the cared-for person?

	Doctor	Public Health Nurse	Social Worker	Home help	Priest or Clergyman
When sent for	1	1	1	1	1
Weekly	2	2	2	2	2
Monthly	3	3	3	3	3
Few times a year	4	4	4	4	4

F.   CARED-FOR PERSON: GENERAL STATE OF HEALTH:

76. How would you describe cared-for person's health?

        Generally good 1   Fair only 2
        Varies a lot   3   Poor   4
        Very poor   5

77. Does cared-for person suffer from any particular disease?

        Yes 1   No 2

78. Can you tell me what it is? _____

79. Is cared-for person bedridden?

        Yes 1   No 2

80. If NO, for how long does cared-for person get up each day?

        For an hour or two 1   For 6 or more hours 2
        For normal day   3

81. Does cared-for person leave the house for a short walk or to sit in the garden?

                  Never 1   Very rarely 2
      At least once per week 3   Most days   4

82. Could cared-for person do so more often, do you feel, if he/she really wanted to do so?

        Yes 1   No 2   Not Sure 3

83. Are there things which cared-for person does for himself/herself which while good for independence, end up by giving you more trouble than if you did them for him/her?

Yes 1   No 2

84. If YES, what are these? _____

85. If you were not available to look after cared-for person, what do you suppose would happen?

_____

86. How does the cared-for person usually spend the day?

_____

87. What does the cared-for person most enjoy?

_____

88. Do you take the cared-for person out sometimes?

Yes 1   No 2

89. If YES, where do you go? _____

90. Does the cared-for person go to Church?

Yes 1   No 2   Very Rarely 3

91. Did the cared-for person vote in the last General Election?

Yes 1   No 2   Don't Remember 3

92. Do you think that you do things for the cared-for person which he/she could do for self?

Yes 1   No 2   Not Sure 3

93. If YES, do you think this maybe makes the cared-for person less independent than he/she might otherwise be?

Yes 1   No 2   Not Sure 3

94. How do you think the cared-for person would feel about going into a residential home for the elderly/handicapped?

Would fear it   1   Would resent it   2
Would feel hurt   3   Would not mind   4
Would like it   5   Don't know   5

95. Would you see it as a good thing if there were residential care for short periods of 2 or 3 weeks to give the carer a rest/break?

Yes 1   No 2   Not Sure 3

96. How do you think the cared-for person would react to being placed in such a setting for a few weeks each year?

Would resent it 1   Would refuse to go 2

97. Do you think that a time may come when you will not longer be able to look after the cared-for person and so will <u>have to</u> seek a place in a home for him/her?

Yes 1   No 2   Not Sure 3

98. What do you think would <u>force</u> you to seek fulltime residential care for the cared-for person?

_____

_____

G. VISITS FROM PUBLIC HEALTH NURSE & RELIGIOUS MINISTERS:

99. If public health nurse visits, what does she usually do for the cared-for person?

_____

100. Does public health nurse help you, the carer, in any way?
   Yes 1   No 2

101. If YES, please explain:

_____

102. Would you rate the contribution of the public health nurse as:
   Essential 1   Very Important 2
   Important 3   Not Important   4

103. Does priest bring Communion on First Friday or on one day each month?
   Yes 1   No 2

104. Do you think that this visit is important to the cared-for person?
   Yes 1   No 2   Not Sure 3

105. If YES, why would you think so?

_____

106. How do you feel about it? Does it help in anyway?

_____

107. Does it create any difficulties or extra work for you?
   Yes 1   No 2

108. Would you suggest any changes in manner or frequency of priest's/clergyman's visits?

_____

_____

H. MANAGEMENT OF CRISIS:

109. Has there ever been a crisis such as serious illness or sudden illness on the part of the cared-for person?
   Yes 1   No 2

110. If so, who came to the rescue?

_____

111. Should a crisis arise now or in the future, to whom would you turn?

_____

112. Were you ever forced to stay in bed yourself through illness while caring?

    Yes 1   No 2

113. If YES, how did the cared-for person manage?

    _____

114. Is there somebody outside the household on whom you can call readily in a crisis such as illness?

    Yes 1   No 2   Not Sure 3

115. If YES, who is this person?

    _____

116. How would you feel if you were forced to place the cared-for person in a residential setting for good?

    Lost   1   Very disappointed 2
    Somewhat disappointed   3   Relieved   4
    Guilty   5

117. What do you think of residential homes for the elderly and for the handicapped?
    (Ask carers of elderly about elderly and carers of handicapped about handicapped)

    _____

I.   BREAKS FOR PRINCIPAL CARER:

118. Do you get away on your own regularly?

	For a Day	For a Night
Yes	1	1
No	2	2
Rarely	3	3
Never	4	4

119. If YES, about how often do you leave the house?

    Daily   1
    Every two days   2
    A few times per week   3
    Once per week   4

120. Where do you go? _____

121. For about how long can you be away without upsetting the cared-for person?

    _____

122. Do you have a regular holiday away from home and from caring?

    Every   1   Most years 2
    Some years 3   Never   4

123. If YES, for how long?
       A few days 1   A week   2
       Two weeks 3   More   4

124. Do you suffer from:

	YES	NO	NOT SURE
Loss of sleep	1	2	3
Exhaustion	1	2	3
Emotional strain	1	2	3
Worry about future	1	2	3
Sense of being trapped	1	2	3

125. Do you have a hobby or pastime?
           Yes 1   No 2

126. What is your favourite hobby?
_____

127. How often do you enjoy this pastime?
       Daily 1   Few times per week 2   Monthly 3

128. When you leave home for a few hours, who looks after the cared-for person?
_____

129. When you leave home for a whole day, who does so?
_____

130. If and when you go on holidays, who looks after the cared-for person?
_____

131. When you come back to the house after being out, do you feel better yourself?
       Yes 1   No 2   It varies 3

132. What about the cared-for person, how does he/she feel?
       Feels better   1   Feels much the same 2
       Feels neglected 3   Feels annoyed   4

133. Do you feel you would like to get the opportunity to go out more often?
           Yes 1   No 2

134. If YES, why do you not do so?
_____

135. What do you most like about caring for the cared-for person?
_____

136. What do most dislike about it?
_____

137. When do you feel best about it?

_____

138. What would you say contributes most to keeping you going?

_____

139. Would you say overall that you get a sense of fulfilment from it?
    Yes 1   No 2   Not Sure 3

140. What is the first thing you would do to help and support a friend in your own situation if you were able yourself?

_____

141. Do you think that other people within the family should share the burden of caring more?

<table>
<tr><td>Those in household</td><td></td><td>Those living outside household</td><td></td></tr>
<tr><td>Yes</td><td>1</td><td>Yes</td><td>1</td></tr>
<tr><td>No</td><td>2</td><td>No</td><td>2</td></tr>
<tr><td>Not Sure</td><td>3</td><td>Not Sure</td><td>3</td></tr>
</table>

142. Do you think that your social life has suffered because of your caring role?
    Yes 1   No 2   Not Sure 3

    If YES, is it: Very seriously affected 1
                          Seriously affected   2
                          Not seriously affected   3

143. *(Ask married)*
    Would you say that caring has put a strain on your marriage?
    Yes 1   No 2   Not Sure 3

144. Is the cared-for person always in the house?
    Yes 1   No 2

145. Does the cared-for person ever go on an outing without you?
    Yes 1   No 2   Rarely 3

146. If so, who takes him/her? _____

147. For how long is the cared-for person away? _____

148. Does the cared-for person ever go overnight to any other house?
    Yes 1   No 2

149. Does the cared-for person ever go away from home for more than one day?
    Yes 1   No 2

150. If YES, please say where the cared-for person goes and how long he/she stays:

_____

151. How is the cared-for person generally affected by such trips, days out or holidays?

        Much improved 1   Improved   2

        No change   3   Seems to feel worse 4

J.   EMPLOYMENT AND HOUSEHOLD:

152. Do you work outside the home?

        Yes 1   No 2

153. If YES, is your work –

        Fulltime? 1   Part-time? 2

154. What is the nature of this work? _____

155. If you do <u>not</u> work outside the home, is it because you are too taken up with caring role?

        Yes 1   No 2   Not Sure 3

156. Were it not for the caring role, would you be seeking work outside the home?

        Yes 1   No 2   Not Sure 3

157. Are you worse off or better off financially because of caring role?

        Better off 1   Worse off 2   Not Sure 3

158. Do you think there are many people who sacrifice a job in order to look after an ageing parent or handicapped child?

        Yes 1   No 2   Not Sure 3

159. Did you have a job outside the home before you began to care fulltime for the cared-for person?

        Yes 1   No 2

160. Do you sometimes regret that you cannot work outside the home?

        Yes 1   No 2

161. *(Ask women)*

Suppose a good friend of yours came to you with this problem. She had a job as a secretary in an office in town, but now her mother has got a stroke and needs continual care for the foreseeable future. Should she give up her job and mind her mother? Or should she seek some other way out?

How would you advise her in her dilemma?

---

162. *(Ask men)*

Suppose a good friend of yours came for advice. His mother has had a stroke and needs continual care for the foreseeable future. He works in a drapery shop. Should he give up his job and mind his mother? Or should he seek some other way out?

How would you advise your friend in his dilemma?

K. RELATIONSHIP WITH CARED-FOR PERSON:

163. Would you describe the cared-for person as

	YES	NO
a very good companion?	1	2
very close to you?	1	2
someone you like to be with?	1	2
someone you look forward to returning to?	1	2
someone with whom you get on well yourself?	1	2
someone with whom you can have a disagreement or falling out, but can easily restore friendship once more?	1	2
someone who can often be very demanding?	1	2
someone who is difficult to get through to?	1	2
someone who is just not happy and cannot be cheered up?	1	2
someone whom you just could not please?	1	2
someone who never shows any signs of thanks or appreciation?	1	2

164. Does the cared-for person have bad moods?

Yes 1   No 2

165. When he/she is in a bad mood, how do you handle things?

_____

166. Do you sometimes lose your patience with the cared-for person?

Yes 1   No 2

167. What annoys you most about the cared-for person?

_____

168. Would you say you are closer now to the cared-for person than you were when you took up caring for him/her?

Closer   1   As close   2
Less close 3   Don't know   4

169. Would you say that the cared-for person has changed much since those early days?

Yes 1   No 2

170. Over the last few days, did you have any disagreement with the cared-for person?

Yes 1   No 2   Don't remember 3

171. If YES, could you say what the problem was?

_____

172. How did you react? _____

173. Does the cared-for person confide in you, share his/her worries, secrets?

Yes   1   No   2
Don't know 3   No answer 4

174. Does the cared-for person entrust you with financial matters and personal business?

    Yes   1   No   2
    Don't know 3   No answer   4

    (Note: If there is no-one else in household, go to Section L)

175. Has the presence of the cared-for person had any effect on the other members of the family?

    Yes 1   No 2

176. If YES, what do you think the effect is?

    _____

177. Would you think that the presence of the cared-for person has had some good effects on the family?

    Yes 1   No 2   Not Sure 3

178. If YES, please explain further: _____

179. Are there some harmful effects also?

    Yes 1   No 2   Not Sure 3

180. If YES, please explain further: _____

181. Do you think that some of the family may feel a bit shy or embarrassed before their friends at the presence of the cared-for person in the house?

    Yes 1   No 2   Not Sure 3

182. Does it prevent them inviting their friends around?

    Yes 1   No 2   Don't know 3

183. Does the cared-for person's presence mean you have more or less visitors coming to the house?

    Yes 1   No 2   About the same 3

184. Does the cared-for person make visitors feel uncomfortable, do you think?

    Yes 1   No 2   Not Sure 3

L. MOTIVES FOR CARING:

185. Do you think if you failed to carry out this task that you would be severely criticised by:

	YES	NO
Family	1	2
Neighbours	1	2
The priest/parson	1	2

245

186. Do you do the caring out of a sense of duty to the cared-for person?
              Yes 1   No 2   Not Sure 3

187. Or is it a sense of duty to someone else?
              Yes 1   No 2

188. If YES, to whom? _____

189. If YES, how do you account for this sense of duty? Where does it come from?
_____

190. Would religion and family be important sources of this sense of duty?
              Yes 1   No 2   Not Sure 3

191. Of the two, religion and family, which would be the more important source in your opinion?
    Religion 1   Family 2   Both equally 3

192. If I were to ask you the crucial question "Why do you do it, and why do you continue to do it when it becomes very difficult?" how would you answer?
_____

193. Do you sometimes feel lonely?
              Yes 1   No 2   Not Sure 3

194. If YES, would you say you were
    Often lonely 1   Sometimes lonely 2   Rarely lonely 3

195. What in your opinion is the greatest need of someone in your position?
_____

196. Do you think you have benefited personally from your caring role?
              Yes 1   No 2   Not Sure 3

197. If YES, in what way? _____

198. Do you think your contact with the cared-for person has taught you anything?
              Yes 1   No 2   Not Sure 3

199. If YES, could you tell me what? _____

200. When you grow old, how would you like to be looked after, presuming that you needed fairly fulltime care?

	Yes	No	Don't know	No Answer
In own home alone	1	2	3	4
In home of a son	1	2	3	4
In home of a daughter	1	2	3	4
In residential home	1	2	3	4
Other (specify)	1	2	3	4

201. Which of these would you most prefer?

To be with son	1
To be with daughter	2
To be alone in own home	3
To be in residential home	4

202. Do you think that the next generation will be as willing as this one to look after their ageing parents, parents-in-law, and handicapped members of families?

Yes 1   No 2   Not Sure 3

203. Do you think that young people should be taught their duty to respect and care for the old and handicapped in their families?

Yes 1   No 2   Don't know 3

204. Can people derive benefit and satisfaction from caring for elderly and handicapped?

Yes 1   No 2   Don't know 3

205. Suppose a friend of yours who was caring fulltime for an ageing parent or handicapped child came to tell you that she was at the end of her tether and felt she could no longer cope, how would you help with her problem?

_____

206. Would you consider that men or women are better at caring for an elderly feeble person or a handicapped child?

Men	1	*(Ask carers of elderly about*
Women	2	*elderly and carers of handicapped*
Both equally	3	*about handicapped)*

207. Why do you think this is? _____

208. Should men be doing more in these kind of situations where a feeble elderly or handicapped person is being looked after in the home?

Yes 1   No 2   Don't know 3

209. Do you think that the care of an elderly feeble person or handicapped child always falls on a woman – with nobody else really doing very much to help?

Yes 1   No 2   Not Sure 3

247

M. TRANSPORT AND COMMUNICATION:

210. Do you have a telephone?
                    Yes 1   No   2

211. If you need help in a crisis, what do you do to call help?

_____

212. Do you have a car in the household?
                    Yes 1   No   2

213. If Not, do you have someone who is willing to give you a lift to town or to the shop?
                    Yes 1   No   2

214. How far away is your nearest neighbour?
                    Yards ....   Miles ....

215. How far away is the person you usually contact first in a crisis?
                    Yards ....   Miles ....

216. Who does shopping for household usually? _____

217. Is there a bus from near your home to take you to town?
                    Yes 1   No   2

218. How far are you from the local post office?
                    Miles ....

_____

N. FINANCE

    How do you mind if I ask you a few questions about State Benefits?

219. Does the cared-for person receive the Old Age Pension?
                    Yes 1   No   2

220. Do you yourself receive any financial help?
             Yes 1   No   2   Don't know 3

221. If YES, please specify: _____

222. Does the Prescribed Relatives Allowance apply in your case?
             Yes   1   No   2
             Don't know 3   No answer   4

223. If Yes, do you regard it as
             adequate 1   inadequate 2   very inadequate 3

224. Why do you say this? _____

248

225. If you do not get any allowance, do you feel that you and people like you should be entitled to an allowance from the State?

Yes 1   No 2   Not Sure 3

226. Does looking after the cared-for person make life more expensive in some ways?

Yes 1   No 2

227. In what ways mainly? _____

_____

O. **SOCIAL STIGMA:**

    (i)   *(Applies only where the cared-for person is handicapped;*
            For carers of elderly skip to O (ii)

228. Does the cared-for person attend a school?

Yes 1   No 2

229. If YES, how does the cared-for person get to school?

_____

230. If adult, does cared-for person go to a workshop?

Yes 1   No 2

231. Does cared-for person go out with you to local town, to Church and to shop?

Yes 1   No 2

232. How do people react to the cared-for person?

_____

233. How do people you meet react to you when the cared-for person is with you in public?

_____

234. Are people still a bit uneasy when in the presence of the cared-for person?

Yes 1   No 2

235. Do you feel any shyness when you go with the cared-for person to public places?

Yes 1   A little 2   No 3

236. Do you feel that people are more understanding nowadays about handicapped children and their parents than they used to be?

Yes 1   No 2

237. Do you think that the handicapped person/child has a useful purpose in life?

Yes 1   No 2   Not Sure 3

238. How would you see this? _____

(These questions apply only to cases where the cared-for person is an elderly person)

239. Do you believe that the old are less or more respected in to-day's world than in the past?

    Less respected 1   More respected 2

240. Do you think that old people still have a contribution to make in the modern world?

    Yes 1   No 2

241. If YES, what is this contribution do you think?

    _____

242. If NO, why do you say this?

    _____

243. Do you feel that children have a duty to look after their ageing parents?

    Yes 1   No 2   Not Sure 3

244. Would you, yourself, like to live to be old?

    Yes 1   Yes, if in good health 2
    No 3   No, if in poor health 4
    Not sure 5

245. Is there an age beyond which you think you would not wish to live regardless of health?

    Number of years ....

P.   MORALE

246. Would you say you are a naturally good humoured person?

    Yes 1   No 2   Not Sure 3

247. If so, have you remained so since you took on the caring task?

    Yes 1   No 2

248. Has fulltime caring changed you in any way?

    Yes 1   No 2   Not Sure 3

249. If YES, in what way? _____

250. Would you say you are more or less irritable now than when you started?

    More 1   Less 2   About the same 3

251. Are you more patient now or less patient than you used to be?

    More 1   Less 2

252. Do you tend to tire more easily now than before?

    Yes 1   No 2   Not Sure 3

253. Do you sometimes feel very much alone and isolated because of your caring task?

              Yes 1   No 2

254. If YES, please explain? _____

255. Do you sometimes have fears for the future?

              Yes 1   No 2

256. Why is this? _____

257. Are you bored very often by your work of caring?

              Yes 1   No 2   Sometimes 3

258. Is there anything you would like to add – anything you think important which I have not asked about?

              Yes 1   No 2

259. If YES, what is this? _____

Q.   INTERVIEWER'S COMMENTS:

260. Please write down your own impressions of the carer and how you think he/she is coping with the task

_____

261. Would you say the carer is generally:
- not finding task particularly difficult   1
- coping very well   2
- not coping too well   3
- being got down   4
- not finding task extremely difficult   5

262. Personality of carer:
- generally cheerful   1
- not really cheerful   2
- a bit discouraged   3
- very discouraged   4
- other (specify)   5

263. Are there any special problems which the carer has to face?

_____

264. Any present need which should be looked after by Social Services or other body?

_____

265. Likelihood that carer can continue to care?
    Very likely 1   Likely 2   Not likely 3

266. Likelihood that carer would be willing to continue to care?
    Very likely 1   Likely 2   Not likely 3

267. Did anything in particular impress you about the carer?

_____

268. Did anything in particular put you off, surprise you or shock you about the situation?

_____

269. Any comments you may wish to make:

_____

Index

Rabbins, P.V., 29
reciprocity, 20, 32, 59, 66, 106, 110
relatives, 4, 13, 20, 25, 30, 33, 39, 44, 56, 57, 71, 88,
        147, 158
religion, 106-107
religious practice, 42, 43
Report on services for the Elderly (1988), 153, 163, 165
residential care, 4, 8, 9, 10, 11, 14, 19, 20, 21, 26, 27,
        30, 34, 45, 60, 70, 73, 75, 80, 81, 100,
        106, 125, 126, 148-153
respite care, 153, 165
rewards, 4, 21, 27-28, 29, 34, 80, 108, 109, 111, 114, 121,
        122, 126, 130, 131, 135, 160
Richardon, A., 119, 149, 153
Rimmer, L., 27
Ritchie, J., 119, 149, 153
Robb, B., 19
Runciman, W.G., 147

Sainsbury, S., 42, 44
self-sacrifice, 10, 15, 29, 33, 34, 128, 132, 160, 162, 163
self selection (of carers), 43
sense of duty, 34, 48, 103, 106-108, 109, 131, 160
sense of satisfaction, 113, 114, 126
senility, 75
Shanas, E., 39, 41
Shakespeare, W., 132
sheltered housing, 167
siblings, 39, 53, 57, 75, 85
Silverstone, B., 132
schools (for handicapped), 46, 56
Social Administration, 1, 2, 4, 5, 33, 34, 42
social control, 107
social policy, 2, 21, 34, 42
  Irish 7-9, 165, 163-168
social justice, 4
social services, 2, 15, 21, 23, 25, 47
  Irish, 7-10, 12-13
Social Service Councils, 10
social stigma, 2, 40, 41, 107, 113, 148, 167
sons, 46, 56, 71, 85, 149
Southern Health Board, 44
spouses, 4, 23, 25, 39, 40, 45, 47, 53, 55, 56, 83, 87, 100,
        147, 157, 158, 169
St. Columbanus Home, 73, 74
St. Francis, 128
St. John of God Brothers, 148, 167
St. Mary of the Angels, 4, 41, 167
St. Vincent de Paul Society, 4
State, 14, 22, 24, 27, 47, 125, 136, 137, 162-163, 166, 168
  benefits, 136, 137, 138, 140
Stewart's Hospital, 8
Stone, R., 56
stress, 22, 48, 119, 122, 123, 163, 164